ID0206236

RADICAL BEGINNINGS

RADICAL BEGINNINGS

Richard Hofstadter and the 1930s

Susan Stout Baker

Contributions in American History, Number 112

Greenwood Press
Westport, Connecticut ● London, England

Library of Congress Cataloging in Publication Data

Baker, Susan Stout
  Radical beginnings.

  (Contributions in American history, ISSN 0084-9219; no. 112)
  Includes bibliographies and index.
  1. Hofstadter, Richard, 1916 – 1970.   2. Historians—United States—
Biography.   3. United States—Historiography.   I. Title.   II. Series.
E175.5.H55B35   1985   973′.072024   84-27930
ISBN 0-313-24713-7 (lib. bdg.)

Library of Congress Catalog Card Number: 84-27930
ISBN: 0-313-24713-7
ISSN: 0084-9219

First published in 1985

Greenwood Press
A division of Congressional Information Service, Inc.
88 Post Road West
Westport, Connecticut 06881

Printed in the United States of America

10 9 8 7 6 5 4 3 2 1

Contents

Acknowledgments

Thanks are due to many people who helped in the preparation of this book. The Department of American Studies at Case Western Reserve University offered generous financial support. The Educational Foundation of the American Association of University Women made it possible to extend substantially the investigation. Morrell Heald and Linda Kirby supported, encouraged, and constructively criticized the project at various stages of its development. David Van Tassell and Carl Ubbelhode read the manuscript and offered many helpful suggestions for its improvement. James Richardson also read and reread this manuscript with a variety of helpful comments.

Several busy people made time for interviews: Selig Adler, Marvin Chodorow, Betty Goodfriend, Alfred Kazin, William Miller, Julius Pratt, David Riesman, Irving Sanes, and Kenneth Stampp. Others took the time to write extensively in answer to my questions: Henry Steele Commager, Merle Curti, Frank Freidel, and Bette Swados. I appreciate this help.

I am especially indebted to those who allowed me to view or to take into possession correspondence from the early years of Richard Hofstadter's life: Merle Curti, Alfred Kazin, Irving Sanes, Kenneth Stampp, and Bette Swados.

The staff of the Columbia Rare Book and Manuscript Library was infallibly gracious and helpful in my efforts to uncover materials. Catherine Emerson, archivist at the University of Mas-

sachusetts at Amherst, took warm and personal interest in the
project. I am also grateful to the archivist at the State Historical
Society of Wisconsin for gracious help.

Merle Curti's warm support of this project has encouraged
me in many ways, as has that of David Kyvig. David Blackbird
perused, edited, and offered helpful suggestions for the final
revision of this manuscript. I am indebted to him for his incisive
remarks.

Susan Baker and Maureen Melino of Greenwood Press have
been unfailingly patient and helpful throughout the process of
editing and printing this book. I am indeed grateful.

This book is dedicated to Naomi and Sarah, who have been
with me all along and who benefited from my work.

Abbreviations

AAA	Agricultural Adjustment Administration
AAUP	American Association of University Professors
AHA	American Historical Association
CCNY	City College of New York
FERA	Federal Emergency Relief Administration
ILGWU	International Ladies' Garment Workers' Union
LID	League for Industrial Democracy
NSL	National Student League
ROTC	Reserve Officers' Training Corps
SLID	Student League for Industrial Democracy
STFU	Southern Tenant Farmers' Union
UCLA	University of California at Los Angeles
YCL	Young Communist League

Introduction

Richard Hofstadter has often been seen as the leading figure in the "Consensus School" of historians, which developed in the late 1940's and continued into the 1950's. The school, historiographers have observed, emphasized the ironies and ambiguities of history rather than the linear progression of an earlier period. It muted the clear outlines of conflict and resolution between political parties and it looked to literature for evidence of symbols and myths affecting and even creating people's attitudes. It attempted to delineate a "climate of opinion" rather than to narrate a literal story of what occurred. The school has often been coupled with the conservative turn taken by intellectuals after World War II.

Hofstadter was a particularly receptive, reflective individual, sensitive to new ideas around him and quick to incorporate them into his own thinking. Although he committed his life to historical scholarship, he was hardly representative of a stereotypical historian immersed in the past and blinded to the present. Hofstadter's was an elastic history, flexible, pliant, thoughtful, and responsive to the criticisms of his readers.

In 1933 when Hofstadter was just a freshman at the University of Buffalo, a leading figure in the field of history offered a challenge to the members of the profession. This challenge might be taken as a blueprint for the general orientation of Hofstadter's career. It was made by Charles Beard in his presidential address to the American Historical Association of that year. He said in part: "The supreme issue before the historian now is the determination of his attitude to the disclosures of contemporary thought. He may deliberately evade them ... or he may proceed to examine his own frame of reference, clarify it, enlarge it by acquiring knowledge of greater areas of thought and events." Whether Hofstadter was put immediately in touch with this challenge is hard to say but that Beard became his most cherished intellectual guide is well known.

In Hofstadter's subsequent work—nine major books and numerous shorter writings—it is clear that he took up Beard's challenge. He did enthusiastically enter into "the disclosures of contemporary thought." He did "examine his own frame of reference, clarify it, and enlarge it." Especially was this true for new insights from the social sciences. Applications of the lessons learned from recent research in political science, sociology, and anthropology sparkle among Hofstadter's pages. From the beginning of his career in 1942 to the end in 1970 his histories demonstrated these "disclosures of contemporary thought."

But while this is true in a methodological sense, it is quite different from placing Hofstadter in the consensus school on a substantive basis. He has only very loosely been so categorized and those who have applied this label have been subject to some sharp criticisms. Indeed, over the years, a rather heated debate has arisen centering on just where and how Hofstadter should be categorized. The questions incorporated in this debate often refer to how much Hofstadter differed from the Progressive historians who preceded him and who were so important to him. These questions include the following: " Just how conservative was he—in a political and/or a cultural sense?" "How critical was he of American Society?" "Was he an elitist?" "Did he form a new school or was he simply an idiosyncratic historian pursuing his own course?" and "Did he have more in common with those others of his own generation labeled similarly or did he link the Old Left with the New?" Increasingly, also, in recent years, critics have tended to ask just *how* he reflected those influences from the social sciences.

Two main lines of interpretation appear to have developed about Hofstadter's place and contribution to American historiography. Some observers have placed Hofstadter among those emerging after World War II with a new attitude toward the American experience. These young intellectuals emphasized the dominant idea of the irrationality of humanity and the ironic nature of life as well as the validity of classic liberal freedoms. This assessment of Hofstadter focuses upon the introduction to his book *The American Political Tradition* where Hofstadter asserted that Americans have always agreed upon more than they have disagreed upon and that fundamentally there has been little change in American society. Because of all that agreement in American life, proponents of this view argue, the historians who documented that agreement have developed, themselves, a "terror" of the clear, sharp outlines of "ideological politics."[1]

On the other side of this debate, an opposing point of view has taken shape. Proponents of this interpretation tend to see *The American Political Tradition* as a reaction against the re-embracement of traditional American values after World War II. It interprets Hofstadter's position in this book as detached, critical, and even alien to these traditional American values. He should be placed, therefore, according to these observers, in a tradition of alienation begun by intellectuals of the 1910's and continued through 1948.[2]

A new chapter in this debate occurred at the 1982 meeting of the Organization of American Historians. The evaluations of Hofstadter put forward there serve to define more sharply the nature of the preceding debate. Lawrence Goodwyn, author of *The Populist Movement*, presented a new and intriguing concept of periodization in American historiography. Nothing much changed, he maintained, in American historical preconceptions between J. Allen Smith and Daniel Boorstin. The "Progressive Paradigm" lasted much longer than has traditionally been conceived. Moreover, when it did die, the "times" shattered its underlying rationale rather than the work of any one historian. It died because it had come under pressure after World War II. By the time of the *Brown vs. Board of Education* decision in 1954 and the Montgomery bus boycott in 1955, when it became clear that "there was a Second Reconstruction," the Paradigm fell of its own dead weight.

In the meantime, however, a new perspective had slowly de-

veloped among American historians: this perspective took as its
basic assumption the notion that it was no longer possible to
write about American history alone. It put the Progressive Paradigm under attack. With the challenge to its hegemony mounting, the Paradigm needed a "great historical mind" to defend it
against its challengers. This defender—the last supporter of
American uniqueness and progress—was Richard Hofstadter.
Hofstadter managed, according to Goodwyn, to carry on the
defense in most of his books. Hofstadter's battle was waged from
the bastions of elitism, from the position of the old American
Brahmins, from the heights of intellectual superiority and tradition with which Hofstadter identified. The battle was best and
most carefully presented in *Anti-Intellectualism in American Life*
but ran implicitly under the surface in Hofstadter's other books.[3]

Countering Goodwyn's interpretation at the session was Lee
Benson, who avoided any mention of *The Age of Reform*, but
offered a rebuttal of Goodwyn's assessment based on the famous
introduction to *The American Political Tradition*. Siding with the
minority of readers who interpreted that book as critical of
American traditions, Benson contended that Hofstadter wrote
the book as a Marxist who had realized the full limitations of
Turner and Beard and that both the introduction and the book
as a whole could be read as a gloss on "something Engels wrote
in 1890." The Marxist basis for the first full-blown statement of
the consensus thesis thus provided an important lead for American radical historians. If one studies history, Benson affirmed,
to find ways in which to change the world and theories to support
those methods of change, then Hofstadter's view of America's
"quintessentially conservative" society was one inescapable step
in moving from "conflictual capitalism to democratic and communitarian socialism."

George Frederickson, moderator of the session, added his own
summation, connecting the two points of view by pointing out
that Hofstadter certainly did miss incorporating the *full* nature
of Populism in *The Age of Reform* as Goodwyn had contended,
but that just as certainly his consensus theory took shape from
the Left and thereby provided an essential link between the Old
Left and the New, a link which is especially evident in the work
of a historian of the succeeding generation: Christopher Lasch.[4]

Who is right? I would like to suggest that to date all the evidence for determining the answer to this question is not in. No adequate resolution to this debate and to the meaning and placement of Hofstadter's history can be made until more is known about his life in general. Although some excellent biographical syntheses have been developed, no one has to date examined Hofstadter's earliest years in order to follow his development from its origins. Because the process of identity formation is crucial to any intellectual's development, and because Hofstadter's total opus is rich and elusive, and because the period in which he came of age was one of ferment and international upheaval, it is important to attempt to understand thoroughly his coming-of-age process.

Of those who have dealt biographically with Hofstadter, most have passed over his early years quickly and superficially. Arthur Schlesinger, Jr., noted Hofstadter's debt to the social sciences in his article "History and the Social Sciences" but concluded that the ideological battles connected to the social sciences in the 1930's "exposed him to Marxism but ... he was too explicitly a Beardian (and too implicitly a pluralist) to capitulate for very long to the Marxist system." Lawrence Cremin called attention to Alfred Kazin's description of their group life in New York led by a "trouble-laden generation" which was "dominated by crises." Stanley Elkins and Eric McKitrick observed that although Hofstadter had been well exposed to Marx's writings in the late 1930's and early 1940's, "as with anything else he allowed to 'influence' him, Marxist ideas were admitted selectively—and here [they were discussing *The American Political Tradition*] one may suspect that it almost required Mannheim to activate Marx and to make Marx usable for him." In each of these accounts, the very crucial period of Hofstadter's identity formation was passed over with a brief nod and his works treated more or less from the perspective of the 1950's and early 1960's, as if Hofstadter had developed his basic orientation in those periods instead of earlier.[5]

One observer, however, has laid out more thoroughly the New York Left of the 1930's as background for a consideration of Hofstadter's work. Christopher Lasch reminded his readers of the hard "third-period" of Communism, in which puristic CP members adhered to an elitist, exclusive party line eschewing alliances with other left-wing groups. Lasch then pointed out that when the change from hard-line to the softer approach of the Popular Front came in 1935, the Left readopted the old Progressive approach to history. This old approach consisted of an attempt to make "armed raids" on the past for elements from which to develop arguments for the present. Whereas, however, in the earlier period of Progressivism proper, in the 1910's, historians had raided the past for critical interpretations, they now were raided it for the supportive, celebratory re-embracement of American values during the Popular Front era. Like the editors of the *Partisan Review*, in this period, Lasch suggested, Hofstadter had searched not for a "usable past" in line with the social concerns of the moment but for "an accumulation of experience." *Partisan Review* editors had asserted that "each generation is formed by its predecessors, and the problem for historical analysis is not to invent a past relevant to the needs of the present but to become critically conscious of those influences." This critically conscious state was what Hofstadter pursued and achieved, according to Lasch.[6]

Although Lasch indicated only Hofstadter's reaction *against* the radical influences of the Left in the 1930's, enough other comments—such as those of Benson and Frederickson—have been made to lead to the bona fide question of what sort of positive influence, if any, the so-called "Rad Decade" did have on Richard Hofstadter's mind and work. The answer appears crucial for the resolution of several of the questions which have arisen in the attempt to place Hofstadter in historiographical perspective. It affects the interpretive question regarding *The American Political Tradition*. It affects the assessment of Hofstadter's general political orientation. And it affects the definition and scope of the Consensus school, in which Hofstadter was to have played such a central part.

The answer, it seems is that Lasch was essentially correct in envisioning Hofstadter in the midst of Communist Party shifts in the mid-1930's. From Buffalo, where he grew up, Hofstadter moved to New York City and established himself in a graduate program in the history department at Columbia. Because of his wife's intense involvement with Left-wing politics and because of the own background with the student movement in Buffalo, Hofstadter was drawn into the midst of the movement in New York. His involvement does not appear to have been the fleeting, ephemeral flirtation which observers have claimed but an extended, intensive personal experience lasting from the fall of 1934 to the Nazi-Soviet Pact of 1939. It contained academic, social, and philosophical dimensions which formed the basis of his intellectual and professional identity. Although Hofstadter moved beyond these early influences, they made up the substance of his original intellectual and historical orientation. Thus it is extremely important to understand their impact.

One further aspect remains. In considering how "schools" of historical thought are developed, it is clear that historians, by the nature of their craft, must deal with change and the causes for it. It may be that their varying interpretations of the causes for change create the schools, themselves. However that may be, historians do utilize theories of change, whether simple or complex, explicit or implicit, elaborated or not. Because it is so inherent to the historian's work, the theory of change is most likely dependent upon deeply held social, political, and personal values—and probably also dependent on early experiences in the profession. Gene Wise called such a theory of change an "explanation-form."

Hofstadter has been criticized for jumping from period to period and form subject to subject, not focusing on a single area and making it his "specialty." While reading Hofstadter's books in the order in which they originally appeared and looking for elements that tied his work together, I noticed that Hofstadter did seem to exhibit an identifiable, consistent, underlying structure of change. The structure appeared to be dialectical in nature. Its appearance indicated an apparent prior acquaintance with the philosophical side of Marxist and Hegelian thought. Not only from the perspective of the political interpretation of Hofstadter's works, then, is the experience of the Radical movement of the 1930's important to an understanding of Richard Hofstadter, but also from the perspective of his fundamental orientation to the philosophical question of change in general.

This book, then, is an attempt to present the first period of Hofstadter's career in as much depth as possible. It is an attempt to go back behind the labels later applied to Hofstadter and to ask what he was actually doing. In part, it makes implicit use of Erik Erikson's identity crisis theory, which held that the years between 18 and 25 offer the opportunity for successful integration of native talents, social role, and an intimate relationship. That integration formed for Hofstadter the basis from which he would grow into the "Consensus" historian of the 1950's and 1960's, the historian which contemporaries came to know well. But it is my contention that early integration left an indelible mark on Hofstadter's scholarship. And so this book is also an attempt to bring to light that fundamental theory of change, which developed early, stayed late, and served to give unity to Hofstadter's life work.[7]

Notes

1. John Higham, "The Cult of 'American Consensus,'" *Commentary* 27 (February 1959) pp. 93–100, Gene Wise, *American Historical Explanations* (Homewood, Ill., Dorsey, 1973) p. 242; Robert Skotheim, *American Intellectual Histories and Historians* (Princeton N.J., Princeton University Press, 1966) pp. 280–84; Arthur Schlesinger, Jr., "Richard Hofstadter," in Marcus Cunliff and Robin Winks, eds., *Pastmasters* (New York, Harper and Row, 1969) pp. 278–315; Marion Morton, *The Terror of Ideological Politics* (Cleveland, Case Western Reserve University Press, 1971) pp. 109–23. The article of greatest importance on Hofstadter's intellectual development, which also pictures him in light of his critics, is Stanley Elkins and Eric McKitrick, "Richard Hofstadter: A Progress," in *The Hofstadter Aegis* (New York, Knopf, 1974) pp. 300–367. The above all present Hofstadter as a member of the 1940's and 1950's "school."

2. Christopher Lasch, in "On Richard Hofstadter," *New York Review of Books*, March 8, 1973, pp. 7–13; Richard Gillam, "Richard Hofstadter, C. Wright Mills, and the 'Critical Ideal,'" The American Scholar, XLVII (1977–78), pp. 69–85.

3. Lawrence Goodwyn, "Hicks, Hofstadter, and the Continuing Legacy of Consensus," Paper given at the Convention of the Organization of American Historians, Philadelphia, April 1, 1982.

4. Lee Benson and George Frederickson, Commentary on Goodwyn, Philadelphia, April 1, 1982. The most recent addition to this debate is an article by Daniel Singal which does not fit either of these established categories but argues that Hofstadter is the godfather to a new school which followed and built on his approach: a group which Singal labels

the "ideological change" writers. Daniel Joseph Singal, "Beyond Consensus: Richard Hofstadter and American Historiography," *American Historical Review* 89, no. 4 (October 1984) pp. 976–1004.

5. Schlesinger, "Richard Hofstadter," p. 279; Lawrence Cremin, *Richard Hofstadter (1916–1970): A Biographical Memoir* (National Academy of Education, 1972) p. 3; Elkins and McKitrick, "A Progress," p. 319, n. 12.

6. Lasch, "On Richard Hofstadter," pp. 7–8. The quotation is from William Phillips and Philip Rahv, "Some Aspects of Literary Criticism," *Science and Society* (Winter 1937) p. 217. The date and publication are directly applicable to this study.

7. Erik Erikson, *Childhood and Society* (New York, Norton, 1950) pp. 261–63, 263–66. See also his *Youth, Identity and Crisis*.

PART I

1

Skeletons in the Closet

Among the waves of immigrants coming to America from Eastern Europe in the last quarter of the nineteenth century appeared a family by the name of Hofstadter. The family numbered five and came from the city of Cracow in what had been Poland. Along with the thousands of other Jews escaping pogroms, discrimination, and impressment in Russia and Eastern Europe, the Hofstadter family probably made its way from Cracow to Berlin and then to Bremen, or one of the other major ports in Holland or Germany. It was 1896 when the family left its native city.[1]

The history and location of Cracow suggest reasons for the date of the family's departure. Located between the Oder and Vistula Rivers, on the southeastern border of Poland and bordering both Prussia and Austria, Cracow had been pulled and tugged between these nation-states after the Congress of Vienna had dismembered Poland in 1815. An independent Republic during the first half of the century, Cracow was ceded to Austria in 1846 and remained an Austrian possession at the time of the Hofstadter family removal.[2]

Cracow was surrounded by the wide open plain of Galicia and its inhabitants lived in fear of invasion, even though there existed a tenuous alliance between Austria and Russia at the time. The Galicians had wielded some control over their destiny. As any weak state tends to do, the province played one power off against another, opting for Austrian control over that of Russia or Prussia. Austrian policy toward Jews was also much to be preferred to Russia's; limitations on basic civil rights for ethnic and religious minorities had been removed in 1870.[3]

Cracow itself served as a haven of refuge for Russian and Prussian Poles, and the University of Cracow, an ancient medieval institution, functioned as the center for underground Polish nationalist agitation. It spawned secret political societies working to further the reestablishment of the Polish state. Although the majority of inhabitants were Polish, Galicia as a province incorporated a large Ukrainian population. In Cracow itself, "a large Jewish colony dwelt amidst poverty and squalor in the Casimirski district, set apart from Cracow proper." It was most likely, then, that the Hofstadter family emigrated from Casimirski, although parts of the family had also lived in Lemberg, Tarnow, Warsaw, and Vienna. The date of the departure of the family may have been due to the intensifying discrimination under Czar Alexander III, Cracow being a stopping place for those fleeing the new Czar.[4]

The family underwent the newly imposed physical examination, given by steamship companies responding to tightened immigration restrictions in the United States. They were probably received en route by the Hebrew Emigrant Aid Society, which was then devoting itself to the cause of bringing Jews out of oppression. Perhaps they crossed borders illegally on foot in the dark of night. Perhaps they even underwent the indignity of delousing before boarding ship. In any event they reached London and remained there for three years.[5]

In 1899 the family crossed to New York. Passing through the ordeal of steerage, they arrived to face the inevitable series of inspections on Ellis Island. Urged by friends or relatives who had preceded them, they either boarded with others or found rented lodgings on Manhattan's Lower East Side. Meyer Hofstadter, the head of this family, was a furrier by trade and fortunately was able to find a position upon arrival in New York. Meyer and his wife, Emma, had three boys. Emil, who was to become the father of Richard Hofstadter, had been born in 1888. William was the second born. Samuel, not born until 1894, was only two years old when the family left Cracow. Four years after their arrival, in 1903, another son was born. This son, Benjamin was delivered by a midwife, a newly rediscovered distant cousin.[6]

The family's progress was atypical compared with the usual Jewish assimilation pattern. Irving Howe has contended that, regardless of accepted theory, most Jews achieved the professional positions ordinarily attributed to them after two generations, not one. Geographically, Jewish families tended to move from the Lower East Side of Manhattan to "colonies" in Brooklyn. This type of move was made by the first generation. The second generation remained "proletarianized" at the working level of its parents, and the third achieved the distinct change in socioeconomic and financial status that the original immigrants had dreamed of when first crossing the Atlantic. For whatever reason, the Hofstadter family did not follow the rule. William and Samuel worked their way through law school. Of the two, Samuel was the more successful. After entering law practice in 1913, he rose swiftly to the positions of deputy state attorney general, Republican state assemblyman, then state senator, and arrived finally at the state supreme court. William handled the campaign work for Samuel's election as state senator and supreme court judge. No father could have asked for more. Benjamin established himself in the field of real estate, also achieving a comfortable degree of financial and social success.[7]

Emil, the oldest brother, proved an anomaly to the family pattern but more typical of Howe's average. Howe has demonstrated that growing up on the Lower East Side was nearly overwhelming for some. The process of deracination and readjustment in one of the major migrations of modern times often involved intergenerational conflict of unbearable proportions. Not only were the young subjected to a "gray, stone world" and overcrowded conditions, but the twelve-hour days of their parents, the basement heder with its worn-out schoolmaster dependent on his stick, their own early employment in the sweatshops, and the ordeal of continued financial restrictions each took its toll on the psychic energy of young people.[8] The adjustment may have been most especially difficult for children born in the old-world conditions of the Pale, and required to meet the demands of Western urban conditions, when their education had been Eastern, Orthodox, and communitarian. It may have been especially difficult for the oldest boy who had received a good part of that education before arriving on the American scene with its striking changes in tempo, freedom, and future expectations.

Emil Hofstadter was eleven years old when his family arrived in New York. For him the tensions of life on the East Side appear to have been burdensome. At sixteen he ran away, a move he later explained to his daughter as having been caused by the extreme religious orthodoxy of his parents and his own rejection of them. This was a typical reaction for a second-generation child, but Emil was caught in the throes of occupying both first-*and* second-generation positions at the same time. Having assimilated the cultural lessons of Cracow and London, he was now being asked to throw them over in New York. In the five-year span of his experience in New York, he would have learned that dominant American mores did not call for religious orthodoxy or the Polish language and accents of his parents. These colliding expectations evidently caused him great strain and the break with his family ensued.[9]

A unique tension also existed between his mother and himself. Emma, his mother, was the type of woman, he later said, "to step out of her clothes and leave them on the floor for someone else to pick up." He remembered her as extremely self-centered.[10] Whatever the other motives for Emil Hofstadter's departure may have been, it is clear that at the height of adolescence, his rebellion against his family and home was stronger than many. In contrast to his younger brothers William and Samuel, who began law school in their teens, fulfilling parental hopes, Emil at the same age left home, evading family expectations.

Some of the East Side sons of immigrants of this period demonstrated their rebellion by joining the budding labor movement and turning to Marxian Socialism to express the outrage and unrealized hopes attendant upon the process of adjustment. Some sons participated in rent and meat strikes and generally proved themselves combative when faced with social injustice. Emil's brothers did not fit this category. They actively affiliated with the Republican Party—the party of German Jews, Taft, and Teddy Roosevelt—rather than with the Socialists. They worked their way up patiently and adapted themselves to the process of

Americanization with little enough combat. Howe has remarked that the "Galitzianer Jews," from Galicia, were thought to be traditionally passive. Perhaps these members of the Hofstadter family can be understood from this viewpoint. But to call them passive without modifiers is misleading. Passive in the face of social concerns enraging their neighbors, they were active in the personal initiative demanded by American society. They accepted the process of acculturation and identified with the dominant values in America. In contrast, Emil, made of different materials, reacted along the more combative and aggressive lines of the East Siders, rebelliously striking out, though in a personal rather than political sense.[11]

Emil's whereabouts between leaving home in 1904 and celebrating the birth of his son in 1916 are not altogether clear, but we know that sometime during this period he worked his way back to Europe. He also learned the fur trade of his father, most likely through establishing an apprenticeship to a furrier in Buffalo. Eventually he settled down, set up a shop, bought a home and a car, and began housekeeping. His business consisted of repairing and remodeling furs; at the peak of the season, in the fall, he hired a few employees. Whether or not he enjoyed the work remains questionable, but he stayed with it the rest of his life. That it brought him an adequate income seems apparent from the fact that in 1919 he owned a car, that before this he had traveled to Europe first class on a dare from his brothers, that he annually traveled to Florida for the horse races, that he was able to present his son a car upon graduation from high school, and that he put both children through college without help. In the 1920's and 1930's, in any city of the United States, these were marks of middle-class status. Emil Hofstadter appears eventually to have fallen into the pattern established by his brothers.[12]

But vestiges of Emil's atypicality remained under the surface. The secularization process, through which American Jews proceeded after they came to the United States, usually occupied three generations. For Emil, however, it occurred all at once, funneled perhaps into the act of running away. After leaving home, he never practiced Judaism again actively. Even more difficult for his parents, undoubtedly, he married out of the faith. Of course he was not able to shrug off his past as effectively as he might have believed he could. Telling vestiges of his original religious culture remained. He found great pleasure in reading. He yearned on occasion for a taste of delicatessen food. He insisted on being married by a rabbi. His son was circumcised. Emil Hofstadter was, in his life, pulled between the old and the new, between an anti-traditional and rebellious stance, on the one hand, and a resigned, assimilationist approach, on the other. He ended somewhere between cultures—a Jew who ignored his birth, a craftsperson of middle-class status, an American of Polish-Austrian birth. He appears to have lived out a variety of incongruities in his life.[13]

Emil's shop was on Huron Street in Buffalo, two miles from his home. Two blocks east of Main Street, dividing the city in half, ran a little two-block road named Welmont Place, inhabited by Germans. It was here that Emil settled, making his home with his new German, Gentile wife, Catherine Hill.[14]

The Hill (originally Hell) family's roots went deeper into American soil than those of the Hofstadter family. Catherine's maternal grandparents had arrived in the United States shortly after 1848, from the principality of Hesse-Darmstadt in the Rhineland. The family was one unit among a number of economic refugees fleeing Europe in the years of upheaval in Berlin, Vienna, and Paris. Catherine's paternal grandparents, the Hill family—also arrived as German immigrants. Her father, Dick Hill, had been first mate on a Great Lakes liner. He has been described as a very handsome man with "shining blue eyes, a strong nose, and long, thick-curled mustachioes." After leaving the sea, he came to be known as "the most daring steeple painter in Buffalo," at one time taking a fall from the roof of a steeple into the water. Clearly a daredevil, he died at a young age, sometime before 1916, "killed on a little pleasure yacht."[15]

Mary Newman, Catherine's mother, and Dick Hill were married in the 1880's. They had six children, five girls and one boy— a direct contrast to the four boys of the Hofstadter family. The fourth child, with two sisters younger than she, was Catherine, a handsome girl with an angular German face who grew up surrounded by siblings, her strong mother, and her renowned father.[16]

Buffalo had begun to thrive after the Civil War. By the late nineteenth century, because of its prime location as a commercial center, it was divided in focus between its lake traffic and its inland railway connections. It was a major livestock center and developed tanneries and a meat-packing industry to complement that in Chicago. In the 1890's and early 1900's, Buffalo was becoming an "industrial Behemoth." The steel industry was burgeoning. Socially it showed all the signs of Victorian America: increasingly differentiated social strata, newfound wealth for some, a quickened pace of life due to increased industrialization. Here Catherine grew up, prized for her appearance and perhaps the favorite child of both her father and mother. Here too, perhaps, where she knew everyone and the environment seemed tame, she was a bit restless. However that may be, she was drawn to Emil Hofstadter when he found her in Buffalo. Having traveled, being different from her family and surroundings, perhaps he reminded her of her dashing father, already dead for some time.[17]

It was, then, this large, sprawling German family, with its roots two generations deep in Buffalo soil, which Emil Hofstadter adopted as his own. Perhaps in contrast to his own mother, the women of the family appeared to him open, "warm and generous." Perhaps they were not so demanding, more matter-of-fact, easier to live with than his own striving and demanding parents. In any case, he appears to have responded enthusiastically to the tone of family life with them. Appreciation extended to him from the Hill family as well, lacking in male members as it was.[18]

In spite of Emil's appreciation for his future family-in-law, he wished to be married by a rabbi. So, unusual as it may have been for that day, Catherine and Emil were married in the Jewish tradition. Despite the gesture, Catherine was never accepted by Emil's family in New York. She was Gentile, she could not continue the Orthodox Jewish line; in practical terms for Meyer and Emma Hofstadter—perhaps especially for Emma—she did not count.[19] One feels here the germ of high family tensions and intense, perhaps bitter, recriminations.

The story of Emil Hofstadter and Catherine Hill clarified Richard Hofstadter's familial roots in the Progressive period. In his maturity Hofstadter would write about a "status revolution" covering the period of his father's youth. And in the picture of the dominant Progressive mind that he drew, he would assign a special place to urban immigrants. The experiences of his family were not without significance in shaping and molding that scholarly interpretation.[20]

Catherine and Emil celebrated the birth of their first child on August 6, 1916, and soon after he was christened in the Lutheran Church as Richard Irving Hofstadter. Three years later, a daughter was born. She was named Betty Marie and made an adoring younger sibling for her older brother. The family lived in a small, two-bedroom home, across the street from Catherine's sister and two blocks away from the local high school. Emil's shop on Huron Street was not far from home. In many ways, this was a small, cozy community, ideal for children—close-knit, bounded by family members, secure. Catherine and Emil had evidently combined their divergent religious backgrounds satisfactorily for both. Although Emil appears to have joined the Hill family, he insisted at times upon recognition of his own cultural and religious heritage. In return he accepted the leadership of the Hill family in matters of everyday religious observations.[21]

The family knew periods that were less than tranquil, however. One of Catherine's younger sisters died during Richard Hofstadter's childhood, and Catherine's daughter remembers the pain of her mother's grief. Also, Emil and Catherine did not always see eye to eye. Emil possessed a "terrible temper" and vented it on his family. Major concerns were not always the cause of an uproar; often problems such as what to do with young Dick's scratched finger kindled differences of opinion. Later in life, however, Emil became known for his kindness toward the children on the block, never leaving the house without gum or candy for them. The same warmth was undoubtedly extended to his own children in the periods between crises, although affection for his own children was naturally complicated by his parental role and his own primary family experiences.[22]

Although both children were originally baptized in the Lutheran Church, the family later became Episcopalian. Gertrude Hill Chapman, Catherine's older sister, had married an Englishman, and when Gertrude began to attend church with her husband, she took Catherine and her family with her. The children were confirmed in the Episcopal Church, close to their home. Emil attended occasionally. Dick Hofstadter became a choir boy.[23]

For outings in the summer, the family rented a house, without electricity, on Grand Island, an area close to Buffalo and at that time entirely rural. The children also visited their relatives in New York, traveling separately with their father to visit their uncles. On lesser occasions, when Emil wanted a taste of delicatessen food, he took his children to a special shop on Elmwood Avenue. There they feasted on lox and herring.[24]

When Hofstadter was ten, however, the security and basic organization of his life were shattered. The family had not been ignorant of death; in 1926 it faced another, larger dose. Catherine, sick for some months, was hospitalized and came home to die of intestinal cancer. The family was broken up. Mary Hill, better known as Grandma Hill, had been living with another of her children. Now she moved into the Hofstadter home, permanently. Young Dick remained at home. Betty moved across the street to live with her Aunt Gertrude. Emil began to make a new life with his mother-in-law as housekeeper.[25]

One can only speculate about the ultimate impact of this event. The new living arrangements, though not ideal for his sister, were fortuitous for Hofstadter. His grandmother "doted" on him, and his sister remembers that she and Dick used to sing while they washed and dried the dishes. Yet, Richard Hofstadter himself later testified that after his mother died, "his childhood became so difficult ... [he] no longer remember[ed], or care[d] to remember much before his high school years.[26] His sister has confirmed that Hofstadter claimed amnesia after the death of his mother. One must wonder in this context if anyone in the family was particularly equipped or prepared to help the children through this trauma. Although Mary Hill had held home and family together from an early point in her life and is remembered as a strong person, her energies were taken up by the physical necessities of life. While she certainly gave of her spirit to the new challenges of the deprived household, it is quite likely that in some important ways she was quite different from her grandson. Emil, who perhaps was more similar to his son, was undoubtedly burdened with his own grief and the residue of his own problems. Also, at the same time as he lost his mother, Hofstadter also—although only partially—lost his sister. The separation of brother and sister at this particular point deprived them both of that distraction and sharing that a close sibling relationship can bring. Still close in terms of neighborhood, they could not share the constant interaction in off-moments that comes to people who live together under the same roof.[27]

An anecdote from a later period may shed some light on the ordeal. Emil was said to have appreciated the matter-of-fact qualities of Mary Hill. When she was an old woman in her eighties and her parakeet died, Emil asked her what she was going to do. Her answer: Go downtown with you and buy another.[28] Her attitude in this mini-tragedy was indicative of her attitude in the major one: down-to-earth, realistic, lacking in histrionics, stoical. The other side of this attitude toward life and its trials, however, is the tendency to shut away from conscious awareness the pain, grief, or guilt that may be arising from the traumatic situation. If Hofstadter himself tended to react in this way, it would have been perfectly possible for him to have remained resigned and reconciled to this tragedy on the surface of his mind while deeply longing for a resolution on another level.

Whatever the answers to speculations such as these, it does appear that the substitute care of his mother's mother—certainly the best surrogate imaginable—brought Hofstadter through the period healthy and psychologically intact, for by his high school years, he led a full, energetic life, effectively expressing his talents. Only one side of his life changed permanently after the death of his mother. He lost interest altogether in religion.[29]

Several years before Hofstadter entered Fosdick-Masten High School, Frank S. Fosdick had established an emphasis on the principles of liberal education. Known as an "accomplished scholar in the . . . tradition of Renaissance learning," Fosdick had done much to increase the academic standing of the school. The building itself, newly rebuilt after a fire in 1914, was "gleaming white." Dick Hofstadter was an attractive and scholastically outstanding young man. "Everyone liked Dick," his friends said. He served as a cheerleader in his freshman year, the same fall as the stock market crash. He played tennis and golf and eventually joined a fraternity, which, it was generally acknowledged, did not admit Jews.[30]

Under the general atmosphere created by Fosdick, and popular among high schools and colleges in general, the debate team attracted widespread attention. Hofstadter joined the team and came under the influence of its coach, Miss O'Meara. At one point, he debated the question, "Should We Recognize Russia?"—a question that must have occupied several debates just prior to Franklin D. Roosevelt's official recognition in 1933. Hofstadter had kept abreast of what was going on in the world since his father took the *New York Times* daily and advised his children to read it regularly. In addition to sharpening his wits, the debate team also served to attract the admiration of the young women in his age group, and one concludes that he was at no loss for friends of the opposite sex.[31]

Having thus aroused his critical awareness and been trained to keep up with current issues, it is not likely that Hofstadter missed the controversy over the banning of *The Merchant of Venice* by the Buffalo Board of Education in 1931. The rabbi of Temple Beth El had requested that Shakespeare's classic be banned from the schools in Buffalo. A furor resulted from the acquiescence of the Board, with Professor Willard Bonner writing caustically to the *Buffalo Evening News* asking whether there would be more such disallowals. This was, Bonner felt, a misplaced feeling of intolerance. At this time, it appears, Hofstadter's Jewish identity had not fully flowered. Yet one wonders how the reflective and sensitive side of Hofstadter was responding to this ambiguous issue. He had been taken under the wing of the head of the English Department, Miss Starr, as a promising student, and as a second-semester sophomore or a first-semester junior in 1931, his was the very class to be deprived of Shakespeare's drama.[32]

At home things were not so rosy as they were at school. Emil, a father alone, was understandably attempting to overcompensate by becoming very protective. He, with others, was worried about tuberculosis, taking Hofstadter's sister out of college one winter because of a threatening epidemic. Emil also pushed Hofstadter to do well in school. What would become of his son professionally was a topic of early discussion, and Hofstadter's sister recalls that he was "brainwashed" about the idea of law school, based on the hypothesis that Uncle Samuel in New York would help Dick there.[33]

In the winter of 1933, Emil took his two children, aged sixteen and thirteen, to Florida with him—their first visit. A picture of the two of them, "playing" on the beach, shows them making a pyramid, laughing into the camera, brother and sister clearly having fun together.[34]

In this same year, Hofstadter was elected president of his class. On graduation day, he brought home virtually all the honors. He was valedictorian of his class, although he did not make the student address. He won a state scholarship to the University of Buffalo. He also won a silver pin for maintaining a grade average of 95 percent for two years. But it did not seem to Emil, sitting in the audience, that his son could possibly win the coveted Dartmouth Award for outstanding scholarship, character, and achievement. When it came time to announce the recipient of this award, Emil poked his daughter and said, "If only Dick hadn't been fooling around [cheerleading] during his freshman year he might be getting this now." As Hofstadter's name was announced, Emil's eyes filled with tears. The efforts of the long struggle he had waged during his son's teenage years, and perhaps the hopes of the parents he had rejected, were finding their rewards and he was justifiably proud.[35]

One example of Hofstadter's written work remains from his senior year in high school, an illustration of the joint influence of the drama coach and the head of the English Department. It is a play, written for school—and radio—presentation. It has no title but should be named "The Skeleton in the Closet." Much later, at Hofstadter's memorial service in 1970, a fellow historian would say, "The history profession robbed the stage of one of its most gifted mimes."[36] This play is evidence of the early fruits of Hofstadter's mimetic and dramatic talents. It will not be remembered for its literary merits, as his histories will, but it offers an excellent glimpse into the sixteen-year-old's mind.

Set in the sitting room of an upper-class Englishman, the plot deals with the past re-creating itself in the present. Lord Eliot and his servant, Jeeves, are alone on a typical morning in Lord Eliot's establishment. While reading the morning newspaper,

Lord Eliot requests things for his breakfast—coffee, toast, grapefruit. Jeeves continually finds that the establishment has run out of the requested item. Eliot, irritated but resigned, settles for something less than desirable or nothing at all. Then, with an abrupt switch, Eliot asks Jeeves, "Did you ever have a skeleton in your family closet?" Jeeves quite characteristically replies that his family never had closets in their home. Eliot continues to relate how he once had a twin brother—Jeeves interjects, "When you were born sir?" with typical deadpan ignorance. The twin disappeared "very mysteriously" when he was three months old. Eliot, apprehensive about his twin returning to rob him of his fortune, hears the doorbell ring. In walks the twin. Jeeves is dismissed, and the stranger/twin accuses Eliot of having had him kidnapped, pulls a knife, and tells Eliot he is going to kill him. Eliot coolly retorts, "If you are my twin brother and if I look like you, then I am ready to die." He delays the twin by reminding him of the "mole on his right wrist." Showing the mole, Eliot informs the twin, "The one that was kidnapped was the one with the mole on his wrist. I am you and you are me." The twin jumps to his feet and exclaims, "Nevertheless I intend to kill you." Eliot again circumvents the act by more mental gymnastics: "Before you stabe [sic] me why don't you strike me? If you feel the pain, you will know that what I am saying is true." The twin tries this, "immediately jumps back, puts his hand to his face and says 'Ouch!'" Eliot comments, "You see? . . . if you kill me you will only be committing suicide." The twin responds, "And to think that all my plans, my dreams, my hopes of killing you have come to this: Oh bitter life! Oh irony of fate!" Eliot comments aside that this twin would "put the ham in Hamlet."

But the twin has another brainstorm: "I can . . . kill you by committing suicide." Eliot, alarmed, argues that he has just saved the man's life. Jeeves reappears under command to get the fellow some nuts. The stranger takes a pill. Eliot laughs and informs him, "I am really myself and you are really you. . . . I did it with mirrors. Don't you think that's clever?" Eliot watches the last death throes of the unfortunate twin, quoting "To be, or not to be . . ." but breaks into his monologue to ask, "What's the matter? You're supposed to be dead." "Well," responds the twin, "I feel much better now." Jeeves pops his head in, announcing, "There's a gentleman to see you Sire." Eliot has had enough and orders Jeeves to tell the stage crew to pull the curtain. Jeeves demurs characteristically, "But there is no stage crew, Sire." Eliot rejoins, "Well Jeeves, do it yourself," and offers a game of chess to the revived twin. The play is ended.[37]

Written for his high school colleagues, this piece shows Hofstadter in his role as comic—a role his friends have consistently testified was essential to his personality. Several traits of both humor and mind are revealed here. First, the domestic Victorian relationship between server and served—stock material for a teenage dramatic effort—was muddied and undercut by the wit of Jeeves. By position, Jeeves as servant was subservient; by behavior he dominated. In each instance he thwarted the desires of his employer by passive aggression—a secondary theme of the play. Asked to bring toast, and appearing with butter, he explained, "I cawn't very well bring you three pieces of no toast with butter on them, so I brought you the butter alone." Asked to bring grapefruit, he asked, "Which hawlf?" When there wasn't any at all, he explained, "I cawn't very well bring you the lower awf of no grapefruit." This pattern continues until the end of the play, when his explanation is "I cawn't very well tell *no* stage crew to pull the curtain."[38]

In addition to thwarting his master's plans, Jeeves's answers are, in themselves, a comment on logical absurdity. His logic breaks things apart until they are no longer meaningful. Is the position of this individual also a comment on logical absurdity? It may very well have been Hofstadter's unwritten contention. It is clear that Jeeves had the upper hand, ran things for the helpless Eliot who could not do for himself, and was the more interesting character of the two. Here is a fascinating precursor to Hofstadter's later, unpainted, unsung anti-heroes.

Second, the relationship and dialogue between the two brothers show four reversals in fortune. Jockeying for power, each has tried to outdo the other, with the family fortune as the ostensible goal. The first reversal is verbal only: The story of the mole on the right wrist is offered by Eliot as an obstacle to the intentions of his twin. The second, the twin's strike that hurts only himself, does thwart his intention to kill Eliot, but turns that intention on himself, since the twin believes that he is now really Eliot. In the third reversal, Eliot reveals that he is really himself and that he has tricked his twin again, this time as the twin is dying. The fourth reversal thwarts Eliot's effort to have his twin commit suicide by the twin's (unexplained) revival. At that point, as if his success in outwitting Eliot has made the twin acceptable to the household, Eliot offers to settle down with him in a game of chess. This series of reversals in fortune—and dominance—through cleverness, trickery, and cunning presents a series of unexpected consequences and characterizes the interactions of the brothers just as it would characterize the process of politics in Hofstadter's later books.

Third, the image of the skeleton in the closet evokes other images of long-submerged or repressed secrets—the major theme of the play. What those secrets are is never defined, but the two men fighting and attempting to outsmart each other over the issue of the secrets is indicative not only of 1930's gangsterism and violence but of the same period's Freudianism. The wrestling and the struggle are not merely between members of the same family but between protagonist and his alter ego. As the skeleton emerges from the closet in the form of the protagonist's mirror image, Eliot is forced to wrestle with his other self and, finally, to incorporate his twin into his establishment, just as in Hofstadter's later histories actors on the stage of the past would be obliged to incorporate contradictory impulses in order to proceed effectively.

The play, although geared to a small-town sense of humor, is not merely a "corny" youthful attempt at comic wit. It is a statement of the sixteen-year-old Richard Hofstadter's own personality and his sense of inner dialogue, underling's wit, and unexpected consequences. It is, as his histories would be later, a drama of dialogue and relationship before it is a drama of action. It shows the salient marks of his later work, from the internal tensions in the mind of the protagonist to the external challenges presented by a new social reality, here so strikingly represented by Jeeves. The play also shows Hofstadter on the threshold of his venture into a university education: a process that would stimulate, sharpen, and toughen his outlook, but would not essentially change it.

One other element of Buffalo life was significant in Richard Hofstadter's development. Although Buffalo was predominantly a conservative, Republican city in the first quarter of the twentieth century, the hold of its Anglo-Saxon leadership was tenuous. As the need for industrial labor grew, Italians and Poles continued to flock to the city and other ethnic minorities grew up rapidly. One of these was the Eastern European Jewish community, overlapping with Poles and Russians in national origin but distinctive in culture and cohesion.[39]

Eastern European Jews had reached Buffalo in two waves: one between 1875 and 1900, the other between 1900 and 1915. They came to Buffalo from Lithuania, Poland, and the Ukraine because the city was "the most convenient western railhead from New York City" and the national Jewish refugee agency was dispersing people from the New York City area.[40]

They came with many various local customs that they attempted to reproduce as completely as possible. They established numerous, very particularized synagogues, called shuls, each of which possessed its own blend of traditionalism, rigidity, and attachment to Yiddish as a folk language. Each embodied the intense desire, born of nostalgia and homesickness, to reestablish the old familiarity, continuity, and stability in a world that was new, free, and strange. They also established for a time a variety of picturesque old-world customs, which provided the "ethnic chaos" that Anglo-Saxons would attempt to reduce to order. In Buffalo these customs were exemplified by the *mikvah*, or Russian-Turkish bath, and the *shohet*, who "slaughtered fowl in his front yard." As new refugees crowded in beside older arrivals—increasing sixfold on the East Side of Buffalo between 1900 and 1915—they created what came to be called the William Street Ghetto, named for the major east-west thoroughfare dividing the city and creating the boundary to the east of which the newly arrived groups settled.[41]

That ghetto has been described in some detail:

William Street itself was the business hub of the ghetto. Its shops were generally small, and only a few of them imitated the glitter and display of the downtown stores. Some pawnshops and second-hand stores with dark interiors and sombre occupants recalled the pictures of the ghettoes of Europe. A step below one could see the rag peddlers in wagons

or behind handcarts who emerged from the neighborhood and scat-
tered all over the city.[42]

Human movement, a combination of old-world ways in new
surroundings, close quarters, an active population on its way up
and out—the picture is a replica of Alfred Kazin's Brownsville
as he grew up in Brooklyn or of Irving Howe's Lower East Side.[43]
    The William Street Ghetto was compact in size and although
marked by many local antagonisms operated as a unified community before the prosperity of the 1920's prompted many to
move out. The neighborhood functioned as a tightly knit center
for Jewish activity and the social thought that Eastern Europeans
brought with them to America. The social thought, as we have
seen in New York City, centered in the left-wing politics learned
by many in Germany and Eastern Europe before coming to the
United States. The second generation arriving in Buffalo did
not fight the religious battles of their parents between Orthodox
and Reform approaches to Judaism; it was torn, instead, between
religious faith in general and the new secular faiths of Marxian
Socialism, Jewish secular nationalism, and Labor Zionism. It was
indeed the totality of these religiopolitical quarrels that kept this
area in intellectual ferment and that aided the general education
of its younger generations.[44]
    One issue separated the entire area from its more assimilated
German counterpart that represented dominant American values on the other side of Buffalo. The problem of financial aid
to the new immigrants weighed on older, more established Jews.
The form this aid took and the method in which it was given
presented substantial concerns to the two Jewish communities.
The German Jews had followed the precepts of Andrew Car-
negie's "Gospel of Wealth," precepts that put forth the expectations of the free enterprise system in this country: Money from
successful business ventures should be voluntarily donated for
meeting the needs of indigents through private welfare institutions. In return, recipients should absorb and retain basic
American values such as cleanliness, straightforward honesty,
family pride and national patriotism. In Buffalo these values
and the approach to financial aid they embodied were represented by the Sisters of Zion, an affiliate of the powerful Jewish

Welfare Federation, staffed by wives of leading members of the major German synagogue on the West Side of Buffalo. The Sisterhood ran a Hebrew religious school, conducted an Americanization program, and administered a night school for adults at its Zion House. Their goals for quick assimilation along the lines they as Germans had followed forty years earlier ran counter to the deeply ingrained attempts to re-create local culture that the East Siders were making. Religiously the Germans possessed what appeared to Jews from the Pale as a vapid, watered-down version of Judaism, offensive to Orthodox religious criteria. Linguistically the Germans stressed Hebrew and English, while ignoring the Yiddish culture from which Russian and Galician Jews came. Socially the Germans wished to avoid embarrassment by association with the non-Western habits of the Eastern Europeans.

In resistance, the East Side Jews developed a "rather loose and careless structure" to care for themselves. The organization, known as the Jewish Aid Society, consistently refused incorporation into the Jewish Federation, despite the obvious financial benefits that would have accrued if they had cooperated. Their resistance was based on two counts in addition to the more general concerns already mentioned: Germans were in control of the Federation and these Germans were the "bosses in the establishments that hired and fired the East Siders." In addition, the memory of the police state, from which they had escaped, haunted the East Siders. For them decentralized control coincided with a freedom they had just begun to enjoy.[46]

One of the widely known institutions caught in the cross-fire of these antagonisms was the Hebrew School, better known as the Talmud Torah, erected in 1904 and located in the very middle of the William Street Ghetto. The Talmud Torah offered the East Siders' alternative to the educational program prepared by the Sisters of Zion. It offered Hebrew as a living language and classes held in Yiddish. The school was free, Orthodox, nationalist, and progressive educationally. At night it offered its facilities to the Labor Zionists and the Workmen's Circle.[47]

By the 1920's an individual by the name of Israel Swados—known as a "fiery autocrat"—dominated the school. He has been described as the "virtual dictator of the school." Swados oversaw many of the problems of children growing up in second- or third-generation Jewish families in the William Street neighborhood. He also headed a large, sprawling family of his own, which continued to make a name for itself in the area.[48]

The Swados family was enmeshed in the cross-currents of the Jewish community in Buffalo. But it was unique in one respect. For most Jews, "a disproportionate number of the second generation turned to economic radicalism as a sort of substitute value system for organized religion." This turn marked the gap between first and second generations in most instances. In the Swados family, however, it was the third generation that turned to economic radicalism, the causes stemming from both local culture and the American economic picture in general.[49]

Israel had produced one son from his first marriage. This was a boy named Aaron, a lonely "only" child who lost his mother early, as had Richard Hofstadter. Aaron's father remarried and sired five other children. But Aaron grew up older than and partially estranged from his five half-siblings. He seems to have felt rejected as a result of the situation. He made the most of himself, however, growing up to go to the medical school at the University of Buffalo and to marry a woman from a well-known New York family. He became a small-town doctor who "administered to the poor." Personally he has been described as "cold and tyrannical" and "dour." Perhaps he deserved these epithets. Quite probably, he inherited some of his father's domineering and autocratic ways.[50]

By the mid–1930's at least, and probably well before, Aaron Swados had settled with his family five blocks north of William Street and perhaps fifteen blocks south of Welmont Place. The Swados home was in the heart of the Jewish community in Buffalo. It was an especially warm, open home—inviting to the friends of Aaron's children. Those young people learned there a free-thinking approach to social problems that gave their later political activities intellectual support. They also obtained a taste for art, music, and literature. Aaron himself was an admirer of German literature, especially Goethe.[51]

Here Aaron's two children grew up. The oldest, Felice Swados, was two years ahead of Hofstadter in school. As a child she was a girl scout for a time. She rapidly became known for her quick intelligence, her extroverted personality, her large size, and eventually her politics. Her brother, Harvey, six years her junior, followed in his sister's footsteps, never to reject the trail she blazed for him. He became a dedicated exponent of the Left, a novelist, and an organizer.[52]

The major reason for the popularity of the Swados home was undoubtedly Aaron's wife. Originally Rebecca Bluestone of a New York medical family, Rivi, as she was familiarly known, has been compared with Nora in Ibsen's play *The Doll's House*. She was fun-loving, gay, and babied by her husband, who adored her. "Lively and animated most of the time," she exhibited real talent for her avocation of painting. She joined her artistic talents with a scientific background, for her father, Joseph I. Bluestone, had served as a New York physician and a brother, Michael, became a hospital administrator, active in both New York and Jerusalem. Another brother, Harry, became a social work administrator, serving in Buffalo between 1940 and 1943 as executive director of the newly established Jewish Center. Rivi inherited artistic talents, a scientific point of view, and twentieth-century social concerns, all of which she worked actively to pass on to her children.[53]

It was this family, with its roots deep in the East Side Jewish experience, which was to welcome and succor Richard Hofstadter from the early days of his career at the University of Buffalo, and into which he was eventually to marry. He identified strongly with the family as a whole. The reasons for this were undoubtedly multiple, but one of the most important was certainly the death of his mother at an early age. He found in the Swados family warmth, acceptance, and stimulation, not because he had not found these at home but because he was young, in need of a sympathetic, intellectual, and cultural community, searching for an identity he had almost forgotten, and intensely drawn to Felice. In identifying with the Swados family, Hofstadter was also picking up the strand of family life his father had abandoned when he left the East Side of New York. He was returning to the roots his father had rejected. The identity Richard Hofstadter found when he met and joined this family circle—Jewish, intellectual, creative—was a permanent one. In adopting it, Hofstadter completed the circle his father had begun by leaving New York at the age of sixteen and situating himself in Buffalo.

NOTES

1. Samuel Hofstadter to Robert Hofstadter, March 29, 1967, Richard Hofstadter Papers, Columbia University, New York, N.Y.

2. Arthur C. May, *The Hapsburg Monarchy 1867–1914* (Cambridge, Harvard University Press, 1960) pp. 18–21, 52–53; Frederick G. Heymann, *Poland and Czechoslovakia* (Englewood Cliffs, Prentice-Hall, 1966) pp. 98–102; F.S. Bridge, *From Sadow to Sarajevo: The Foreign Policy of Austria-Hungary 1866–1914* (London, Routledge and Kegan Paul, 1972) p. 2.

3. May, *Hapsburg Monarchy*, pp. 53, 176–78. Discrimination rose in Austria, however, due to the policies of the Christian Socialist Party. See p. 180.

4. Ibid., pp. 53–57. For quotation see p. 57. Hofstadter to Hofstadter, March 29, 1967. Also see S. M. Dubnow, *History of the Jews in Russia and Poland from the Earliest Times Until the Present Day, II* (Philadelphia, Jewish Publication Society of America, 1918) pp. 244–50, for increasing victimization.

5. Irving Howe, *World of Our Fathers* (New York, Harcourt, Brace, Jovanovitch, 1976) pp. 25, 29, 44–45 and especially pp. 36–39, "From Border to Port"; Hofstadter to Hofstadter, March 29, 1967. Howe emphasizes the mixture of "mounting wretchedness and increasing hope" in Jews after the death of Alexander II.

6. Howe, *World*, pp. 39–46; Betty Goodfriend, Personal interview with the author, May 26, 1981; Hofstadter to Hofstadter, March 29, 1967.

7. Howe, *World*, pp. 143, 163; *New York Times Biographical Edition, I* (New York, n.d.) p. 1647; Betty Goodfriend, Personal interview, May 26, 1981.

8. Howe, *World*, pp. 71, 154–59, 180–87, 200–204. Howe's story of a boy threatened by his religious teacher who was about to hit him with his ever-present stick and who thereby shocked the boy into running away conjures visions of Emil.

9. Goodfriend, Interview, May 26, 1981.

10. Ibid.

11. Howe, *World*, p. 125 and Chapter 9; Goodfriend, Interview, May 26, 1981.

12. Richard Kostelanetz, "Richard Hofstadter: Historian's Indomitable Skepticism," in Kostelanetz ed., *Masterminds* (New York, Macmillan, 1967) p. 167; Goodfriend, Interview, May 26, 1981.

13. Goodfriend, Interview, May 26, 1981.

14. Ibid.

15. Ibid.; Felice Swados to Harvey Swados, September 2, 1942, Harvey Swados Papers, Courtesy of the Archives of the University of Massachusetts, Amherst, Mass.

16. Goodfriend, Interview, May 26, 1981.

17. Selig Adler and Tom Connolly, *From Ararat to Suburbia* (Philadelphia, Jewish Publication Society of America, 1960) p. 167; John Horton et al., *The History of Northwestern New York, I* (New York, Lewis Historical Publishing Co., 1947) pp. 222–27, 358. There exists a fictionalized account of Catherine's younger years and the reasons for her attraction to Emil, written by Felice Swados in 1940 or 1941. Felice was not successful in her fictional attempts, and the piece is not to be trusted for accuracy. Nevertheless, she does describe Catherine as restless and searching as well as being especially attached to her father. See Swados Papers.

18. Goodfriend, Interview, May 26, 1981.

19. Ibid.

20. See Richard Hofstadter, *The Age of Reform* (New York, Viking, 1955), Chapter IV.

21. Goodfriend, Interview, May 26, 1981.

22. Ibid.

23. Ibid.

24. Ibid.

25. Ibid.

26. Kostelanetz, "Indomitable Skepticism," pp. 167–68.

27. This facet of Hofstadter's life needs more careful attention in light of the literature on grief in children. This is outside the scope of the present study.

28. Goodfriend, Interview, May 26, 1981.

29. Kostelanetz,"Indomitable Skepticism," p. 167.

30. Horton, et al., *Northwestern New York*, p. 364; Goodfriend, Interview, May 26, 1981; Irving Sanes, Personal interview with the author, March 26, 1981.

31. Goodfriend, Interview, May 26, 1981.

32. Ibid.; Horton, *Northwestern New York*, p. 404.

33. Goodfriend, Interview, May 26, 1981.

34. Ibid.

35. *Program, The Thirty-Fifth Annual Commencement of the Fosdick-Masten High School,* June 28, 1933, newspaper clipping, n.d., in Hofstadter Papers; Goodfriend, Interview, May 26, 1981.

36. C. Vann Woodward, "Richard Hofstadter 1916–1970," *New York Review of Books* XV (December 3, 1970) p. 10.

37. High School Play, Hofstadter Papers. For quotations see pp. 3–6.

38. Ibid., pp. 1, 6.

39. Horton, *Northwestern New York*, pp. 314–15; Maxine Seller, "Ethnic Communities and Education in Buffalo, N.Y.: Politics, Power and Group Identity, 1838–1979," Buffalo Community Studies Graduate Group, Occasional Paper #1, 1979, the Archives, State University of New York at Buffalo, p. 38.

40. Adler and Connolly, *Ararat*, pp. 164–218. For quotation see p. 169.

41. Ibid., pp. 187, 188–200, 220, 224; also see Horton et al., *Northwestern New York*, pp. 318, 159, for increases among the Polish population.

42. Adler and Connolly, *Ararat*, pp. 224–25.

43. Alfred Kazin, *A Walker in the City* (New York Harcourt, Brace, 1951) pp. 5–8; Howe, *World*, pp. 69–70.

44. Adler and Connolly, *Ararat*, p. 164.

45. Ibid., pp. 229–38; Ralph Gabriel, *The Course of American Democratic Thought* (New York, The Ronald Press Co., 1940) pp. 160–64.

46. Adler and Connolly, *Ararat*, pp. 230–32.

47. Ibid., pp. 238–42.

48. Ibid., p. 239.

49. Ibid. It is pertinent to point out the contrast between generations in the Swados family, for they give us an insight into three generations rather than two, as noted by Howe. Israel had invested himself in the "progressive" aspects of Jewish education, in the Eastern European sense. His son Aaron, becoming a doctor, appears more conservative, although he must have given of himself unstintingly to his patients. [See Harvey Swados' portrait of "Irv's" father, the doctor, in *Standing Fast* (Garden City, Doubleday, 1970).] Aaron's children were to turn to economic radicalism. Thus, a conservative middle generation interceded between the efforts of the first and the third in this family. It seems apparent that external factors, i.e., the Depression, made the difference.

50. Bette B. Swados, Personal correspondence to the author, May 3, 1981; Goodfriend, Interview, May 26, 1981.

51. The term "free thinking" is Selig Adler's. Personal interview with the author, March 26, 1981. Marvin Chodorow has related that he visited the Swados home many times but never went to the Hofstadter home. Personal interview, May 17, 1981.

52. Felice lived in this home while she was at the University of Buffalo, *Directory of Students and Faculty at the University of Buffalo, 1934–1935*, p. 38.

53. Bette Swados to the author, n.d.; Adler and Connolly, *Ararat*, pp. 215, 380; *Who's Who in World Jewry: A Biographical Dictionary of Outstanding Jews* (New York 1955).

2

The University of Buffalo: Two Sides

At the University of Buffalo, Hofstadter's education took two different and semiindependent forms. On the one hand, he learned from his peers. On the other, he learned from several of the outstanding academic figures who had recently been hired by Chancellor Samuel Capen. The combination of the two formed the background for Hofstadter's later statement that he went into history out of an engagement with contemporary problems. These two sets of influences also served as the basis for his later concern with the tensions between past modes of thought and current realities.

Socially, the University of Buffalo reflected the conservative nature of reigning opinion in the city itself. Student apathy was high, more attention was given to sports and social events than to anything else in the school newspapers, and most students— sons and daughters of working families—looked forward to the added luxury of a white-collar position as a result of their college education. A street-car school, the University of Buffalo had to fight all the centrifugal forces of homes, families, and outside work for students whose lives were not campus oriented. In addition, the school itself was rooted historically in an ethic of practicality. Begun as a medical school in 1846, it had added the School of Pharmacy and School of Dentistry before the turn of the century. Only in 1913 did the School of Arts and Sciences become a reality and begin to give a broader, liberal basis to the practical aspects of the professional schools. Most students then were "quite narrowly concerned with their own careers." The dominance of the business administration curriculum over the minds of the undergraduate population was reflected in an advertisement for school activities made in the student newspaper. The editors said; "Activities give you the kind of practical education that businessmen demand in their employees." The editor of the 1937 yearbook—Hofstadter's original, intended date of graduation—offered another example of the dominant attitude at the University, citing the prime class achievement: "The supreme innovation . . . [in making the Arts School more active] was daily luncheon-dancing in the Norton Hall lobby." In Buffalo these students were still catching up with the innovations of the 1920's.[1]

There was a minority of students, however, who looked beyond its own horizons and met together to carry on long and spirited discussions of political problems in the Iron Room of the Student Union. Irving Kristol has written about his own experiences in a similar group that met at "Alcove #1" in the lunchroom at City College of New York (CCNY). The Buffalo students, like those in New York, represented all shades of political opinion left of center, from the main-line Socialist position to the Socialist Labor Party to splinter groups such as the Lovestoneites. They debated the changes in Communist Party leadership both in the Soviet Union and in the United States. They debated Communist Party activities in Germany. They debated much that occurred in local, national, and international left-wing politics. While others played contract—or auction—bridge, these politically precocious few, arriving at the University of Buffalo from first-generation, Eastern European families, developed a group of talkers and thinkers a good deal like their counterparts in other cities.[2]

One issue of special concern in Buffalo was how active one wished to become in the practical activities of the parties whose positions were so deftly analyzed. Some thought it would be useless actually to join any of these political sects. Nothing could be accomplished by the miniscule efforts of such groups, even if they were correct. To others, it appeared a matter of principle to unite one's energies with one's intellectual convictions and take a stand. Both Socialists and Communists had student organizations that, by 1933, were active on the Buffalo campus. The Student League for Industrial Democracy (SLID) and the National Student League (NSL) competed for the active participation of students, while cooperating in promoting activities.[3]

This small coterie of Left-minded intellectuals was a group of old friends by the time Hofstadter became acquainted with them. Many were two or three years ahead of him and almost ready to leave the University. Felice Swados had entered the University in the fall of 1931 and had been a member of this informal Iron Room group long before Hofstadter appeared on the scene. Rooted in the potential economic radicalism of the East Side William Street Ghetto, Felice had eventually been introduced into University politics by Edward Braunlich, an indefatigable organizer on campus. Felice, herself no introvert, soon aggressively adopted the movement for her own. She and Braunlich often worked as partners in joint organizing efforts.[4]

By the time of Hofstadter's entrance, Felice had made a name for herself at the University. She was a philosophy major and had distinguished herself with several faculty members, among whom were Marvin Farber, head of the Philosophy Department, Richard Boynton, Philosophy Department member, Henry Perry, popular head of the English Department, and Nathaniel Cantor in the Sociology Department. A picture of her as a member of the Glee Club, taken for the yearbook in 1932 at the end of her freshman year, shows Felice as a first alto standing in back, a tall, large woman with hair pulled back severely into a bun. She appears older than eighteen or nineteen and seems almost matronly.[5] She was a powerful woman, an extrovert who made an immediate impact on people when she met them, liked to organize everyone, and knew her own mind. She has even been described as "taking up more space than she deserved." She impressed people by her confidence, by her convictions, by her absolute manner. That she did not identify with other women goes without saying, but she once commented on the fact herself—"I have never liked women." She was often the sole member of her sex to populate the particular Iron Room circles we have been discussing.[6]

Felice took up the secular radicalism that marked Buffalo's

second- and third-generation Jews. When the NSL established
a branch on campus, she quickly became involved. It was as a
committed member of this organization, as an active participant
in the Philosophy Club, and as a woman of high intellectual
standing in the campus community that Hofstadter first knew
her. Because of her striking qualities of mind and presence, some
have said that Felice overshadowed Hofstadter and even dominated him in the early years of their relationship.[7] However that
may be, it was in the shadow of the NSL on the campus of the
University of Buffalo that both were gaining their identities and
learning the lessons of active participation in social and political
affairs.

The NSL had first come into being in December 1931, as a
result of the New York Student League's battles with Depression-
era educational retrenchment and its efforts to impose left-wing
political and social solutions on those problems. Beginning as a
local organization centered at CCNY the group attempted to
define the role of the student for those times. Since the student
had only bread lines instead of jobs to anticipate after school,
they argued, his task now was to "understand the causes for
economic disintegration," to "organize, attend group meetings
to supplement the classroom . . . join with workers, oppose race
discrimination." Formed at a variety of schools in response either
to local dissatisfactions or to the original call for national organization, the NSL came to be represented at schools as different
as the University of California at Los Angeles (UCLA), Reed
College, Ohio State, and the University of Buffalo. Under changing leadership, the movement roughly followed changes in Communist Party agenda. The mood pervading the atmosphere has
been summed up by one former member: "Participants in the
student left of the thirties," he said, "lived life intensely; they
enjoyed the battles; they were part of a brotherhood of like-
minded persons." Said another, those were days of "glory and
high romance. . . . Perhaps it was because we were young, could
believe, and were committed."[8]

The members of the NSL on the campus of the University of
Buffalo were committed individuals. They picked up on the
national call for attention to concrete and immediate issues, but
they did not forget the necessity in their own hometown to ed-

ucate their fellow students in respect to the pressing issues at stake in the world. By the end of 1932, national leaders had redefined revolutionary student action as "the relationship between student and worker organizations. It is dialectical and the issues are one." The future for both students and workers, it appeared, lay in the process of building a new economic structure from the shambles of Capitalism.[9] Many of the activities in Buffalo reflected these ideas. The story of those activities is the story of the growth of influence, visibility, and acceptance of the Left in relation to the general student population. Through the intensive efforts of a very few people, the NSL and its Socialist counterpart, the SLID, brought about a changed outlook at the University of Buffalo by the spring of 1936.

During the first year of Hofstadter's attendance, the NSL helped to sponsor groups or individuals brought into the area to speak about a variety of concerns. Sometimes, the NSL was directly responsible, sometimes only indirectly. Always, its members were active and present. Several radical speakers visited Buffalo between October 1933 and April 1934. On Friday, October 13, for example, Tom Mann, English labor leader, spoke under the auspices of the Buffalo Committee for the U. S. Congress vs. War. Known as a dangerous character, he was able to obtain only a two-week visa to the United States. He spoke against war and Fascism. On October 22, the NSL delegate to the Paris Youth Conference vs. War and Fascism, which had been held during the summer, spoke at Liberty Hall in Buffalo. On November 3, as part of a lecture series at the University, Max Eastman, well-known translator of Trotsky and independent Marxist intellectual, spoke on poetry and the growth of science. On November 10, for Armistice Day—the traditional day of demonstrations for left-wing activists—Dr. Leon Godshall of Dickinson Junior College spoke to the International Relations Club in connection with the anti-war movement; his subject: "The Situation in the Far East."[10]

In the spring of 1934, the activities continued apace. In March, another speaker of note arrived. Reinhold Niebuhr of Union Theological Seminary spoke on the question, "Is Germany an Omen of the Course of Western Civilization?" He spoke at the First Presbyterian Church in conjunction with the well-sup-

ported community peace group in Buffalo and also in conjunction with the second annual Conference on World
Interdependence, sponsored by the joint efforts of the NSL and
the SLID. The same month Walter Relis, a delegate to a student
conference in Cuba during the Christmas holidays, spoke at the
Social Science Club, reporting his visits to the sugar mills and
refineries of Cuba, his glimpses into the poverty of the country,
and his eventual imprisonment there. Relis had also written up
his experiences for the February edition of the *Student Review*,
the national publication of the NSL. In April, the Round Table
Club at the University discussed war, Dr. Olive Lester and Reverend Braunlich taking leading parts, the latter suggesting a
national secretary of peace.[11]

Thus, the NSL was active behind the scenes of several community and campus events during Hofstadter's first year at the
University of Buffalo. But it appears that it was operating against
some intense student antipathy. Its activities were not featured
in the student newspaper, its sponsorship buried at the end of
an announcement. By the fall of 1934, however, a change had
begun to appear. The group began to hold meetings of its own.
Braunlich had joined the editorial staff of the student newspaper. Coverage was more central and more sympathetic.

The first NSL meeting of the fall presented Michael Gold,
renowned editor of the Communist *New Masses*, visiting Buffalo
from New York. To the student reporter covering the event,
Gold presented a "very meaty talk," addressing forty people on
October 18. The reporter had been primed to get in a push for
the NSL, for interjected into the report was the declaration that
the organization was determined to "break through the unsocial
attitude of students." The organization could also boast fifteen
new members present at this meeting. The NSL in Buffalo, it is
clear, was beginning a new year with high hopes and new confidence. On November 1, the group sponsored a political sym-
posium in which members of five parties spoke: Socialist,
Republican, American Workers Party, Democrat, and Communist. The event was followed by "heated discussion," especially in relation to munitions industries and the recent Nye
Committee disclosures. The industrial complexion of Buffalo
had led to an increasing supply of war goods to France and

England prior to World War I, and this subject was one of recurring concern to Buffalonians. It had been discussed at the Conference on World Interdependence. Not only the NSL, then, but other peace-loving and forward-looking Buffalonians were deeply concerned about the issue.[12]

From this point the intensification and increasing confidence of the NSL in Buffalo are evident. At the Cornell Peace Conference in November, Edward Braunlich, Howard Wiedemann, graduate assistant in the Philosophy Department, Ben Kalish, graduate assistant in Sociology, and Felice Swados represented the NSL chapter of the University of Buffalo. Braunlich and Swados both conducted seminars, the former on "Nationalism and War," the latter on "Education and War." All seminars at the Conference adopted resolutions suggested by the national NSL, proposals ranging from a statement against compulsory Reserve Officers' Training Corps (ROTC) programs to condemnations of Presidents Robinson (of CCNY) and Moore (of UCLA) for their restrictions on student activities. The NSL branch at Buffalo was, then, in direct contact with branches in other parts of the country.[13]

In December, two students represented the Left at the University Round Table Club meeting on "Students in Politics." These were Edward Braunlich of the NSL and William Chamberlain, former field organizer for the League for Industrial Democracy (LID). Both came out against the organization of Student Council heads known as the National Student Federation, labeled as largely conservative and business-oriented. Both also spoke enthusiastically of the approaching National Conference on Students in Politics, to be held in Chicago during the Christmas vacation. Heading the delegation from Buffalo, they announced, would be Felice Swados.[14]

It was in the middle of this hectic fall of 1934 that Hofstadter became involved with left-wing politics, met and began to see Felice Swados, and identified himself with the cultural aspects of his nearly forgotten Jewish heritage. He was drawn to the political discussions in the Iron Room as an intellectual, from his own experiences with the debate club in high school, as an idealistic, concerned young man who was not able or willing to identify with the majority of students at the University of Buffalo. As he was finding himself, he appears to have been turning away from the majority of students—with whom it would appear he had identified in high school—and turning *to* some older students who had actively taken their education into their own hands and were making of it this politicized experience. Aware of the world from the proddings of his father, with a mind precocious and eager to grapple with the challenges of current crises, he moved into this group, made of them his intimates, and took on an attitude that was critical and biting at the same time as it was exuberant and intense.[15]

There can be little doubt that Hofstadter would have been present at most if not all of the NSL activities held during the fall of 1934. He may well have been among the fifteen who were new members attending Michael Gold's presentation in October. He must be given some credit, then, under the leadership of Braunlich, for participating in the extension and intensification of NSL activities, no small accomplishment for what must have been a tiny group of students in a "provincial" school in an overwhelmingly conservative community.

During the winter, NSL activities gained momentum. John Strachey had created a mild sensation with his book, *The Coming Struggle for Power* (1933). Reviewed in the *Student Review* as one who could not take his dialectical materialism straight but had to Anglo-Saxonize it, Strachey had been scheduled as one of the University of Buffalo Fenton Foundation lecturers. He spoke on January 25, 1935, arguing that Capitalism need not be abolished but only radically altered to take care of the problems of surplus and distribution. Whether it was due to the inspiration of this talk, the reading of his book, or his articles then appearing in the *New Masses*, Felice later recalled her "Strachey period" in which she and Hofstadter went to Fort Erie, across the Niagara River from Buffalo, to read and discuss the innuendos of Strachey's outlook.[16]

Early in 1935 the NSL and its contributing members and affiliated groups reached a crescendo of activity. On January 12 and 13, they cooperated with other local organizations to sponsor a Niagara Frontier Regional Youth Congress. Again, Braunlich and Chamberlain of the SLID were active in organizing the effort. The two-day Congress featured Nathaniel Cantor, a well-known sociology professor, as speaker on war and round-table discussions on unemployment, "fascism education," industry, and agriculture. "At least a dozen" students were expected to attend this Conference, which was aimed at an audience larger than the University's. Those twelve students undoubtedly came from the NSL and SLID chapters at the University of Buffalo. Here was the perfect opportunity to put into practice the worker-student axis called for by the national NSL. Student friendship with working youth could create an umbrella of the young, a strong coalition ready to plan and work for the future. When interviewed on the subject, Chamberlain affirmed, "I think it is a wise idea for the students of this university to seize this as an opportunity to acquaint themselves with the opinions of less tutored and cloistered youth."[17]

In March the Norton Union sponsored another Peace Conference. This time Braunlich worked with someone new on organization. In addition to lectures, round-tables, and informal forums, a semiformal dance was featured—an allurement to the more conventional Buffalo students. Indeed, other students, from a radius of 150 miles, were expected. Dr. Leon Godshall of Dickinson Junior College, who had appeared in the fall of 1933, was again featured. Now, in 1935, with Hitler's conscription program inaugurated, he spoke on "Peace Machinery and the War Scare in Europe." Stressing the failure in Europe of diplomatic efficiency in general and the World Court and League of Nations in particular, Godshall called for peaceful change.[18]

Three days after this weekend Conference, the NSL held its own meeting, hosting Dr. Wilfred Kerr of the History Department who spoke to the question: "Do Capitalists Make War?" Dr. Kerr's answer was a resounding "no." Instead, he proposed the thesis to his doubtless dubious audience that "sentiment, aided by propaganda . . . and encouraged by patriotism, motivates all wars." Napoleon and Bismarck, he argued, had opposed business interests, the Spanish American and the World War were fought against disapproving business concerns, and Hitler came to power entirely on the basis of popular sentiment. When asked about the economic motivations of munitions makers, he answered: a very small percentage of the Capitalist population. Clearly, Kerr had decided to take the Marxist view to task at this meeting. Perhaps piqued by the theoretical positions taken at the Peace Conference, he had decided to argue down the approach of the NSL. He addressed a "small assembly." Whether the members of that assembly were restrained or heated in their responses is unknown.[19]

Two weeks later the NSL entertained another speaker with views opposed to its own. John Horton of the History Department discussed two classes of historians: those who sought to record a vast array of events and details as a chronicle of what happened, like Von Ranke, and those who sought to impose a pattern or system on events, like Marx. Horton saw the dialectic as Marx's "means to an end," "as a result of his emotional urge upon viewing the economic and social conditions of his time." When the dialectic did not work, a historian should be thrown back on the idea of "gifted rulers," Horton said. To many NSL members, with a strong belief in an active dialectical pattern pervading history, Horton's point of view would have been anathema.[20]

Here, if he had not met him before, Hofstadter was encountering the future historian of Buffalo. Horton, who was in the midst of completing his Harvard Ph.D., was then teaching medieval history and early colonial American history. The approach, views, and assumptions that he showed in his later book on Buffalo, published in 1947, ran against the grain of current radical ideas. There is a story that Hofstadter, uncharacteristically insulted Horton while they were both at the University. This NSL meeting would have presented a likely occasion for a verbal duel between the two. The event would have been just one of many potential conflicts on college campuses in those years, events in which the Marxist dialectic offered a focal point for the tug of war between points of view.[21]

Hofstadter took his first visible and active part in these activities during the April student strike for peace in Buffalo. As the *Student Review* sent out a call for tens of thousands to participate in a "united front" approach and dispatched a paid student organizer to build support for the event, organizations in Buffalo banded together to create a successful meeting. The Norton Union Peace Committee, the NSL, and the SLID put together the demonstration in Buffalo. Important in the success of both longer- and short-term goals was the strike publicity committee. Hofstadter worked on this committee and took responsibility for the preparatory letters sent to all faculty members requesting them to dismiss classes for one hour on the morning of April 12, a technique that was aimed to win them the cooperation, if not the support, of the faculty and that was to be used with great success the next year on a national scale. Interviewed together about the preparations for the affair, Braunlich sounded the ideological note:

The struggle for peace must be carried to its logical conclusion. This conclusion is that the present economic system must be drastically changed. War can be averted only in a totally socialized world where there will be no violent economic rivalries.[22]

Hofstadter was silent. One must conclude that Braunlich spoke for both of them. As ever, he was active, enthusiastic, committed.

This strike, like the Peace Conference in March that preceded it, was not a success. Even though other strikes on campuses around the country proved more successful than ever before, in Buffalo the attempt failed. It featured the militant Reverend Herman Hahan, who had recently been expelled from the Socialist Party for an overly militant stand. The radical note of the strike did not sit well in Buffalo, and the effort turned into a "fiasco." Most students were still under the powerful influences of the business administration curriculum.[23]

For the Philosophy Club things were different. It had periodically featured presentations, by both students and faculty, on philosophies of history. Edward Braunlich had presented a paper. Professor Farber had spoken. Now it was Felice's turn. Dovetailing with a talk on "The Psychology of Revolution" by another Club member, Felice, this April of her senior year, discussed "Facts Concerning Materialism." Her talk was a direct presentation of Marx and Engels. She discussed productive relations as determining the social structure, the cause for revolutions, the relationship between the economic forces and the "ideological superstructure," and state oppression in the class struggle between bourgeoisie and proletariat. Here was the NSL's counterpart to those presentations by Professors Kerr and Horton.

And here Felice felt free to present her ideas in the spirit of true academic freedom. This was an academic milieu within which she could bring her political and intellectual interests together with integration and without camouflage. One is forced to attribute the opportunity to the head of the Philosophy Department, Marvin Farber, who was the Club's advisor. One month later, at the May meeting of the Club, Howard Wiedemann, outgoing president, turned over his responsibilities to two new chairpeople: Richard Hofstadter and William Spring. One month later still, on June 12, 1935, at commencement exercises in the Elmwood Music Hall, Felice graduated at the top of her class, summa cum laude.[24]

Hofstadter's interest in the Philosophy Club indicates his own strong original impulse. His election as co-chairman in his sophomore year also indicates that those around him thought his own proclivities in the field of philosophy were strong. His active participation further indicates his early, close association, outside the classroom, with Professor Marvin Farber.

The spring of 1935, then, was full of activities on many levels. From Youth Congress to Norton Hall Peace Conference and the student strike, from the presentation by John Strachey to arguments with University History Department members, NSL members were involved with the attempt to create at home a new consciousness and ultimately a new social order. Often they were not successful, but their determination does not seem to have flagged. This was, it must be remembered, the militant "third period" of Communist Party policy, in which the membership pushed for "immediate revolution" and adopted the doctrine of "Social Fascism," i.e., no alliances with the political parties immediately on the Right. How closely the Buffalo groups followed these lines is unknown, but that they were affected at least indirectly is certain. Being small, they would have had less opportunity to be fastidious about their alliances, as those at CCNY were. In any case, it seems that Hofstadter, personally, made no effort to limit his personal relationships to those within Communist ranks, although those relationships did become a way of life for others.[25]

We know very little about Hofstadter's first involvement with the NSL except that it appears to have developed in conjunction with several other new aspects of his life: his identification with those Iron Room intellectuals who were so avidly discussing the problems of their world, his developing relationship with Felice, his decision to major in history, and his desire to be linked with Jewish culture, symbolized by his learning some Yiddish. Left-wing politics was thus inextricably intertwined within a social and cultural identification process that Hofstadter was undergoing during his first two years at the University of Buffalo and that came to some visible fruition by the spring of 1935.[26]

The discussions with History Department members that spring were probably not the most pressing concerns occupying the minds of student activists, but in long-range intellectual terms they did serve to bring into focus the issue of causation in history as well as to highlight the question of point of view. A student with a budding interest in both history and philosophy would have found those interests combined by the dialectical underpinning of Marxism. A student who had taken his stand for radical change in the economic and social system of the United States would have found his opponents in Professors Horton and Kerr and their respective views on causation. A student who had begun reading Marx would have been drawn more to Marx's and Engels's vision of the structure of society and change than he would have been to the older, scientific, Anglo-Saxon or Romantic ideas expressed by Horton and Kerr. A student who had seriously involved himself with a woman who gave as her presentation to the Philosophy Club a paper on dialectical materialism would have had a stake in this argument. It is also of import to recall that it was during this academic year in 1934 that Hofstadter first read the Beards's *Rise of American Civilization*.[27] The interpretations in that book would have fallen in line with other views of history and society that Hofstadter was developing at the time.

Hofstadter, as seen from his high school play, was sensitive, subtle, and critical. As will be clearer later, his opinions on political matters were made in the same vein. Many people were drawn to Marxism in the 1930's, as they had been in Europe in the late nineteenth century and as they would be in the 1960's. Not all accepted the ruthless and vulgar form of Marxism that was just then beginning to be portrayed blatantly by Stalin in the Soviet Union. Many did decide that Marxism represented the best possible political solution to what appeared to be the wreckage of Capitalism in the United States. One suspects that even this early, Hofstadter took his Marxism without illusions— as he took much else and as, perhaps, his grandmother had taken his mother's death—matter of factly trading one imperfect solution for another. One suspects that he saw the Communist movement as one concrete politicoeconomic alternative diametrically opposed both to the European form of Fascism as it was appearing full-blown on the Continent and to the native American style that many thought was beginning to appear on the scene by the mid–1930's.

The University supported and encouraged some of these budding tendencies in several different ways. Chancellor Capen, by assuming a determined position in favor of academic freedom at all costs, gave those on the Left the intellectual breathing space to develop and articulate their views. The members of the Philosophy Department helped both Hofstadter and Swados academically and personally. Professor Julius Pratt provided encouragement and stimulation in the area of history and served as a model for the detached and coolly objective scholar which Hofstadter may have rejected in other History Department figures.

The University of Buffalo was academically innovative in the 1930's. The source of this innovation was Chancellor Samuel Capen—"a liberal-minded and level-headed Yankee educator"— known throughout administrative circles as an advocate of complete academic freedom. Capen had begun his tenure as chancellor in 1922, just nine years after the opening of the School of Arts and Sciences. Characterized as an "intellectually exciting man," he worked especially hard to develop the new school. He established a nondiscriminatory hiring policy when women and Jews were systematically limited on faculties. He strengthened departments by hiring strong figures on a national basis. He inaugurated an honors system whereby promising students were ensured a close and intimate relationship with a faculty member in their major departments by work on a tutorial thesis. He cooperated with faculty members while pushing at the same time for innovations. He was able to call forth the trust of the members of the community.[28]

Capen's unswerving policy of total academic freedom at a time when many other administrators around the country were pulling back in fear of student protests had earned him recognition on a national scale. In fact, Chancellor Capen defended as "cheap" his support for radicals in the 1930's when it cost him some funding from the business community. Capen's address at the opening convocation of Richard Hofstadter's first semester at the University exemplifies the spirit of his perspective.

> The University does not waste energy policing people. There is no censorship. The privilege of academic freedom is consistently observed but one must [also] observe the good name of the University....
> At the outset, the University is a complex instrument with all its possibilities for the student to use. He may use it to acquire a better future and financial independence, but if this is his sole purpose at the University, he will miss the best that a University has to offer. If his first purpose is to learn to understand the world with all its complicated jumble of forces and men of which he is a part, if he wishes to cultivate some dominant intellectual interest, he will become a master in his field and a leader among men.[29]

Hofstadter and his group appear to have been following in the spirit set for them by Chancellor Capen.

In 1933 the Philosophy Department at the University of Buffalo consisted of two people only: Marvin Farber and Richard Boynton. Boynton, distinguished in his own right, had moved from a position as minister in a local Unitarian Church to a full-time teaching position at the University. He became the administrative head of the honors system and an affectionately remembered faculty member to ex-students.

It was the head of the Department, however, who made, during his long academic career at both the University of Buffalo and the University of Pennsylvania, a national and international reputation for himself. Farber had studied at Harvard and then with Edmund Husserl in Germany. It was to this German philosopher, the originator of the school of philosophy known as Phenomenology, that Farber devoted his life work. From his first full-blown work, *Phenomenology as Method and as a Philosoph-*

ical Discipline, published in 1928, to the end of his career, Farber concerned himself with explicating Husserl, whose influence he believed too significant to be ignored or forgotten. In 1940 he founded the *Journal of Philosophy and Phenomenological Research*, dedicated to expanding the implications of Husserl's work and to dissemination of the tenets of Phenomenology.[30]

During the years of Hofstadter's attendance at the University, Farber taught classes entitled "Logic and Scientific Thinking," "The History of European Philosophy," "Symbolic Logic," "The Philosophy of Evolution," and "Phenomenology and Related Theories of Knowledge." Only two courses were offered by Professor Boynton. As a major, it is probable that Hofstadter took as many as fifteen hours of philosophy, or five courses in the Department. There is no doubt that Marvin Farber was a primary influence on Hofstadter at this time.[31]

Farber was a powerful influence because of the clarity and nontraditional nature of his ideas. One student summed up his position as that of "a critical materialist, an evolutionist and a historical naturalist." Farber unrelentingly emphasized the external and independent existence of the natural world, the historically bound nature of all philosophies, and the necessity for any philosopher to explicate and become hypothetical about his biases. The idealist tendency in philosophy, he thought, led to "a self-generated web of confusion" that was opposed to empirical clarity.[32]

As a teacher, one student recalled that "[Farber's] knowledge of social and economic history and its causal relations to philosophy often made discussions in his seminar some of the most illuminating I have engaged in." Farber led students to do their own thinking, to question their presuppositions, charging the "fallacy of illicit ignorance," and making philosophy "once again ...a function of social beings in pursuit of concrete historical goals." Another student remembered Farber's tough-minded approach and his scorn for those philosophers who had based their thought on "emotive" positions. Farber's criticisms of these philosophers became almost "gleeful," this student remembered. At the same time, Farber's influence was positive and beneficial.[33]

Phenomenology itself treated the epistemological question, How do we know? It was a reaction against the so-called "formal-logical" method—the use of language and language systems to answer this question. Phenomenology instead would establish an "adequate critique of knowledge from the starting point of radical empiricism." In the cognitive process itself, in Farber's view, the outside world could be "bracketed" so as to reduce experience to the immediate level of sense perception, a process by which the functions of the mind would be reduced to a limited number—perceiving, remembering, imagining, judging, believing—so that the essence of the function would be clear and "could not be changed without changing the *nature* of the things under study." These several functions of the mind made up what Farber called the "preconstituted essences" of human experience. By dealing with them alone, Phenomenology became "the most fundamental science and the absolute ground of all knowledge." Through those functions all knowing took place and all relationships between the person and the outside world were understood.[34]

In a closely related corollary, Phenomenology also held that these essences could never be conceived in any disembodied state. Farber argued that essence should and could be conceived only in its embodied, active, empirical, and contextual state. Nothing really existed for him without a form or in time. The world, then, did not depend on one's perception of it. The human lived enmeshed in physical, physiological, psychological, social, and cultural facts. All philosophers were historically bound, and so was all philosophy.[35]

The implications for Farber's approach to the history of philosophy are clear. He rooted the thought of all philosophers in concrete, sociohistorical conditions and viewed all systems relativistically. He eschewed idealism in all its forms. He was a materialist and perhaps an atheist.[36]

There is no doubt that the influence of Farber and the tenets of Phenomenology helped direct and form Hofstadter's thinking at this crucial stage in his life. Some of the tenets of Phenomenology coincided with those of Marx and Engels. The materialist notions that all thought and all action were rooted in necessity and developed out of biological, social, or cultural concerns and not out of spheres that were transcendent or preexistent were congenial to Hofstadter's larger point of view. In addition, that philosophical materialist position supported the study of history. Indeed, the very decision to go into history enabled Hofstadter to pursue in empirical fashion the "scientific" data that would fill out the Phenomenological hypothesis. Hofstadter's was a dual major at the University of Buffalo. He decided only later to pursue history to the exclusion of philosophy on the basis that he did not have a "natural bent" for the latter.[37]

The third important, long-standing, and perhaps most immediate academic influence on Hofstadter at the University of Buffalo was Julius Pratt. A Chicago Ph.D. with experience teaching at Rutgers, Julius Pratt had been appointed Emanuel Boasberg Professor of History at the University of Buffalo, a newly endowed position, in 1926. His dissertation, *The Expansionists of 1812*, had been published in 1925, and he came to the University as department head and one of Chancellor Capen's strongest appointments. Keeping a hand in teaching lower-division courses, Pratt taught each year the second required history course, "The Survey of U. S. History," mostly to sophomores. He also taught "U. S. from the Civil War to the Present," and in addition, two new courses added in the academic year 1935–36: "New Points of View in American History" and "Territorial Expansion of the U.S." In later years, Hofstadter remembered Pratt's influence with appreciation, calling him "a thoroughly professional historian, which I think I'll never be," and saying, "He always kept bringing me back to the problems of history and the facts of life."[38]

"The Territorial Expansion of the U. S." represented Pratt's primary focus during these years, a focus backed by intensive research. His doctoral thesis on the unsuccessful efforts of expansionists to acquire Canada and East Florida in 1812 had been published by a commercial publisher. It was a clear, well-written, and persuasive discussion of sectionalism as a motivating force in American history. In the 1930's he had been working on another phase of expansionism, the establishment of an island empire in the Pacific in the 1890's. Published in 1936, *The Expansionists of 1898* was a remarkable combination of classical historical detachment and current applicability. In one sense it was the story of the American annexation of Hawaii, but that story tied in so many aspects of American life in the 1890's that the book became—without ever losing its narrative line, close focus, and tight construction—an exposure of small groups of political agitators, of business opinion, of religious lobbyists and the roles they played in bringing about the policy of expansion. Everything in the story of Hawaii—from the interests of sugar planters, to the fomented revolution by a band of local merchants, to the long debate over annexation and the relative advantages and disadvantages of American holdings beyond the shores of the Pacific—culminated in the victory of the ethic of expansionism. But Pratt, a superb narrative historian, made no statement beyond what the story itself told.[39]

While one's professional writings may differ markedly from one's behavior in the classroom, it is not likely that Julius Pratt's did. Nor is it likely that he presented his students with a role model any different from that which he presented in his books—classic historical detachment, thorough research, balance in consideration of all factors likely to be involved, and a sober, nonexaggerated conclusion.[40] It is also quite likely that Pratt's subject and his assumed quasi-scientific role toward the data of history were perceived by young radicals passionately engaged in the issues of their day as fuel for their arguments. Pratt, himself no ideologue, was providing documented, factual ammunition of American imperialism that was appearing daily more appropriate in the mid–1930's. As a figure of authority and expertise, he also would have seemed a useful figure for those agitators setting up forums for discussion on war and international politics.

Hofstadter's undergraduate education was to this point a mix of sociopolitical activities aimed at changing his society and a sampling of the best offerings the Liberal Arts School could give him. He had arrived by the spring of 1935 at an identity quite different from that of the high school senior who had written "The Skeleton in the Closet." He had absorbed much of worth that was offered him at the University of Buffalo, but he had not yet put himself forward to take the responsibility for which his mind qualified him. After the spring of 1935, when many of his friends had left the University, he would be forced himself to take the lead.

NOTES

1. Marvin Chodorow, Personal interview with the author, May 17, 1981; Selig Adler and Tom Connolly, *From Ararat to Suburbia* (Philadelphia, Jewish Publication Society of America, 1960) pp. 181–82, 348; *Buffalo Bee*, (September 22, 1933) p. 1; *Buffalonian* (1937) (n.p.), Courtesy of the Archives, State University of New York at Buffalo.

2. Chodorow, Interview, May 17, 1981; Irving Kristol, "Memoirs of a Trotskyist," *New York Times Magazine* (January 23, 1977) pp. 42–56.

3. Chodorow, Interview, May 17, 1981.

4. Ibid.

5. *Iris* (1932) p. 127, the Archives, SUNYAB.

6. Chodorow, Interview, May 17, 1981; Betty Goodfriend, personal interview with the author, May 27, 1981; for quotation, Alfred Kazin, *Starting Out in the Thirties* (New York, Little, Brown, 1962) p. 99.

7. Chodorow, Interview, May 17, 1981; Alfred Kazin, *New York Jew* (New York, Vintage Books, 1978) p. 25; Alfred Kazin, Personal interview with the author, November 19, 1980.

8. Joseph Clark, "Introduction," *Student Review* (Greenwood Reprint Corp, n.d.); Joseph Lash, "Introduction,"*Student Advocate* (Greenwood Reprint Corp., 1968) p. 1; "Role of the Student," *Student Review* (December 1931) p. 1.

9. Donald Henderson, "Building a Student Movement: On the Second National Student League Convention," *Student Review* (December 1932) p. 5. Henderson goes on to say: "It is precisely because these immediate conditions now facing wider numbers of students, and more fully facing them after they graduate, are integrally connected with the conditions facing the worker, that their interests lie with the revolutionary working class" (p. 6).

10. *Buffalo Bee* (October 13, 1933) p. 1, (October 20, 1933) p. 2, (November 3, 1933) p. 2; (November 10, 1933) pp. 1, 6.

11. Ibid. (March 2, 1934) p. 6; *Buffalo Express* (March 3, 1934) a clipping in Elizabeth Smith Papers, the Archives, State University of New York at Buffalo, *Buffalo Bee*, (March 23, 1934) p. 2, (April 13, 1934) p. 1; Walter Relis, "A Cuban Diary," *Student Review* (February 1934) p. 25, and "The Cuban Student Movement," *Student Review* (April 1935) p. 18.

12. *Buffalo Bee* (October 26, 1934) p. 1; (November 9, 1934) p. 3.

13. Ibid. (November 16, 1934) p. 3.

14. Ibid., (December 19, 1934) p. 3.

15. Hofstadter's sister has testified that he did not meet Felice until

his second year at the University of Buffalo. If he did not meet any of her Iron Room friends until then either, he adopted them very quickly when he did meet them. Goodfriend, Interview, May 27, 1981.

16. *Student Review* (March 1933) p. 22; *Buffalo Bee* (January 18, 1935) p. 1, (February 8, 1935) p. 2; Felice Swados to Harvey Swados, October 17, 1937, Harvey Swados Papers, Courtesy of the Archives of the University of Massachusetts, Amherst, Mass.

17. *Buffalo Bee* (January 11, 1935) p. 1.

18. Ibid. (March 5, 1935) pp. 1, 3, (March 22, 1935) p. 1, (March 29, 1935) p. 3.

19. Ibid. (March 22, 1935) p. 1; (March 29, 1935) p. 3.

20. Ibid. (April 12, 1935) pp. 1, 3.

21. Selig Adler, Personal interview with the author, March 26, 1981.

22. *Buffalo Bee* (April 5, 1935) p. 1; (April 12, 1935) pp. 1, 3, for quotation see p. 3; *Student Review* (April 1935) pp. 3, 13.

23. *Buffalo Bee* (April 5, 1935) p. 1; (November 1, 1935) p. 2.

24. Ibid. (April 5, 1935) p. 3, (May 10, 1935) pp. 1, 3; *Program, The University of Buffalo 89th Annual Commencement,* June 1935, the Archives, State University of New York at Buffalo.

25. See James Wechsler, *The Age of Suspicion* (New York, Random House, 1953), for his own experience of a closed group and vilification after leaving the Party.

26. Richard Kostelanetz, "Richard Hofstadter: Historian's Indomitable Skepticism," in Kostelanetz, ed., *Masterminds* (New York, Macmillan, 1967) p. 168, quotes Hofstadter as saying: "I spent a lot of years acquiring a Jewish identity."

27. Ibid.

28. Selig Adler and Shonnie Finnegan, Interview with Julius Pratt, March 3, 1973, the Archives, State University of New York at Buffalo.

29. *Buffalo Bee*, (September 29, 1933) pp. 1–2.

30. Ibid., (October 26, 1934) p. 4; Adler and Finnegan, Interview with Julius Pratt; Dale Riepe, ed., *Phenomenology and Natural Existence: Essays in Honor of Marvin Farber* (Albany, State University of New York Press, 1973) pp. 1–18.

31. *The University of Buffalo Arts and Sciences Catalogue,* 1927–28—1935–36, Course Listings for 1933–34 academic year.

32. Riepe, *Phenomenology,* p. 5; James E. Hansen, "Marvin Farber as Teacher," in Riepe, *Phenomenology* p. 43.

33. Hansen "Farber as Teacher," pp. 44–45; Chodorow, Interview, May 17, 1981; Roy W. Sellers, "Reflections on the Career of Marvin Farber," in Riepe, *Phenomenology,* p. 24.

34. Marvin Farber, "The Function of Phenomenological Analysis,"

Philosophy and Phenomenological Research I (June 1941): 431–32; D. C. Mathur, "Marvin Farber and the Program of Naturalistic Phenomenology," in Riepe, *Phenomenology*, p. 30. For quotation see the latter (emphasis in original).

35. Mathur, "Naturalistic Phenomenology," pp. 31–32.

36. Phenomenology fits into the development of Western philosophy as distinct from but a definite precursor to Existentialism. The line of influence moves from Husserl to Martin Heidegger to Jean Paul Sartre. See Wilson H. Coates and Hayden V. White, *The Ordeal of Liberal Humanism, II* (New York, McGraw-Hill, 1970) pp. 358–59, 391–92; Roland N. Stromberg, *An Intellectual History of Modern Europe* (New York, Appleton-Century-Crofts, 1966) pp. 402–3.

37. David Hawke, "Interview: Richard Hofstadter," *History*, 3 (September 1960) p. 140. Hofstadter told Hawke that he had originally been more interested in philosophy than in history.

38. Hawke, "Interview," p. 140; Adler and Finnegan, Interview with Julius Pratt; *Univeristy of Buffalo Catalogue*, 1927–28—1935–36.

39. Julius Pratt, *The Expansionists of 1898* (Baltimore, Johns Hopkins University Press, 1936).

40. I am basing these remarks on my own impressions of Professor Pratt, who was, in May 1981, 94 years old and a perfect gentleman—courteous, diplomatic, reserved, amiable, and detached.

3

Out of an Engagement

Between the spring of 1935 and the summer of 1936, Hofstadter matured to make some crucial decisions for his life. He decided to get married and he decided to go to law school. At the same time, he began what would be his lifelong academic career in the field of history. These stepping stones along the path toward full identity were always made against the backdrop of the radical campus activities in which he was becoming more completely engaged.

Hofstadter was seeing a lot of Felice during this time. He had begun to visit the Swados home regularly as others of Felice's friends did. She, on her part, despite the leadership role she played on campus, was made to suffer some indignities at home. Her father, used to old-world ways or nervous about his daughter's interest in a young half-Gentile, subjected her to his own parental anxiety. She later remembered that he made it a point to sit around the living room while she entertained male callers, perhaps snoozing in his chair but present and forbidding nonetheless. At one difficult point, when she and Hofstadter had been out half an hour later than expected, as they reached home, Aaron walked out on the porch to meet them and gave her face a slap. That this did not subdue Felice's buoyant spirit need hardly be emphasized. It probably cemented the feeling between Felice and Hofstadter by providing them a foil against which to ally. In any case, by the spring, perhaps not long after the abortive student strike in April and certainly by May when Hofstadter took over as co-chairman of the Philosophy Club, the couple had made the decision to get married.[1]

But they knew they would have to wait. Sometime that winter or spring Felice had applied for and been awarded a Trustee Fellowship at Smith College for work toward her M.A. in the Philosophy Department. The Fellowship was a real mark of distinction, as only seven existed to be distributed among the various departments for graduate work. For this award she was competing with graduates of Smith as well as graduates of a variety of other leading universities. It was worth $500, $250 of which was to go for tuition. It required that she live in Graduate House, the center of graduate social life, and that she enroll for full-time work. These stipulations allowed Felice to concentrate upon the 24 hours of course work necessary for the Master's degree and to complete all requirements in one year.[2]

By the fall of 1935, Hofstadter was resigned to life without Felice for a while. Perhaps he attended summer school during the summer of 1935, as he hoped to finish a year early. Perhaps plans had not then congealed to that extent. In any case, he found himself with much to do when the University opened in September. Edward Braunlich, former executive secretary of the local chapter of the NSL, had also graduated, leaving the presidency of the NSL to Hofstadter. Also, in comparison with the previous two years, the campus appears to have been activated "overnight." The student newspaper was full of interviews with professors and other community members on the subject of the recent Italian invasion of Ethiopia. It also ran a poll on student opinion about the action and U. S. responsibility in light of it. During the summer, a new philosophy had been initiated among members of the Left. The Popular Front approach was just then taking shape, replacing the "Social Fascist" line and reversing the policies of immediatism and—more gradually—the pacifist, anti-war policy. The accepted positions now were support for the New Deal, coalition politics, and collective security against the menace of Fascism. The local NSL in Buffalo would have been looking for new alliances while still keen to stir up student awareness.[3]

In addition to their attempts to arouse student opinion, the

NSL hosted an important representative of the student movement that fall. Celeste Strack had been a student at the University of Southern California and at UCLA. She had won national awards as a woman debater. In the summer of 1934 she had worked with the longshoremen's strike at San Pedro, California, demonstrating many of those qualities that also characterized Felice: energy, intelligence, extroversion, militancy, ambition, fearlessness. Later, she and four others had been expelled from UCLA for insisting on maintaining "open forums" for student discussions of ROTC programs. In the summer of 1935 she had gone to Cuba with an investigation committee headed by Clifford Odets and there, with others, was arrested and deported. Described as a "cool young woman," she was making a three-month coast-to-coast tour for the NSL to discuss the Ethiopian situation and NSL policies. One of her stops—an engagement for October 18—was at the University of Buffalo.[4]

Strack spoke at a well-publicized NSL meeting and was an immediate success. She discussed the increased likelihood of war, the student congresses against war, the broadened (Popular Front) approach of the student movement, and the possibilities for action among all students. Apathy, she said, was "the most alarming of all tendencies on college campuses." As NSL president Hofstadter made the arrangements for her appearance.[5]

Two weeks later Armistice Day plans began to be publicized at the University of Buffalo. Working as co-chairman of the Committee for Peace Mobilization, Hofstadter and two others represented "the result of [a] stimulus toward concerted student action in the face of Italo-Ethiopian crisis ... conducted by a *united front*." Even the Norton Union Board of Managers, who represented those students who had instituted the luncheon hour dancing, was included in these organizing plans. A dramatic skit was planned by the campus dramatic society, and university figures—the former editor of the school newspaper, a representative of the NSL, and two professors—were to speak.[6]

Hofstadter was working with Frank Miller, editor of the campus humorous publication the *Bison*, on these plans. Possibly in relation to this connection and surely indicative of his increasing involvement, Hofstadter wrote, in the middle of these preparations for November 8, a letter to the student newspaper, taking to task an anonymous writer who had contributed a satirical article on relief recipients to the *Bison*. The letter is a good demonstration of Hofstadter's early prose, smooth and flowing when he was personally engaged with his subject. It read in part:

> Unfortunately, the talent of the writer was badly misdirected. The import of his little piece is that the people on reliefe [*sic*] are primarily a group of parasites whose chief function in life is to extort high luxuries from their benefactor, the government. Now the suggestion that there is parasitism in modern society is not without its merit, but it is obvious that the writer has not sought for it in the right place. It seems quite unnecessary, when there is so much genuine parasitism to be satirized to exaggerate the admitted fact that there are a group of unfortunates who are forced to live at a bare subsistence level because our economis [*sic*] system cannot find sustained employment for them at a decent living wage.
>
> Typical of the cynicism and the political illiteracy of the writer is the remark to the effect that conditions are better in fascist Germany.
>
> Wholesome satire of any group or movement is always welcome. But why pick on the unfortunate? Human suffering is not funny. There are plenty of subjects of real humor. Why not a satire on the social snob? Or the American policeman? Or the American politician? Or the American red-baiter?
>
> Why not a satire on the superficial American college student?[7]

The letter was signed "Dick Hoffsteher." In light of later jokes about the mistranslation of his name, there is little doubt that the writer was Hofstadter. He had just come from a newly acquired knowledge of Mencken and was thus perfectly aware of satirical possibilities on the American scene.[8] Here one sees him deeply involved in the insensitivity of his more conventional peers. Reasonable, to some degree measured, he nevertheless was pitting himself against "political illiteracy" and against the untested biases of his student colleagues.

At the same time as Hofstader was working for a new united front approach to the peace movement, then, he was also continuing the attack on unfeeling, apathetic, and narrow attitudes on the part of his fellow students at the University of Buffalo. The position established his own marginality there and in relation to the dominant ethic of American society as a whole. It would not decrease over the years.

Owing in large part to the extended and inclusive plans, the demonstration of November 8, coordinated with many others around the country, was a huge success. Some 375 students enthusiastically attended the activities. Julius Pratt, undoubtedly invited by Hofstadter, spoke in favor of an embargo against all nations at war, a position he had acknowledged would be increasingly difficult to maintain during a major war, when the demand for even nonmilitary products would soar. When it came to endorsing the Oxford Pledge against all war, the University of Buffalo students were less enthusiastic, however. This was a petition widely supported by the student Left in the period before 1935. Having discussed the possibilities of both aggressive and defensive wars, the students voted 335 to 40 against the pledge. Hofstadter made a plea for the pledge on the basis that, since it was unlikely the United States would be invaded, any war it might wage would of necessity become a trade (or imperialist) war. His argument fell on deaf ears at the University. It was one of the few times, however, that he had felt moved to make a public pronouncement to his peers.[9]

Some students on campus, influential on the school newspaper, did not agree with the idea of holding student strikes at all. Two editorials preceding the November demonstration had noted the negative reaction to the strike during the previous spring and had applauded the inclusion of a more varied student representation on the planning committee and the choice of campus figures to speak at the demonstration. A third statement, in article form, argued that peace demonstrations were in themselves "war-like"—i.e., hostile—maneuvers, that the "frankly Communistic" student organizations fomented them in order to create a platform and heighten agitation, and that this was "not an American way of bringing this about, especially when their [sic] is no danger of war." A fourth article pushed this position further, advocating education and other "non-excitable alternatives" to strikes.[10]

These articles were answered by two long letters from Benjamin Kalish and Howard Studd, representatives of the political Left. They took issue with the editors, one of whom had also written the articles in question. Kalish and Studd argued that war was indeed imminent and that the editors should correct their inconsistent "social policy." That inconsistency had come, the writers believed, from the change from an initially lukewarm endorsement of the demonstration to an increasingly critical attitude toward it. In view of the threat of war, and in view of the nationally aroused student opinion, Kalish and Studd challenged the editors to a clarification and a reply.[11]

The editors did reply, assigning items labeled as "social" concerns a place in the "Soap Box"—a column devoted more or less to gossip. They added, "We would like to know to just what particular social policy the noted writers are trying to convert us." The editors' conception of their role did not include the development of a "consistent social policy." And they were wary of what their radical opponents were attempting to carry out. As business administration majors who also happened to have become editors of the school newspaper, they undoubtedly considered themselves practical men of affairs rather than philosophers or intellectuals. Thinking through a "consistent social policy" was not within the confines of their outlook; they had inherited the uncontested social policy of laissez-faire Capitalism. Such theoretical speculation was much more characteristic of the thinking of Kalish as a graduate assistant in the Sociology Department.[12]

The issue of the imminence of war ultimately also brought the NSL into this exchange. A letter outlining what it stood for—lower student fees at the University, pacifism, anti-Fascism—as well as a denial of its Communist foundations appeared at the conclusion to the exchange between the editors and Kalish and Studd. It was signed by "R. Volk, etc." for the NSL. It stressed that "everyone who is at all interested in these issues is interested in the NSL and the ASU [the American Student Union—soon to be known as the merger between the NSL and the SLID]." The exchange, the accusations, and the denials bring out some significant perspectives.[13]

In the growing polemic, two points of view are clear. From one, that of the editors, it appeared that the status quo was being threatened by a group of "trouble-makers" deliberately fabricating issues in order to gain attention and ultimately control of the sources of power. To these people, the basic American economic system seemed sound. They were looking forward to taking their own places within it and therefore did not wish to see it challenged. Perhaps, in those Depression years, they were also beset by a nagging subliminal fear that in some fundamental sense they were wrong, but they had not thought far enough about it to come up with any "consistent social policy" except for that attitude castigated by Hofstadter in his letter to the newspaper.

From another point of view, the Depression proved that the American economic system was indeed fundamentally unsound. This was a widespread opinion in most cultural centers by the mid–1930's. These people hoped for an alternative system, Socialistic in nature, whereby government control and planning and worker participation and eventual control in those processes would alleviate future suffering and future aggression based on the expansion of business enterprise.

The term "Communist" held a loaded significance, of course. For the first group it meant the threat of an external agent and a foreign system different from that that most Americans had accepted as natural. Those thoughts were frightening in their implications. The same term for the second point of view meant a series of tactics proposed to facilitate the inauguration of a new social order in which justice and equality would exist at a higher level than they did currently. From this point of view, the negative implications of the first definition had to be manipulated in order to make people understand the benefits and desirability of the proposed new order. From this point of view, also, it hardly mattered whether members of the NSL were Communists or not. What did matter was the commitment to social change among its members. The anti-war movement, as a fundamental criticism of the government/industry partnership, which appeared to have led to war in the past, was a central part of that commitment. Despite the clash between these perspectives, it is significant that Hofstadter, as president of the NSL, did not sign the official publication of the organization denying its Communist orientation. By not doing so, he was maintaining his personal detachment while at the same time allowing other voices in the organization to represent it as they saw fit.

In the spring of 1936 Hofstadter wrote his tutorial thesis. As has been pointed out, Chancellor Capen had introduced the tutorial system at the University of Buffalo. At first an honors system only, by 1931 it had become a true tutorial system for everyone. This was presumably due to the size of liberal arts enrollment at the time. Most students, as preprofessional or business administration majors, were not liberal arts majors, and fewer still were likely to become liberal arts majors in these years of economic decline. In any case, the system appears to have been designed for a two-year period, in which, at least in the field of history, juniors were asked to read and respond to seminal works in the field and seniors were enabled to complete independent research projects.[14]

It is not clear just how long Hofstadter spent on his thesis. He may have worked on it during the fall of 1935 as well as during the spring of 1936. He also may have traveled to New York for some of the materials he used. He went once, during March, to New York to see Felice. Most likely he spent some time pursuing his research then. The finished project remains *in toto*, fortunately for the field of historiography.[15]

This project, dated May 1936, shows the impact of both aspects of Hofstadter's education at the University of Buffalo, that of his peers and that of his elders. As an investigation of the evidence for Charles and Mary Beard's reinterpretation of the Civil War, in *The Rise of American Civilization*, it was entitled "The Tariff and Homestead Issues in the Republican Campaign of 1860" and was a response to his elders. In the logic of its analysis, in its choices of evidence, in its urgent underlying tone, it was a reflection of his active engagement in the contemporary world around him and a response to what he had learned from his peers. Here we see some of the marks of Hofstadter's later histories: economic causation, the connection between deep-seated states of mind and their expressions in political issues, a deft handling of resources.

In *The Rise of American Civilization*, the Beards had contended that the Civil War could best be known as the "Second American Revolution"—a "social cataclysm in which the capitalists, laborers, and farmers of the North and West drove from power in the national government the planting aristocracy of the South." The causes for this profound social upheaval were to be found in the economic interests of the population rather than in sectional differences of a geographical or topographical character. The humanitarian and anti-slavery sentiments of some portions of the population never caught fire enough to make them the major issue at stake in the conflict. Unfortunately, according to Hofstadter, the Beards' thesis was put forth only in "a popularly written general history," was "not a thoroughly documented exposition," and therefore could not be accepted as "definitive proof" by the historian. So, Hofstadter set up his premise and possible conclusion:

> If the economic causes listed by the Beards are held to have been effective in the way in which they are described in *The Rise of American Civilization*, it follows that these issues were *consciously fought for*, by the participants in this revolution. Whether or not they were is the crucial question in the evaluation of the details of the Beardian interpretation.[16]

What followed the introduction was a survey of the homestead and tariff issues as they appeared in the public annals in the 1840's and 1850's. Hofstadter's discussion of the tariff was later rewritten and published as a "note" in the *American Historical Review* for October 1938, his first scholarly publication. That the tutorial thesis as a whole was a remarkably able piece of historical research for an undergraduate has been attested to by Julius Pratt.[17] The purpose here is not to assess the thesis for its ultimate value on homestead or tariff, however, but to draw from it what it reveals of Hofstadter's mind in 1936.

In the 32–page first section, Hofstadter followed the Congressional debate over the homestead issue from its inception in the 1840's to the final successful passage of the Homestead Act in 1862, from the early policy of "pre-emption" to the outright policy of free land to homesteaders. Under the 1841 Distribution Pre-emption Act, preference had been given, among buyers of public land, to those who would till and reside on that land. The policy had been undercut by speculators, and thus agitation for homestead arose. Until 1852 alternative measures for parceling out land obstructed even a vote on the issue in Congress. These alternatives included "graduation"—decreasing costs of land depending upon length of time in the public market, bounty proposals—payment for military service in land, and railway grants.

Despite opposition, especially from Southern Democrats, the issue—at first "regarded by more influential people as a radical notion of the lunatic fringe"—grew in popularity and influence. The chief reason for this growth, as it emerged in Hofstadter's paper, was the combination of numbers, voice, and party alignment of the Northwestern immigrants.[18]

Although the Southern oligarchy was united against the homestead issue, which in its mind threatened to populate the territories with small farms inimical to the extension of slavery, the Southwest, at least in the early 1850's, contained its share of German immigrants. The northern tier of Southern states could also boast its share of small farmers. These elements formed the source of the divided position of the South on homestead, and such division accounted for the early favorable vote of the South on the 1852 bill, so Hofstadter recounted.[19]

New—mostly German—immigrants were greeted with a good deal of nativist animosity. Although it was not Hofstadter's intent to survey the issue of nativism, that hostility did color the debates on the homestead issue and Hofstadter liberally illustrated the fact. From the *Charleston* (S.C.) *Mercury*, he found the following expression:

The hundreds of thousands of foreigners ... reach New York by the shipload, and to the Southerner, one of the strange sights is a train of 30 to 60 cars hauled by one or two locomotives, solely freighted with Germans and their plunder, *in transitu* for the extreme Northwest. We have seen trains with a thousand foreigners aboard.... It is true that this immense influx of Germans and others have [*sic*] populated the great Northwest, and with their agrarian notions and sound ignorance of the genius of our institutions, have vitiated and demoralized the principles of the Democratic party.... Their position on Squatter Sovereignty belie [*sic*] all their professions upon the constitutional rights of the South in the territories concerning slavery, and their advocacy of the Homestead Bill [shows] their acquiescence to a principle that only makes the Abolition forces stronger and the growth of any heresy sanctioned by American demagogues.... We make bold to say that it [the Homestead Bill] is the most dangerous abolition bill which has ever indirectly been pressed in Congress.... With us land is cheap, and the disposition for a planter to take his negroes and go to a distance, where

the Government may own land, is ranked among the novelties of Southern societies.[20]

Hofstadter also noted the similar arguments presented by Senator Wigfall of Texas in Congress:

The only effect of the bill is to fill the country with paupers. We are
under no obligation to provide for your paupers. We are under no
obligation to provide for the paupers of Europe. . . . I believe the effect
of this thing will be to fill up that Territory with a prejudiced, sectional,
fanatical population that will send member after member to this body
to agitate, agitate, agitate, and keep up the sectional question until you
put the feather upon the camel's back. . . . The whole object of this thing
is sectional. It is to free-soil the Territory.[21]

Hofstadter made no comment on these two statements except
to label the latter an "outburst.[22] He had been well trained to
let the evidence speak for itself.

The increasing Southern intransigency against the bill was
matched by the equally increasing fraternal feelings between the
West and East. The alignment had become so clear by February
1859 that Homestead and Cuba were pitted against one another,
and Senator Wade could arise "in considerable heat" to declare
that "the question was one of giving 'niggers to the niggerless
[acquisition of Cuba was desired for its large population of Blacks]
or land to the landless'." Despite the increasing expression of
antagonism between the proponents of these issues, the Homestead Bill was defeated again in 1860, as it had been in 1852 and
1854. This time, however, by Presidential veto.[23]

The Northwestern immigrant vote made the difference. Having gained ground as a state issue in the West in the late 1850's
and increased in strength by the Panic of 1857, the immigrant
role became a decisive national issue for the election of 1860. It
became "inevitable" for Hofstadter "that the Republicans should
have incorporated the Homestead Bill in their platform of
1860. To elect their president, they had to carry the North West
and to do that they had to win the vote of the foreign element."[24]
"Inevitable" or not, Republicans achieved their goal by adopting
the "Dutch" planks (#13 and #14) as put forward by a caucus
of Germans held just before the Republican Convention at Chi-

cago. These planks denounced nativism and espoused the homestead principle as then embodied in a House bill. In response,
the Northwestern immigrants switched party allegiance en masse
and effectively divided the Democratic Party.

In the campaign and the struggle to gain the immigrant vote,
slaveholding and homestead interests were polarized by Republican "propaganda." Carl Shurz worked especially effectively to
create high feelings in the farmers of the Northwest. The effort
worked for the Republicans. But, Hofstadter was careful to clarify, the fact that the homestead issue was antithetical to slavery
did not make the Northwesterners lovers of Black people. In
fact, there was very real dislike of them in the Northwest. Several
states passed laws barring their admittance, and Lincoln was
obliged to tone down his own anti-slavery sentiments for the
benefit of the region.[25]

In conclusion, Hofstadter spelled out again the links he saw
between the issues:

We have seen the necessity of the votes of the foreignborn to the election
of Lincoln in 1860, and the tremendous special appeal which the Republican propagandists made to that vote; we have shown the immense
importance of the homestead measure to this element and have given
some indication of the extent to which it featured in Republican campaign literature. A comparative estimate of the importance of the slavery issue suggests that the differences between the stand of Lincoln and
Douglass on this issue alone cannot account for Lincoln's victory. These
facts lead to the tentative conclusion that the homestead issue was decisive in the campaign of 1860, a necessary even though not sufficient
cause of Lincoln's election. There can be no doubt that this issue was
a factor of the greatest significance in the unity between the East and
the Northwest that lay at the basis of the Republican party and made
possible a victory over the slave power.[26]

In other words, not the slavery issue but the "intimately connected" issue of homestead affected the crucial vote of the Northwest immigrant, divided and lethally weakened the Democrats
and the slaveholders which that Party continued to represent,
swept Republicans into power, and hastened the military phase
of the "Second American Revolution."[27] Homestead was the crucial link in a theoretical chain of interrelating interests and issues,

and the Beards' contention had been borne out. Although Hofstadter let his evidence speak for itself, what he accomplished here was the footwork for the Beards' interpretation—the accumulation of evidence and the analysis of voting records that gave weight to the bare assertion of homestead as the economic cause for voting patterns in 1860.

The second half of the tutorial thesis considered the tariff as a campaign issue in the 1860 election in light of tariff history since 1832. According to the evidence, Hofstadter asserted, a study of the two industries most interested in tariff reduction—wool growing and mining—indicated that the tariff caused the reigning interests in Pennsylvania and certain areas of the West to support the Republican platform in 1860. And although other Capitalist and financial interests in the East were content with the tariff of 1857, the manufacturing interests in Pennsylvania dominated votes in that state and that state was a primary key to success for the Republican Party. Wool growers in the West, Ohio and Indiana, whose protection had been cut by a 23 percent decrease in duties on raw wool in 1857, strongly favored the new protection offered by the higher tariff proposed by the 1860 Republican platform.[28]

Hofstadter's evidence, then, suggested support for the Beardian thesis in a ratio of three to one. German immigrants, Pennsylvania mining interests, and Western sheepherders reacted to their own economic concerns and voted in relation to them in the election of 1860. Other Northern Capitalists and financial powers in the Northeast reacted less directly. With this group, the sociopolitical problem (although Hofstadter did not state it as such) of Lincoln's effect on the stability of the nation took precedence over the simpler, more clear-cut economic interest of other groups. The Eastern magnates, Hofstadter's conclusions imply, wanted union more than they wanted increased protection. They turned to the Fusionist Party and against Lincoln because the larger, political issue superseded and incorporated their purely economic interests.[29]

The tutorial thesis reflects several aspects of Hofstadter's undergraduate career. First, Hofstadter was Julius Pratt's student. In choice of subject matter and partially in organization, Hofstadter showed here the effect of Pratt's teachings. Although following a roughly chronological outline for the development of both homestead and tariff issues, he also moved consecutively through the attitudes of those in different sections of the country. Pratt had approached his material in *The Expansionists of 1812* in the same way. Hofstadter was naturally not nearly so orderly, consistent, or detached as the mature Pratt, but the influence is apparent.

Julius Pratt was a model of scholarly detachment. In language and phraseology—despite some overblown legalisms—Hofstadter here followed suit. He meticulously developed his presentation, even though he had relied on secondary material and remained very close to his sources. He organized his evidence but let it speak for itself. He avoided speculation. The correct approach to a historical research paper was evidently to keep oneself out of the story, except for some interpolation in the introduction.

He was also rigorously logical, and the power of his mind is quite evident even this early. Examples exist in such constructions as "If the economic causes are held to have been effective ... it follows that ... "; his last paragraph on the homestead issue quoted above in which he emphasized homestead as the "necessary" but not "sufficient" cause; and questions such as "the significance of the tariff issue to the capitalists of the North.... Were they strongly opposed to this reductive measure? Was there a heated partisan debate? If these questions can be answered in the affirmative, then we may perhaps assign great importance to this issue as a factor in the support for the Republicans in 1860."[30] He had repeatedly imposed the "if ... then" formulation on his materials. In fact, rarely again in Hofstadter's writings does one sense such a desire to tie up cause and effect or to link so explicitly various related factors.

Indeed, the thinking here, was *deductive*. Hofstadter had established that the issues of homestead and tariff were "consciously fought for" by several identifiable groups. Thus, by his structuring premise, the issues were "effective." The conclusion thus followed *necessarily* from the premise and "proved" it decisively. The fallacies of this kind of thinking—its rigidity and its circularity—are not the point here. What is important is that Hofstadter, in testing the thesis, was attempting to limit himself to the impact of economic issues on voting behavior. He did not allow himself directly to consider other possible types of causation. This is partially because he never defined—tightly or at all—what was economic and what was not. Therefore, he did not end, as he might have, by considering the potential influence of other types of concerns. Miners and sheepherders voted Republican because their occupational interests were directly affected. Eastern financiers voted otherwise because their purely economic interests were affected adversely by the Republican position. For Hofstadter at this point economic interests pervaded the political arena. And, as he came to say much later, the Beards had set the parameters of historical inquiry "even for those who [were] least persuaded."[31]

More apparent than the influence of the Beards on Hofstadter's choice of evidence is the fact that Hofstadter here was making a serious effort to apply some of the Beards' own methods in *The Rise of American Civilization* to his undocumented thesis. In *The Economic Interpretation of the Constitution* and in *The Economic Basis of Jeffersonian Democracy*, Charles Beard had used early forms of statistical analysis to establish the relationship between financial assets and voting patterns among the members of the Constitutional Convention and the later ratifying conventions. He had used materials from newly opened Treasury Department documents.[32] Hofstadter, also, even this early, was attempting to uncover the link between economic issue and political attitude, to look at "economic causes as they affected the minds of people at the North."[33] Moreover—and unlike Beard—he was attempting to do so not for the articulate elite, but for the nameless masses whose interests were truly at stake. So, although he was clearly a Beardian in the historical sense at age nineteen, he also may be categorized on the basis of this thesis, as a critic—to the left—of Beard in a historiographical sense.

Although the tutorial thesis was a tightly constricted, logical, even "dry" presentation of evidence, which did not stray from the central question, and although Hofstadter *wished* to limit himself to economic factors, there is an emotional color with a social basis that haunts the reader on reflection. Hofstadter spent fully four pages on the quotations from the *Charleston Mercury* and Senator Wigfall noted above. These constituted the center of his findings on the Southern point of view. In addition, of his 32 pages total on the homestead issue, he spent the last eleven presenting the changing attitudes of the Northwest immigrants. So whether presenting them directly or indirectly, he spent almost half his time on German or Scandinavian immigrants or ideas about them. Such a focus appears not to have been his original intention, for he began by chronicling the Congressional battles over the issue, not by noting local opinions. The immigrant community, then, by this account, played a central role in the drama of the election of 1860.

The image of this community that evolved from the evidence Hofstadter produced was that of an originally uninvolved and independent group of people, neutral in the great concerns over slavery *per se*,—concerns that were tearing apart Abolitionists and Southern oligarchs, a community finding itself embroiled in the purely American conflict through its own need for land ownership and economic independence. Choice of evidence enabled Hofstadter to give this ostensibly cold and logical presentation a hidden emotional tone. Who could have sympathy for Senator Wigfall's "outburst"? Who could have sympathy with the attitude expressed by the *Charleston Mercury* with its sneering picture of packed cars full of "little people" being transported far distances, a kind of mobility, according to the *Mercury*, which would be "one of the novelties of Southern society"—an image that almost predicts the packed cars of Nazis carrying off Jews to their foreordained fate, an image that could easily also have referred to Jews and other immigrants being transported from New York to the distant hinterland—even Buffalo itself—an image that did directly refer to the very same Germans arriving with Richard Hofstadter's grandfather? One must remember that this was 1936 and the exodus from Germany had begun.

One must also remember that it was Communist Party policy in the middle 1930's to open its arms to the "Negro question." Hofstadter did not look at Black opinion directly here—although Carter Woodson's *The Negro in Our History* appears in his bibliography—but the question of slavery and its demise was necessarily central to his subject. If the Civil War could be labeled a Second American Revolution, or a social upheaval whereby agrarian—and by association feudalistic—forces were overthrown for industrial, then the Third Revolution, which was coming soon, would gather to it as beneficiaries those especially who had benefited from neither previous revolution.[34] Hofstadter was a member of the Young Communist League (YCL). He had read his Marx and his Lenin. He had taken his stand, in the present, for radical social change. As constricted, as logical, as close to his evidence as he stayed in this senior tutorial thesis, his passionate response to his own political surroundings was made known. Indirect as his expression of these feelings was, his choices of evidence are telling. The outburst of Wigfall and the sneers of the *Charleston Mercury* provided the negative keys to Hofstadter's own sympathies. Those negative keys indicated a complicated set of circumstances in the past that reflected inequity, prejudice, and contempt, on the one hand, and simplicity, hardihood, and persevering independence, on the other. Retardative elements for history emerged from the first: from the Southern oligarchy, from the "ruling classes." Propelling elements for history emerged from the immigrant classes in the Northwest. It was the switch from Democratic to Republican allegiance among these immigrants that caused the revolution and the key to the success of the Republican Party in 1860. Similar sorts of social clashes with retardative and propelling elements would also arise in Hofstadter's more mature work.

The Northwest German immigrants made their switch in Party allegiance because, although originally "disposed to enter the Democratic party ... *their presence in that party was a living contradiction.*"[35] This phrase, striking in any case, was not simply a fortuitous choice of words or an offhand observation for Hofstadter. It was a phrase, chosen in the context of the times, that revealed Hofstadter's acquaintance with the Hegelian theory behind Marx.

While many in the 1930's picked up and bandied about the jargon of the political Left, a few of the more dedicated souls of the period made the theory an object of intensive and serious study. Along with Max Eastman and Sidney Hook, Felice was one of these. It is of utmost interest to those studying Hofstadter's early years to learn that just at the point when Hofstadter was writing his tutorial thesis, Felice also was writing her M.A. thesis at Smith. The title for her project: "Two Types of Ma-

terialism. A Comparison of the Mechanical Materialism of Holbach and the Dialectical Materialism of Marx and Engels." The
thesis was an attempt to summarize the history of the theory of
materialism and to pinpoint the nature of the contributions to
it made by Marx and Engels.[36]

Along the way Felice was necessarily forced into summarizing
the contributions of Hegel. These contributions, by her account,
consisted of the concepts of contradiction, opposition, the notion
that nothing is ever lost, the idea of the "negation of the negation," and the notion of transformation of quantity into quality—
all part of Hegel's interpretation of the principle of movement,
or the dialectic.[37]

"Nothing is ever lost" in the Hegelian dialectic, Felice maintained, because each synthesis incorporates the original opposing
tendencies in a higher level. The "negation of the negation" is
another way to speak of the original synthesis, postulated by
Hegel, as being split into positive and negative elements, and
then the negative element split again in order to form once more
with its opposite. Felice took example from Engel's *Anti-Duhring*
to indicate what this meant. In botany, the seed negates itself,
or loses its essence by the process of ripening. In mathematics,
$-a \times -a = a^2$ and $+a \times +a = a^2$. Thus, two roots of a^2
exist, a positive and a negative form. By negating the negative
form, one arrives again at the product.[38]

The abstract elements of Hegel's dialectic illuminate Hofstadter's use of the term "living contradiction," but do not say all.
Marx and Engels stood Hegel on his head, postulating that the
origin of consciousness in humankind lay in human "activity in
the social realm." Furthermore, they said, consciousness was a
product of activity, or "work", and the two interrelated in the
same dialectical fashion as Hegel had postulated in the abstract.[39]

This, then, was the definition of "living contradiction" as Hofstadter used the phrase to describe the German immigrants'
situation in the United States of 1860. Their activities—their
work in the new American environment—outpaced their self-
awareness. The living contradiction existed in the tension, which
marks all of life at any stage according to Marx, between the
current level of economic development (and the social relationships connected to it) and the level of consciousness with which

the participants in that economy viewed their situation. The philosophical underpinnings of Hofstadter's earliest historical work make much sense in the context, both personal and political, of his life situation.

One other point is significant. For Felice, the philosophical strength of Marx's and Engels's materialism lay in their assumption of the *collective* nature of consciousness. It was important for her to point out that the definition of that collective consciousness was taken one step farther by Engels, who identified the essentially ironic aspect of history. Discussing consciousness, he defined it as "passion" or "deliberation" and said that it marked the difference between the natural and human realms. But history, he added, was made up of a lot of crisscrossing purposes and so *what was intended was not always what resulted.*[40] Felice was thus pointing out the ironic consequences of the Marxian view of history and society, a view that Hofstadter retained at the base of his work throughout his life.

Here, then, by the end of his three-year undergraduate career at the University of Buffalo was a newly emerged young man, different from the sixteen-year-old who had written "The Skeleton in the Closet" for the benefit of his high school peers. Not a trace of the natural humor showed through in Hofstadter's tutorial thesis. What did appear was the logicality of the mentally overactive Jeeves. The logicality is now Hofstadter's own and is applied to historical evidence to make it bear on the topic of economic causation. But behind the detachment, control, and logicality of the semiprofessional historian's stance lurked a passionate involvement with his subject and with its meaning for the present. The application of both these powers, logic and passionate concern, in conjunction with the influences and stimuli of his life at the University of Buffalo brought Hofstadter to such observations as he made of the Germans as a "living contradiction" in the Democratic Party.

By the spring and summer of 1936, Hofstadter and Felice were working in their respective and complementary fields, immensely engaged in the political issues of their day and eagerly planning to be married. It is not to be doubted that their relationship was extremely intense, that their mutual admiration and influence were very high, and that they looked on the world as their "oyster." That this was as much due to the opposition of their parents as to anything else is quite likely. In March Felice wrote, referring to Hofstadter, that she knew him "better than I know myself,"[41] as defense in some problems she was having with her family over her future plans. It is not, therefore, insignificant in any way that when Hofstadter and Felice did leave Buffalo in the fall of 1936 to go to New York to be married, it was neither from the Hofstadter home nor from the Swados home that they departed but from the home of Marvin Farber, their friend and personal mentor.[42]

NOTES

1. Felice Swados to Harvey Swados, September 12, 1944, Harvey Swados Papers, Courtesy of the Archives of the University of Massachusetts, Amherst, Mass.; Bette Swados to the author, May 3, 1981.

2. *Bulletin of Smith College*, Catalogue Issue, 1935–36, issued at Smith College, Northampton, Mass., Series 30, #3, January 1936, pp. 157–59, 184–87, 277.

3. *Buffalo Bee*, (October 11, 1935) pp. 1, 4. The opening convocation that year was given by a *Buffalo Evening News* columnist reporting on the Ethiopian crisis. Shortly thereafter a professor recently returned reported on "armed fascistsi" everywhere in Italy. The student poll appeared and reappeared in the student newspaper. Late in October Julius Pratt was interviewed on the problem. It is somewhat surprising with all this new activity on the part of the editorial staff that they should have become embroiled in a polemical battle with the student Left later. The disagreement may have been caused by a sudden turnover in editorship, giving more leeway to a new managing editor who wrote the articles in question. *Buffalo Bee*, (October 25, 1935) p. 1; (November 8, 1935) p. 2.

4. "California's Higher Learning," *Student Review* (November 1934) p. 12, (December 1934) p. 3, "Expulsions at California" (March 1935) p. 17, "Strack on Tour" (October 1935) p. 19; *Student Advocate* (December 1936) p. 29; Irving Howe and Lewis Coser, *The American Communist Party* (Boston, Beacon Press, 1957) p. 358.

5. *Buffalo Bee* (October 18, 1935) p. 1, (October 25, 1935) pp. 1, 4.

6. Ibid. (November 1, 1935) pp. 1, 4 (emphasis added).

7. Ibid., p. 2.

8. Hofstadter later testified: "I soaked up everything of Mencken's when I was an undergraduate at the University of Buffalo." David

Hawke, "Interview: Richard Hofstadter," *History* 3 (September 1960) p. 140.

9. *Buffalo Bee* (November 15, 1935) pp. 1, 4.

10. Ibid., editorials (November 1, 1935) p. 2; "Strike Is Wrong Method of Demanding Peace" (November 8, 1935) p. 2; "Futility of Peace Displays Declared" (November 15, 1935) pp. 1, 4.

11. Ibid., (November 27, 1935) p. 1, (December 6, 1935) p. 2.

12. Ibid., (December 6, 1935) p. 2.

13. Ibid., (December 6, 1935) p. 4.

14. Selig Adler and Shonnie Finnegan, Interview with Julius Pratt; Julius Pratt, Personal interview with the author, May 27, 1981. In this interview, Professor Pratt referred to his "junior tutorial" during the period in question. In this tutorial the tutees read H. G. Wells's *Outline of History* and were expected to respond to it. Professor Pratt did not remember exactly to which year this assignment referred.

15. Hofstadter drops out of view in the spring of 1936. Until December 1935 his name appeared regularly in the *Buffalo Bee*. But a letter to Marvin Chodorow dated February 1936 refers to Hofstadter's address as 134 Montague St., New York. Also a letter from Felice Swados to her brother in March 1936 refers to a trip from Smith to New York City where she saw Hofstadter. Richard Hofstadter to Marvin Chodorow, February 9, 1936, Swados Papers; Felice Swados to Harvey Swados, March 5, 1936, Swados Papers. It is possible that Hofstadter's letter is misdated as to year; it is not possible that Felice's is misdated.

16. Charles A. and Mary R. Beard, *The Rise of American Civilization, II: The Industrial Era*, (New York Macmillan, 1930) pp. 52–54. For quotation see p. 54. Richard Hofstadter, "The Tariff and Homestead Issues in the Republican Campaign of 1860" (Tutorial Thesis, University of Buffalo, May 1936) Hofstadter Papers, p. iii (emphasis in original).

17. Pratt, Interview, May 27, 1981.

18. Hofstadter, "Tariff and Homestead," pp. 1–7. For quotation see p. 6.

19. Ibid., pp. 7–10.

20. Ibid., pp. 15–16.

21. Ibid., p. 17.

22. Ibid., p. 18.

23. Ibid., pp. 18–20. For quotation see p. 20.

24. Ibid., p. 24.

25. Ibid., pp. 24–31.

26. Ibid., pp. 31–32.

27. For the military aspect as a phase of the "Second American Revolution," see the Beards' *Rise*, p. 53.

28. Hofstader, "Tariff and Homestead," pp. 35–40. For quotation see p. 38.

29. Ibid., pp. 41–47, 49–53.

30. Ibid., pp. iii, 31–32, 38.

31. Hawke, "Interview,"p. 141.

32. Charles Beard, *An Economic Interpretation of the Constitution* (1913; repr. New York, Macmillan 1961) Chapters VIII and IX, "The Process of Ratification" and "The Popular Vote on the Constitution," respectively.

33. Hofstadter, "Tariff and Homestead," p. iii.

34. Donnal V. Smith in "The Influence of the Foreign-Born of the Northwest in the Election of 1860," *Mississippi Valley Historical Review* XIX (September 1932) pp. 192–93, which Hofstadter cited, was quick to emphasize that "historians have long recognized the influence of the Northwest in the election of 1860." He contended that the Germans came with preformed political concepts, especially those of personal liberty and universal manhood suffrage, and therefore held a direct antipathy to slavery. Although Hofstadter was not original here, his point is more subtle than Smith's. He was asserting the indirect influence of the immigrants' economic interests despite the restraining power of their antipathy to Blacks. Thus, he shows ambiguity and internal tension from this early age, as well as the more simple elements of Marxist influence.

35. Hofstadter, "Tariff and Homestead," p. 14. Italics are the author's.

36. Felice Swados, "Two Types of Materialism: A Comparison of the Mechanical Materialism of Holbach and the Dialectical Materialism of Marx and Engels" (M.A. Thesis, Smith College, 1936).

37. Ibid., pp. 40–46.

38. Ibid., pp. 60–63.

39. Ibid., pp. 66–73.

40. Ibid., pp. 76–78.

41. Felice Swados to Harvey Swados, March 14, 1936, Swados Papers.

42. Irving Sanes, personal interview with the author, March 26, 1981.

4

The Edge of Catastrophe

In the fall of 1936 Hofstadter and Felice Swados were married in New York, probably in City Hall by a justice of the peace. With the move to New York, the couple entered a new world and began an exciting phase of their lives. New York attracted them. Both had family ties in the area. It was the center for Jewish life, as it was the center for the radical movement in which they were both active. It had already become the intellectual and literary center of their lives. It was the natural focal point for aspiring writers and intellectuals of earlier generations. No other center—not Boston or Washington—could have attracted them as New York did.

They established themselves in a two-room "flat" at 134 Montague Street in Brooklyn Heights, near the docks. They lived down the street from a local sailors' home and were surrounded by the nautical life, a fact that linked them to the atmosphere they had left in Buffalo. At first, life was quiet for them and they had to search for adventure. As time went on and they became acquainted with people and the environment, their lives became very full. In the early weeks, they bought furniture for their little den, went to the Yiddish theater, toured the Bowery on foot. They participated vicariously in a friend's experiences, listening to his stories about relief clients in a Muslim neighborhood. They visited cousins, aunts, and uncles and occasionally even discovered a distant relative of whom they approved.[1]

They were, in these days, imbued with the life of "proletcult"—
the Left-inspired literature of the people that applauded the no-
bility of the worker and his eventual rise to consciousness—literature of the 1930's which has become symbolized by the works of
Robert Cantwell and James Farrell. They were eager and hungry
for good material and a full taste of real proletarian life, and began numerous plays and stories based on their perceptions of
that life. Some they wrote together, others independently. Felice
began a series of stories centered on the life of a sailor named
Ralph. Hofstadter wrote some plays with her and some hilarious
letters of fictional exploits in the Federal Building where he was
in law school. By December, Felice had sent poems to the *New
Masses* and one to *Poetry*.[2] In these first months of life in New
York, external interests took a back seat to these creative ventures. Gradually, however, the exigencies of making a living in
Depression-ridden New York began to be felt.

Finding a place in the external world was not easy. Felice, with
her M.A. from Smith, had a hard time finding a job. Hofstadter,
through his uncle Samuel Hofstadter, then newly appointed State
Supreme Court judge, obtained the position of errand boy at
the law firm of Irving R. Kaufman, Assistant U. S. Attorney and
member of Noonen, Kaufman, and Eagen. His night-school
studies, at New York Law School, were dull and boring, his
daytime activities little better.[3]

Yet the tenor of the times suffused their lives. James Wechsler
has described that tone, in relating his own similar experiences:

With all our sense of urgency and with all our presentiments of im-
pending disaster, we were enjoying life.... We were convinced that,
though we were living on the edge of catastrophe, we had been uniquely
blessed with a knowledge of what was happening to us.... We lived on
a keyed-up plane of continuing adventure and we rather pitied those
who could not share the cosmic fun.[4]

Hofstadter and Felice could share in the cosmic fun, which
more often than not waxed serious enough. In their search for
the "real" people, they invited into their home combinations of
sailors and intellectuals, which made either the "edge of catastrophe" or the new order seem imminently close. One of their

friends was struck by these combinations and described the type
of political radicalism he found there:

[The psychiatrists and physicists] usually had the same harshly left views
that the sailors did, but they expressed themselves more suavely. I was
so used to people who in any political argument reached for the jugular
that the coolness with which Harriet's [Felice's] new friends talked politics surprised and misled me. I came to see that despite their coolness,
some were revolutionaries more fanatical than any of my neighborhood
friends; for their opinions rose not from poverty and social despair,
but from the pure calculation that existing society was finished. The
workers would inherit the earth—if they had the right teachers. These
were hard-core Stalinists whom nothing, in the increasingly treacherous
years ahead, would ever soften and dislodge.[5]

This friend used to recount stories of his own proletarian childhood to Felice, who, deprived of that type of experience herself,
listened "with rapture" and wrote of them in letters to her friends.[6]
   These intellectuals were the people for whom Marxism was
"the science of society." Felice listened to some of them "white
faced with ecstasy." Her preference for people of scientific bent,
"with a great sense of fact," appeared remarkable, and some
attributed her preference to the medical background of her family.[7] There was something more than family background at work
in Felice, however. Her training with Marvin Farber, her M.A.
thesis written at Smith, her identification with the philosophy of
Marx and Engels, and her materialism had all formed her sense
of the concrete and worldly sides of life.
   This social milieu, philosophical orientation, and emotional
involvement eventually entailed the continuation of a working
commitment. Felice tried several lines of political work before
settling down with the National Maritime Union. At one point
during the first fall in New York, during October, she worked
with the International Ladies' Garment Workers' Union
(ILGWU). At another she did "very interesting and rewarding
work" with factory girls and housemaids at the Young Women's
Christian Association. These, presumably, were assignments given
her by the YCL. Eventually, she entered and remained with the
waterfront unit of the YCL branch of the National Maritime
Union, working with Milt Rayfield as membership secretary. Later

she put together the political newsletter that the unit printed and that effectively publicized the YCL.[8]

As Hofstadter was acting as clerk during the day and attending law school at night, there was hardly time left over for voluntary political activity. He did, however, go to meetings with Felice, and a year later, in October or November 1937, he went to see Jay Lovestone about a job for himself. Lovestone had been ousted from the Communist Party in 1929 for "right-wing deviationism" as a follower of Bukharin and an exponent of the theory of American exceptionalism—the idea that the time for revolution in America was not yet ripe. He had formed a tiny party of his own, which took on a variety of names, one of them the Communist Party (Opposition), and he had developed an anti-Stalinist Marxian philosophy of direct agitation within the unions. His followers were especially strong in the ILGWU, headed there by Charles Zimmermann, manager of Local 22. It was about work in this union that Hofstadter saw Lovestone. His observations and reflections on this visit are instructive of his attitude at the time:

His [Lovestone's] version is that the Communists are ruining the UAW [United Auto Workers]. I felt like calling him a liar. Lovestone has been moving toward T'ism for some time. At first his group used to criticize Trotzky as harshly as the CP [Communist Party], and only opposed CP policy on certain trade-union questions. [This was the anti-TUEL (Trade Union Educational League) position of the Lovestone leadership in the 1920's.] (They were probably right at the time. NOW L has a POUM [the Trotskyist faction in Spain] banner on his wall, and CPO [Communist Party (Opposition)] literature is hard to distinguish from T'ite literature. Which is unfortunate, because if L had had a chance to follow his line in 1928 instead of the line of the CI [Communist International], the CP would have a better leader than Browder today. These guys are not rats by nature but by force of circumstance. These splits could be avoided if there were room for legitimate differences over questions of policy.[9]

Although little is known about the outcome of this interview in terms of assignments, the tenor of Hofstadter's thinking is clear. He was committed but critical, searching for ways to combine *legitimate opposition* with the discipline of Party loyalty, lamenting the continual splits that weakened the left-wing movement, but clearly not favoring the opposition—Trotskyism.

Meanwhile, the exigencies of reality were continuing to make themselves felt. Hofstadter's life was far from fulfilling. That he was less than inspired by law school is crystal clear. In a letter written to a friend that fall, he was short and cryptic: "Law school is dull, my work almost as bad. So much for that." While no detailed description of law school emerges from this period, one important aspect of Hofstadter's character does pop out from his correspondence. While Felice and Hofstadter often wrote together, it was more often from Felice that one obtained an empirical account of what was happening in their world. Hofstadter's portions were often parodies, spoofs, or gags. As has been observed, wit and the comic sense played a large part in his life from an early date. In this period the quality showed up in his tendency to play with or distort various facets of experience. Short notes such as the following were common:

dearh/ noanswerfromyouonquestionofscienceandsocietywhatdoyousay orhaventyouseennoblepublicationyet? and
Dear H/ Most amazing thing happened to me yesterday at work. Was going up to the office on 22nd floor. Elevator boy got in friendly tussle with Western Union messenger, neglected his wheel. Elevator (lift) kept going up faster and faster. Floors sped by. Suddenly a loud crack and splintering sound. We see the *open sky* and the lift is still lifting!! Went up several hundred feet. Very exhilirating feeling./ Best, Dick

Hofstadter retained that element of comic relief first exhibited in high school. Here he portrays the same natural inclination to experiment, whether with grammatical style or with a distorted form of experience. It is of note that both these letters were written in response to mildly aggravating experiences. In the first it was his brother-in-law's lack of response to a previous question, in the second a dull and boring job.[10] Some people respond to frustration with anger; Hofstadter responded with humor.

Ultimately, Hofstadter made the decision to withdraw from law school, to abandon preparation for the profession his family had planned for him. The experience was a rough one. He tore against the fabric of family expectations and hopes, something not in his nature to do. His uncle Samuel took offense and did not speak to Hofstadter for twelve years, until after the publication of his first commercial success, *The American Political Tradition*, in 1948. His father was more understanding. While disappointed, he told Hofstadter he wished he could afford to support him as a scholar.[11] But it was really Hofstadter's parents-in-law, Rivi and Aaron Swados, whom he had to convince, for he was taking a risky insecure step, in the days of the Depression, the result of which was unclear and the financial support for which he would have to obtain from his wife—a highly unconventional and even undignified procedure to the mind of a critical father-in-law.

Sometime in December 1936 or January 1937, Felice obtained a position among a pool of copy editors at *Time*, Inc. Her response to the new position was ambivalent. On the one hand, she was ambitious for the opportunities to write and express her own intellectual gifts, which she thought might be forthcoming. On the other, she was officially alienated from the corporate life of America; to be working for a Henry Luce publication disgusted and demoralized her. At this same, precarious moment, Hofstadter announced his decision to withdraw from law school. The information aroused great concern, and even, one suspects, animosity on the part of Felice's family. Felice wrote her brother at this time: "D is leaving Law School and there's hell to pay. Please write in our defense."[12] Hofstadter, for his part, tackled the problem with his own particular skills. In one sense, the young man with his back to the wall, unable to bear the constricting nature of law school, was reduced to his most instinctive coping mechanism: comic relief. The expression of his feelings in this particular situation is too telling a statement of his personality to be paraphrased. He wrote to all three members of the Swados family at once:

Dear RBS, HBS & AMS
    Now I think it can be told.
    About 5 weeks ago today a tall, gawky blond young man without a moustache could have been seen entering 134 Montague St., if anyone

had been there to look. In his coat pocket he carried a mysterious little box.

Had the contents of that box and the identity of the young man been known the whole question of Felice's position at Time and relation to her husband's career would not have caused such family agitation.

But let me continue with the story. The young man entered one of the apartments on the first floor, extracted the box from his coat pocket and went to work quickly. He opened the box and placed it of all places—on the center of the bed.

For a moment nothing happened.

Then slowly and curiously, there emerged from the box a little wing-less, bloodsucking hemipterous insect technically known as *Cimex lectularius*.

In brief, a bedbug.

It is one of the noted characteristics of the bedbug—known already to Lucretius[1]—that it prefers female to male flesh.[2]

It must be apparent to the gentle reader that this was nothing other than a vile plot against the female occupant of the bed.

The insidiousness of the plot would have been more apparent to a naturalist at the time. For skillful observation of the little *Cimex* would have shown it to be a female. And, what is more, a female that was—er—enciente—er—in a family way. Or, as we say, pregnant.

In a short time, there were to be 157 little blessed events in the Hofstadter bed. (Cimex lectularius has been known to produce 330 in one litter.[3])

In short the bed was soon infested.

The young man? *Entre nous*, it was myself. En plein jour, *I* myself committed this deed. Coute que coute, I must tell this story now.

Not only did I do it, but it was only the coup d'essai of a number of endeavors to discomfort and embarrass—I blush to say it—my own wife. This was an attempt to accomplish à la dérobée, what I lacked the courage to do openly.

I was trying to drive her out.

I FAILED.

She stuck. The devices and tortures I resorted to I cannot but conceal.

Do not judge me too harshly for doing this. Tout comprendre c'est tout pardonner. At the same time that it was an attempt to get rid of my wife, it was a test of her loyalty. She has given incontestable proof that she intends to stick *to* me no matter what happens. Tout lasse, tout casse, tout passe, but F. goes on forever.

In the meantime, we are eagerly awaiting Harv's arrival. We are, to use the old idiom, lungsum.

As far as Columbia is concerned I swear by the beard of Allah that I am getting my M.A. Did anybody say anything to the contrary?

And if I will not somehow become a journalist, I will become an historian. Or V.V.

Anything but a lawyer! As they say, bon avocat, mauvais voisin. Nicht wahr?

Au grand serieux, please don't worry about us. Au fond, we are just hard-working, ambitious peasants, eager to make good in a small way.

Tien foi!

Dick

---

1. Lucretius, De Rerum Naturae, VI, 137.
2. CF. Schwanstein & Sonnen, De Insectis, pp. 331–397.
3. Ibid., p. 462, 579.[13]

Along with this marvelous expression of humor went an offer of reward for the capture of " "Deadeye Dick', alias 'Dick the Dip'." The two documents almost defy paraphrase and comment. One is helped, however, to infer certain aspects of the familial situation that lay behind them. Discussion about the change had probably begun at Christmas-time (about five weeks prior to the letter) when Hofstadter and Felice, as well as Harvey, were home for the holidays. At that time, the question of "Felice's position on Time and her relation to her husband's career" had probably come up. If Dick left the promising career that had been opened up to him through law school, where was he going now and how was he going to get there? Was he going to depend on Felice for his support? Her newly obtained position at *Time* seemed shaky enough. Would he continue to clerk for a law firm, in which he now could never hope to rise? Would he be able to find a job as a teacher of history after taking his M.A.? Would he even finish this new venture in graduate school? What kind of man was this, anyway? Had Felice made a good marriage to this younger, introverted, half-Jew? He seemed to be mortifying her by dropping out of law school just as she was beginning to get somewhere. All these questions would have been fermenting in Rivi's and Aaron's minds.

The letter appears to have been an indirect attempt to reassure them first of his devotion to their daughter, second of his drive to succeed, and third of his intellectual repugnance at the taste of law school that he had experienced. It stands out among others as a remarkably apt response to a difficult situation. It is Hofstadter's response to the plight Norman Podhoretz has written of—a common one for many: that of being pulled between ambition and alienation. Hofstadter seems to have been saying, How could someone as clever as this fail to do *something* worthwhile in life, even if it isn't law school and a typical attorney's life? Perhaps he was still trying also to capture completely the affection of his parents-in-law. One undeniable conclusion is that Hofstadter's humor came to his aid in times of trouble, to help him overcome obstacles, as a coping mechanism with emotional distress. Perhaps this was not the only way he expressed his comic sense throughout his entire life, but his use of it here is telling. He would prove his capability without resorting to direct measures.

Also significant here is the contrast between this type of letter and Hofstadter's discussions of politics. His tone in the latter took a far different coloration. With an almost 180–degree turn, he became tough-minded, objective, analytical, logical, and predictive—the other side of a supple mind.

The constant scenario of accelerating political crises in the second half of the 1930's stimulated the couple's sense of living on the edge of catastrophe. The events that paved the path toward European war in September 1939 demanded the continuous attention and analysis of radical observers in the United States. Two especially fed their sense of imminent disaster: the Spanish Civil War and the Moscow trials. In response to these crises, the developing policy of collective security also agitated the Left. It is only within the context of these international issues and the Marxist viewpoint that pervaded his life that one can consider Hofstadter's academic work of the period.

Since July 1936 when it broke out, the Spanish Civil War had provoked intense concern in New York and other intellectual circles. The popularly elected Republican government in Spain, made up of a right wing and the so-called Popular Front, had been attacked by a military rebellion launched in Morocco. The government in Madrid, unarmed, was defenseless. The left wing in Spain—Socialists and Anarchists—demanded arms from the government for self-defense. Once armed, these elements were able to put down much of the military rebellion quickly. But General Francisco Franco, leading the military forces, moved across Spain, badly organized and equipped, and requested aid from Fascist governments abroad. Italy and Germany quickly complied. On its side, the Republican government then asked for help from France and Britain. In the spirit of appeasement, leaders in those countries responded by establishing a policy of neutrality, banning materials to either side. This led to the formation of the "Non-Intervention Committee" of some 22 European nations, including Germany and Italy. The United States joined England and France by establishing an embargo on arms purchases for both sides, at first by executive decision and then through Congressional action.[14]

The response from observers on the Left was one of indignation and growing outrage.[15] To them the forces of Fascism were on the rise everywhere. Soon after the original attack, the liberal government in Madrid disintegrated and the Socialists under Largo Caballero took control. At that point, to observers in the West, it appeared that the two extremes on the political continuum stood face to face and that no alternative existed except to battle it out. To the Marxists it was clear that the Fascists had provoked the ultimate revolution; the moment had come in Spain to do battle for the proletarian state.

As the situation evolved, opinions on the Left began to take shape and cluster around two poles. Some people defended the Communist Party's official policy in Spain, which was to maintain a political alliance with groups to the right—the Popular Front policy—to win a purely military victory against Franco's forces. The policy was broad and based on immediate ends, with little reference to the analogy of the Russian revolution. At the other pole were those who argued that the whole Popular Front approach was too moderate, that the general disorder should be exploited to promote immediate social revolution in the wake of collapse on the part of the old regime. This was the type of thinking which assumed the Bolshevik revolution was the only correct model to follow.

Hofstadter's position, as it had developed by March 1937, lay somewhere between these two poles. He wrote at that time:

Realistically, it seems as though the bourgeoisie of England will not permit socialism to come to Spain *even* if Hitler and Italy can be persuaded to stop sending help. The element of foreign intervention is therefore essential to the situation. But this does not automatically make it a war to save the Republic [a liberal aim] or a war of national liberation. Because if the workers win what they are fighting for—expulsion of foreigners and the crushing of the fascists, there can be no other answer but socialism. Not because the demands of the workers won't be received but because they *will* be received and the structure of Spanish capitalism won't be able to stand it. After all, fascism is a last resort of the bourgeoisie. Juan March and his boyfriends resorted to Fascism because they *needed* its force to crush the peasants and workers. If it should be broken up by the civil war and the old army replaced by an army of the masses, the capitalists and landlords will have lost their last weapon for the repression of the masses.[16]

Hofstadter expressed his youthful and enthusiastic belief in the classic image of Capitalism crumbling while the army vainly seeks to maintain a feeble hold on society by forceful means. But even though he appeared immersed in the Marxist language, he was not simplistic or linear in the way he pictured change. Within the terminology, he was stressing not the forward march of the proletariat, but the contradictions in Capitalism, its decay, its frailty, the fact that it was doomed. In the debate over the definition of purpose among those who sought to intervene in Spain, in the arguments between liberals who sought to save the Republic for freedom and Communists who sought to bring about a way of "national liberation" for equality, Hofstadter took his position on the basis of historical inevitability. Capitalism was so decayed that it could not be expected to last, no matter what its perpetrators did. Juan March, a Spanish millionaire who had fled Spain after the February 1937 elections and then attempted to undermine the currency of the Republic from abroad, had resorted to his last card. That reaction showed only how weak he had been in the first place. What Hofstadter saw happening was a step beyond saving the Republic, the step modeled by the experience of the Soviet Union, the step in which the proletarian revolution occurred when liberal ineptitude became apparent. If this was not *immediate* social revolution in Spain, as Lenin

would have advocated, the Communist policy of a broadbased
military victory was acceptable because it was so *inevitable* that
social revolution would follow in its wake.[17]

Here Hofstadter shows the kind of thinking evident in his
tutorial thesis: the emphasis on a series of theoretically contin-
gent factors and a kind of domino theory that assumed that if
one could find the right key to the political situation, one could
unlock the formula that would activate an automatic series of
related events leading to a foregone, ultimate conclusion—here,
the workers' state.

By October 1937 arguments about the Party policy in Spain
had tightened up. The Popular Front policy had led in May to
some rough conflicts with those traditional enemies of the Communists, the Socialists and Trotskyists. The latter group had been
"disciplined" after a rebellion in Barcelona, news of which shocked
sympathetic observers. To many, however, discipline seemed the
paramount value, as the coalition of political parties continued
to face increasingly powerful attacks from the Fascists. Some
decried the lack of unity among the leftist forces. Among these
Hofstadter took his place.

If the C.P., S.P. [Socialist Party], & F.A.I. [Anarchists] were united on
a proletarian revolutionary policy they might have established a system
in that portion of Spain which they control. [Approximately half of
Spain was then controlled by Republican forces.] But that wouldn't have
put them any nearer to victory over Franco than they "now" are.

For Hofstadter, as for Marxist-Leninist tacticians, winning the
particular civil war in Spain and waging the ultimate social revolution were two distinctly different realities. And he was pessimistic about the latter. It appeared that classical Leninist tactics
alone would not win a military victory.

A genuine prol. revolution in all of Spain would lead to intervention
by Hitler, Mussolini + England and would result in a joint occupation,
followed presumably by a puppet gov't based on reaction. So that there
would be nothing gained by following such a policy now. The P.F.
[Popular Front] in Spain is absolutely ok.[18]

The workers' movement had not yet arrived in Spain simply
because the forces of reaction were too strong. Therefore, cor-

rect policy by the revolutionary party should be a "consolidate gains and hold" approach. Basic realism demanded this technique. England, Italy, *and* Germany combined would be too much even for the Popular Front.

Significantly, Hofstadter mentioned nothing of the policy of appeasement that motivated France and England in these years, nothing of the *fear* of war produced by fresh memories of World War I. His mind was on *class* attitudes. England's major fear, in his mind, was of workers, not of Germans. He was in basic agreement with a journalist of the time who had concluded: "We have come to the end of a period of national ways. There will never again be a united nation fighting against another united nation. War from now on will involve civil war."[19] Class warfare existed everywhere, either in reality or in potentiality, and further political thinking followed from that premise.

Ultimately, both of Hofstadter's statements indicated an attempt to rationalize the Party position. Whether this was a Stalinist position or not is worth some thought. There is a strong case to be made for the difficulty that must have been encountered by those who were initially educated in Communist theory during one ideological period and later requested to switch their basic thinking when the Party line changed. During the purist Third Period between 1928 and 1935, Communist Party policy promulgated the concept of "Social Fascism." Those slightly to the right of the Communist position were conceived not as potential allies, but as archenemies who would undermine the ultimate revolution if included in any coalition of the Left. Social Fascists were defined as those who, by lack of the requisite militancy and immediatism demanded of Party regulars, directly aided the purposes of the Right. With the softening of policy and the Popular Front approach, these former archenemies came to be considered close collaborators. Although they may have considered themselves "good Communists" and given lip service to the Popular Front ideology, those who grew up with Third Period teachings must have remained attuned to the more alienated and extreme—elitist—attitudes of the years before 1935. The earlier attitude was fed also, for those of a literary and sensitive bent and on the fringes of the movement—where Hofstadter was—by the traditional alienation from the materialistic values of bourgeois America. Those alienated on this basis would have found it difficult to swallow the watered-down, moderate alliances of the Popular Front period, even though lip service may have been given to Popular Front policies.

Such a difficulty appears to account for some problems Felice was having at this time. In a unit meeting in March 1937, Felice was reprimanded for advocating a line too militant to please the Party bosses. She had been arguing that "Capitalism knows no boundaries," that the Spanish, German, and Italian Capitalists were all allied and therefore the class warfare in Spain was the same as anywhere else. If the Loyalists were to win there—and here she ended as Hofstadter had—the regime would topple of its own weight. Implicitly, she was declaring the old Social Fascist line: hindering that old regime and making alliances with the liberals who might shore up that regime was not advisable. She was accused of being "incorrect" and "undeveloped" and of having a "fascist chauvinist . . . ideology," of trying to "sneak socialism over on the masses." Somehow, Felice had missed the articulation of the Popular Front line that urged broad coalition for defeat of the Fascists but not immediate social revolution now.[20]

The same phenomenon, in addition to his inability to conform intellectually, may have accounted for Hofstadter's opinions. For him the genuine proletarian revolution was ultimately desirable, but the threat of reactionary intervention made a moderate non-immediatist policy expedient *for the moment.* The Popular Front, as a present political tactic, was acceptable, but only because of the exigencies of external Fascist threats. It seems safe to assume that as members of the YCL, Hofstadter and Felice considered themselves rank and file Party workers. There would, then, have been no overt rebellion against the change in Party line *per se*, as there was about this time by the editors of the *Partisan Review*, for example. Discipline and continuing effort within the movement were of paramount concern. But a change directed from the distant top quarters of the official bureaucracy would not have been very effective, simply because it was not possible to reverse one's thinking completely on the basis of Party directive.

The Spanish Civil War took a back seat in intensity and challenge to the Moscow trials for many American radicals between

1936 and 1938. Breaking out just at the time the Civil War in Spain began, the series of show trials staged by Stalin and his lieutenants dazzled and puzzled the observing Western world. Going back, for their source, to the assassination of Sergei Kirov, the supposed successor to Stalin, in December 1934 the trials disposed of one group after another of "deviationists." On August 16, 1936, Leo Kamenev and Gregory Zinoviev with fourteen others were accused of conspiring to undermine the Soviet regime along with Leon Trotsky and the German Gestapo. They confessed to conspiracy, sabotage, and treason. And they were executed. In January 1937, others labeled the "Anti-Soviet Trotskyite Center" including Karl Radek and Gregory Piatakov came to the stand. All confessed. All were executed. In June 1937 it was the turn of the chief army generals of the revolution including Michael Tukachevsky, who had been chief of the general staff during the revolution. Nine months later, in March 1938, the "Anti-Soviet Bloc of Rights and Trotskyites" including Nicholas Bukharin took its turn. All were convicted, all executed. By this point arrests were also being made by quota in every district throughout the Soviet Union. These included lower officials who sometimes quickly had to learn the nature of the accusations before they could attempt to defend themselves, or even to confess coherently.[21]

In contrast to the situation in Spain, where the antagonists' positions seemed so clear, the Moscow trials muddied the waters for observers on the Left. Responses in the United States varied from enthusiastic endorsement by Communist Party members, to doubts and suspended judgment among neutral but sympathetic liberals, to conviction that the trials were fraudulent among moderates, to outright disgust among independent Marxists. The connected issue of Leon Trotsky and sympathy for his person or his policies often interfered or altered opinions about the trials themselves. It seemed to some that Trotsky should be given his day in court, that since many if not all the allegations involved connections with his activities, his views also should be given an open hearing. Among those who felt this way were John Dewey and a number of others, who formed in 1936 the "Committee to Obtain Right of Asylum for Trotsky" after his house arrest in Norway. After obtaining asylum for him in Mexico, this Committee became the Trotsky Defense Committee, aimed at satisfying Trotsky's own plea for an impartial investigation. The findings of this Committee were publicized in September 1937. It found Trotsky "not guilty," thereby casting greater doubts on the veracity of the trials.[22]

To others not involved with Trotsky, the demanding discipline of the movement was primary and provided the necessary method to counteract the failure of Capitalism, the impact of crisis conditions, and the chaotic condition of the world. In his reports as an eye witness to the first trial in Moscow, Joshua Kunitz described the official version of the cause for the conspiracy and sabotage in the Soviet Union. His account ran along the following lines. Opposition to revolutionary movements is impossible because of the enormous nature of the task and the need for order and acquiescence among those working for change. Anything else holds within it the "seeds of counter-revolution." Nevertheless, people like Kamenev and Zinoviev did form an opposition from the very beginning, even prior to October 1917, argued Kunitz. Thus, little by little they became susceptible to the "flattery and manipulations of the class enemy." Furthermore, it was mainly people who were "excessively egotistical, conceited, ambitious," and "individualistic" who provided material for opposition movements. These people grew increasingly distant from the real desires of the masses. Thus, these trials were an educational tool to make the conspirators themselves realize how they had betrayed the original purposes of the Bolshevik revolution. It was also correct to make of them an example to those who might follow in their footsteps.[23] It is easy to see, with the goals stated like this, how those committed to the left-wing movement in the United States would find it difficult to break away.

Whichever side one favored in this dispute, the pro-Trotsky or the pro-discipline—and the two did not necessarily cancel each other out—many observers in the United States, even when they suspended judgment, did not question the truth of either the accusations or the verdicts. Most, it seems safe to say, assumed some guilt behind the massive accusations and questioned the trials only on the basis of specific connections to Trotsky or the quantity of sabotage evidence put forward by the prosecution.[24]

For Hofstadter, questions first occurred on the basis of evi-

dence and of logic. He was perplexed. The will to believe and
the clarity of his insight into the external situation vied for dominance in his mind. After the second trial, in March 1937, he
wrote:

As for the trials, I tried to convince myself that they were kosher, and
at one point succeeded, but my conscience bothers me. I still don't see
how the confessions could have been anything but true. And yet, how
about the Bristol Hotel? How about the airplane to Norway? Worst of
all, how about Paris and Royan? [These were allusions to the fabricated
accusations in which the accused were alleged to have held conspira-
torial meetings with Trotsky, his family, or his friends around Europe
and which Trotsky painstakingly disproved.][25]

To the historian in Hofstadter, the nagging, unexplained dis-
crepancies meant increasing skepticism. By November 1937, after
the third trial, the questions accumulated.

I am by no means convinced that they were innocent, mistake me not.
Because I don't know why they didn't take advantage of the chance to
TELL ALL during the open trials. As a matter of fact, after the second
trial was over I sat me down and wrote out an analysis of their possible
motives, in which I proved, at least to my own satisfaction that there is
no possible basis of approach to the trials except on the assumption
that the confessions were bona fide.
    The fact remains that the trials contain internal evidence against the
truth of the confessions. I am not referring to the Bristol business which
is quite satisfactorily explained. But I don't believe that Pyatakov or
anybody else flew to Oslo at a time when no planes landed there. And
the hypothesis that a plane could have landed, at some other place than
the airport is pretty thin, especially if you look at a topographical map
of the region around Oslo. Also Trotzky [sic] has pretty good evidence
that he was at Rouen when he was supposed to be in Paree.... I am
not of course referring to that committee of half wits that went down
to Mexico to make sure that T. got a whitewash. I refer to evidence
that came out at the time of the trials.[26]

Despite his lack of sympathy for Trotsky, it appeared to Hofstadter's inexorably logical mind that, at least according to Western judicial standards, the prosecution still had much to account
for. He went on:

Another thing that I find hard to believe is that seasoned revolutionaries (excuse the cliche) like Radek sat around like poor fools waiting to be led by directives from Trotzky. No, it's not exactly outside the pale of possibility, but it's much less than probable.

As for the smaller boys, nobody has yet shown me that the German and Japanese spy systems, particularly WEST of Baikal are so efficient as to enable the [*sic*] to contact so many agents. Moreover, the smaller boys weren't quite small enough. Except for a few cooks and some other nobodies, they were mostly Party or Soviet or Komsomol officials of importance. If they were all guilty, then there is something fundamentally shitty about the entire organization of the USSR. It is as tho dozens of section organizers here were suddenly accused of being police agents and expelled from the party.[27]

Clarity of insight was winning in its battle with the will to believe. Hofstadter divined what others understood only by hindsight. Either the revolution had been carried out with the confidence of its leadership in its personnel, i.e., with *trust*, or at the first sign of opposition, as Kunitz had stipulated, the process of duplicity, counterintelligence, and surveillance had set in. The logical culmination of the second alternative was exactly what the prosecution was attempting to picture—a nation undercut by a network of subterfuge and doubledealing, members of which were plotting with the government's enemies a future treason against the regime it had helped put in power. For American Communists and those still sympathetic to the Russian experiment, the conflict between the values of free expression through a legitimate opposition and those of social equity through disciplined political change defied resolution. On the one hand, Russia looked "totalitarian." (It was to be just one and a half years later that the Committee for Cultural Freedom would publish a statement against "totalitarian" political forms, linking Russia with Germany and Italy.) On the other hand, it also looked completely undisciplined and opportunistic, with "egotistical" and "individualistic" political opposition apparent everywhere. Either freedom existed without discipline and the purpose of the revolution had been undermined, or discipline existed without freedom and human initiative and creativity were being snuffed out. To Westerners this moral conflict between two values of high priority became very painful. Either way one emerged, once one questioned the predicted consequences of the proletarian revolution as it had been foreseen by Marx, a sad and disillusioning reality stared one in the face.[28]

By January 1938 Hofstadter had reached the point at which he could be more explicit. He now joined those who criticized the trials and labeled them "phony and "frameups." He thus set himself apart from other observers, 150 of whom had unfortuitously signed a statement defending the trials in May of that year.

But the movement, for Hofstadter and for others like him, was more significant than Russia and its bureaucratic leaders, and as a whole remained worth defending. As he found the Popular Front policy acceptable because of the Fascist threat, so he concluded that the changing Party line on leadership and its gamble in "throwing overboard" its original Leninism had to be seen in the light of reactionary Europe. After lamenting the trials and their effect on the morale of the workers, after lamenting the pro-Roosevelt stand of the Party in the United States, Hofstadter still concluded that it was best to work along Party lines.

With these issues in the forefront of his mind, Hofstadter attended a party meeting of the Columbia graduate unit in early March. At that point he denied having any intention of joining the Party but wanted "to see how they function[ed]," which he found to be "pretty well." At the same time he was let down by the type of thinking he found among those who attended.

I was appalled at their attitude of mind. Which is like this:
(If) I doubt the correctness of the party line, collective security, the Moscow trials, (or anything else):
Therefore, my education is deficient and I have to go down to the section and talk to somebody who will straighten this out for me, and improve me.
Then I will be satisfied with the party line, coll. sec., the Moscow trials, or anything else.
The underlying assumption, of course, is that the party can't be wrong. This from intellectuals.[29]

Having made these observations and this denial, however, Hofstadter almost immediately reversed his position—at least on membership. By April 30 he was explaining his reason for entry,

aware that the move would appear contradictory in light of his
views on the trials. He wanted to make his position quite clear.

My entrance into the party is not the result of any change of mind. I
join without enthusiasm but with a sense of obligation. Let stand anything I have said about the trials, I still think they are shit, and admit
they are important. But not the most important consideration for me
or you or him in America at the present moment.[30]

He had moved from his own personal position to one that was
more collective in nature. In this decision, Hofstadter joined
many others who were making similar moves in these years.
Discipline and combined work were simply more important than
one's own doubts or political interpretations.[31]
     He continued his rationale:

My fundamental reason for joining is that I don't like capitalism and
want to get rid of it. I am tired of talking. I am ashamed of the hours
I have spent jawing about the thing. . . . Once grant the desire to do
something, what should I do? Join the Trotzkyites, who just finished
conducting a student peace demonstration with the Catholic Workers
Group at Columbia?[32]

Hofstadter could no longer tolerate the strain between the detachment of his cool logicality, which sought to find the key to
the mechanism of society, and the intensity of his commitment
to justice and probity. Spurred on by the velocity of life and
politics in that time, he had moved in the only direction that
made experiential or logical sense—toward commitment, toward
integration, toward concrete work to further industrial
democracy.
     That the move was late and temporary does not mean that it
was not deeply felt. He believed, as much as he probably ever
believed in anything, in the purpose and vision of the American
Party.

The party is making a very profound contribution to the radicalization
of the American people. Whether it is losing its revolutionary character
I don't know. Even if it is, I prefer to go along with it now. If a new

party is someday needed to complete the job of pushing capitalism over I think I will be ready join it. I postpone that question for the future.[33]

At the same time, there is no doubt that he took his Party without illusions. He was never taken in by the obeisance to bureacratic power or the thought control requested by that power. This was clear from the beginning of his serious consideration of membership. In a marginal group, he was always a marginal member—an intellectual first, an activist second. Later, when he had joined, had crossed the line from observer to participant, the ethical and principled grounds for his decision were clear. Within the policy issues at stake, he had been forced to make a practical commitment for what he felt to be *right*, morally and socially. On the question of collective security, the point was particularly striking:

The question then is whether to become isolationist—which after all is wrong . . . or to take no stand on the war question at all—which is out of the question for a CP. Grant again, that we have not enough influence to put over cs[collective security]; that is no argument against advocating it; might as well say that we should not advocate lifting the embargo on Loyalist Spain for the same reason.[34]

Power was not the question. Collective security as a policy meant a united front against Fascism. *Inherently*, this was the ethically and morally correct position to take. A political position, backed by the commitment of Party membership, was an act of principle, not an act of pragmatism. No, one did not wish to remain blind to the realities of any situation, but at a point, after long discussion and much consideration, one felt moved to make an existential act of commitment.

But to some, the old anti-war policy of the united Left seemed more moral and less opportunistic than the apparently war-mongering collective security position that had replaced it. Hofstadter responded to such thoughts by a defense of collective security, extended over several long months. He argued that the next war would involve the United States regardless of whether it pursued an isolationist *or* a collective security policy. Economic entanglement followed its own evolutionary internal pattern and dynamic. War would mean military dictatorship for the United States although not "in the full sense of the word." Could any political movement that fully supported collective security—and thus ultimately war and dictatorship—retain the confidence of the masses? Yes, because war would feed the wish for the defeat of Fascism—or for "anti-fascist revolution." All this in Europe would serve the interests of radicalization in the United States.[35]

The policy of isolationism before war would mean only unnecessarily increased economic distress for the working class, a group which would suffer both before and during the war. And it would not avoid the necessity of war. By taking a collective security position, the Party did not destroy its chances to lead a proletarian revolution, because it was unrealistic to imagine there would be any immediate revolution in the United States in the first place. Furthermore, American Fascists were for isolation. And the American bourgeoisie could make peace with Fascism. The workers could not. The world situation had decreased the chances for improvement among workers. "It is no longer possible to make revolutions under the old straight-forward clearcut circumstances. I share your nostalgia ... But you will acknowledge that nostalgia, like most other sentiments, has no political validity."[36]

These thoughts were written just after Hofstadter had turned in his M.A. thesis and had been an active Party member for about eight weeks. The anti-Fascist policy of collective security appears to have molded his defense of the Party line. His was a commitment to gradualism, American exceptionalism, and the Popular Front notion of temporary coalition for the defeat of Fascism. His Social Fascism, his Leninism, had been by this time abandoned in favor of an iconoclastic Stalinism, which had no respect for Party leaders or the "intellectual discipline" of the Party but was committed to economic change. This view held within it, very close to the surface, the seeds of its own destruction.

These discussions formed the context of Hofstadter's early academic career at Columbia. That he matured considerably between September 1936 and May 1938 is certain. The group of friends who met at the Hofstadter/Swados flat or elsewhere and actively engaged themselves in the "cosmic fun" of political debate served as the primary stimulus for his growth. Without the challenge and discipline of graduate work in history, however, that growth might have taken a very different turn. Graduate school focused and channeled Hofstadter's natural penchant for political analysis and displaced his passion for the issues of the present onto the problems of the past.

NOTES

1. Felice Swados to Harvey Swados, September 22, 1936, October 17, 1936, December 3, 1936, n.d., Harvey Swados papers, Courtesy of the Archives of the University of Massachusetts, Amherst, Mass.; Richard Hofstadter to Harvey Swados, n.d., Swados Papers.

2. Felice Swados to Harvey Swados, October 17, 1936, December 3, 1936, May 11, 1936; Richard Hofstadter to Harvey Swados, n.d., n.d. [May 1937], Swados Papers.

3. Felice Swados to Harvey Swados, n.d., December 3, 1936; Richard Hofstadter to "Fred," n.d., Swados Papers.

4. James Wechsler, *The Age of Suspicion* (New York, Random House, 1953), pp. 72–73.

5. Alfred Kazin, *Starting Out in the Thirties* (Boston, Little, Brown, 1962), p. 105.

6. Alfred Kazin, *New York Jew* (New York, Vintage Books, 1979) p. 25.

7. Kazin, *Starting Out*, pp. 105, 103, 113.

8. Felice Swados to Harvey Swados, October 17, 1936, January 9, 1937, December 3, 1936, March 1937, n.d. [October 17, 1937], Swados Papers.

9. Hofstadter to Harvey Swados, November 7, 1937, Swados Papers; see also Irving Howe and Louis Coser, *The American Communist Party* (Boston, Beacon Press, 1957), pp. 161–74; Bert Cochren, *Labor and Communism: The Conflict That Shaped American Unions* (Princeton University Press, 1977) p. 132.

10. Hofstadter to "Fred," n.d.; Hofstadter to Harvey Swados, n.d.; Felice Swados and Richard Hofstadter to Harvey Swados, n.d. (emphasis in original), all in Swados Papers.

11. Betty Goodfriend, personal interview with the author, May 26, 1981.

12. Felice Swados to Harvey Swados, January 25, 1937, Swados Papers.

13. Hofstadter to RBS, HBS, & AMS, January 24, 1937, Swados Papers.

14. Stanley G. Payne, "The Second Spanish Republic, 1931–1939," in Allen Guttmann, ed., *American Neutrality and the Spanish Civil War*

(Boston, D.C. Heath, 1963) pp. 20–30; Richard W. Leopold, *The Growth of American Foreign Policy* (New York, Alfred A. Knopf, 1962) pp. 507–8, 518–20.

15. F. W. Dupee, "An Interview with André Malraux," *New Masses* (March 9, 1937) pp. 17–18. In this interview Malraux described the reaction to Spain as determination and growing rage and fury. He was speaking from first-hand experience. During his visit in February 1937 to New York, Felice and Alfred Kazin attended one of the fund-raising meetings at which he spoke. Felice donated an entire week's salary to the Republican cause that evening. See Kazin, *Starting Out*, pp. 106–7.

16. Hofstadter to Harvey Swados, October 17, 1937.

17. Payne, "Second Spanish Republic," pp. 26–27; for Juan March, see Hugh Thomas, *The Spanish Civil War* (New York, Harper & Bros., 1961) pp. 64–65, 98, 185.

18. Hofstadter to Harvey Swados, October 17, 1937.

19. John Langdon-Davies, "What It Means to Us," *New Masses*, (January 5, 1937) p. 5.

20. Felice Swados to Harvey Swados, March 1937.

21. Donald W. Treadgold, *Twentieth Century Russia* (Chicago, Rand McNally, 1959) pp. 178–83.

22. For the array of responses, see Frank Warren, *Liberals and Communism: The Red Decade Revisited* (Bloomington, Indiana University Press, 1966) pp. 163–92; for Dewey Committee, see Isaac Deutscher, *The Prophet Outcast* (London, Oxford University Press, 1963) pp. 350, 360–83, 393; Constance Ashton Myers, *The Prophet's Army: Trotskyists in America 1928–1941* (Westport, Greenwood Press, 1977) pp. 134–35.

23. Joshua Kunitz, "Seeds of Counter Revolution," *New Masses* (October 27, 1936) p. 12. Kunitz leads into this explanation of the trials with the following statements: "The history of oppositions in revolutionary movements has amply demonstrated that the first step toward resisting discipline in a revolutionary organization . . . is objectively and inevitably the first step toward counter-revolution." This was the thinking of main-line Communists.

24. This is Warren's judgment in *Liberals and Communism*, pp. 174–79.

25. Hofstadter to Harvey Swados, March 1937.

26. Ibid., November 7, 1937.

27. Ibid.

28. Warren posits a similar-sounding dilemma. "The issues raised by the Moscow trials and the general purges in all areas of Russian life severely challenged the Popular Front. If Trotsky were not guilty and the trials were a monstrous frameup one could not distinguish morally

between Communism and Fascism. And if the Russian system was not only without political and civil liberties, but was also characterized by systematic terror, there remained little basis for including Russia in a 'democratic' anti-Fascist front." *Liberals and Communism*, p. 163. But this describes only one horn of the dilemma. Hofstadter had grasped both horns, without the advantage of hindsight. The larger issue of freedom versus equality is well expressed in Carl Becker, "Liberalism—A Way Station," in *Every Man His Own Historian* (New York, F.S. Crofts, 1935) pp. 91–100.

29. Hofstadter to Harvey Swados, n.d. [March 8, 1938], Swados Papers.

30. Ibid., April 30, 1938.

31. For this general movement, see Malcolm Cowley, *The Dream of the Golden Mountains* (New York, Viking Press, 1980); and Matthew Josephson, *Infidel in the Temple* (New York, Alfred A. Knopf, 1967) especially Chapter 6.

32. Hofstadter to Harvey Swados, April 30, 1938.

33. Ibid.

34. Ibid.

35. Ibid., May 12, 1938.

36. Ibid.

5

The Science of Society

In February 1937, the month that he officially graduated from the University of Buffalo, Hofstadter enrolled as a part-time graduate student in the History Department at Columbia University. He was twenty years old. The year and a half pursuing his Master's degree at Columbia brought Hofstadter to a new sense of himself. He moved away from the old comic to a new and "scientific" definition of the social sciences in general and history in particular. He tested himself against established intellectual figures at Columbia. And he raised his sights and ambitions. The process was an inexorable step in his formation as a historian.

During that first semester, Hofstadter took just two courses: "The Establishment of the American Nation, 1492–1829," taught by Professor John Allen Krout, and in the Government Department, "Contemporary American Politics," taught by Professor Raymond Moley. Both were evening courses. This arrangement perhaps enabled Hofstadter to make his peace with his parents-in-law by keeping his job with Kaufman for a time. As he experimented with graduate school and became acquainted at Columbia, his academic goals became clearer and leaving his job may have become easier. Whatever the case, he had, by the fall of 1937, changed direction. Unlike his commitment to the Communist Party in early 1938, his initially tentative experiment with graduate work in history became a lifelong engagement. And unlike the Communist Party, which offered an avenue for active current engagement in the pressing social issues of his day but asked for intellectual constrictions in return, the field of history offered him vast opportunities for intellectual expansion and diminished the possibilities for social activism. The interplay between the two roles, however, that of observer and that of activist, would mark his life work.[1]

Krout's course for the spring of 1937 covered the "English settlements with the experience of a colonial system seeking to protect and control them," "revolution and organization of the United States," "neutrality," the "development of national parties," and the "problem of expansion." All this was surely ground Hofstadter had covered at the University of Buffalo with Julius Pratt—perhaps in more exciting ways. Krout's course may have been a requirement for undergraduate or graduate majors at Columbia. It appears to have been a broad survey course, and as such would not have challenged Hofstadter. Moley's course may have taken more attention and critical interest, for here he would have had a ringside seat to observe and develop an opposition to one of the leading New Deal minds, a mind that was then becoming critical of Franklin Delano Roosevelt. The course dealt with the "composition and activities of the parties," the "political tendencies and methods of economic and other organized groups," and the "main lines of controversy over public policy." These areas were germane to Hofstadter's concerns, albeit presented from a perspective quite alien to his own.[2]

It is striking that the characteristic which marked Hofstadter's correspondence of the fall of 1936, the light, gay, spoofing gags, almost completely disappeared in the spring of 1937. In its place appeared sharply analytical and political discussions, parts of which have been quoted above. It has been said of this period that "Felice's hearty sense of her own powers tended to put Dick into shadow," and that he felt insecure.[3] Perhaps this was the case in some respects, but in his political criticism, beginning in the spring of 1937, Hofstadter—while sometimes arriving at debatable conclusions from his Marxist premises—hardly appeared timid. In fact, Felice, in her letters to her brother, spoke several times of others having been "intimidated" by Hofstadter on the basis of his hard-headed, logical arguments and conclusions.[4]

Felice's thoughts in this period were the ideas of a disciplined Party worker, devoted to Marxism on practical and philosophical levels and committed in her approach to the massive tasks of organization that seemed to face the Party. Hofstadter's were the arguments of one schooled in Marx and Lenin but possessing an original sense of political reality and therefore a more variegated view of the world and the variety of its possibilities. Whether or not Raymond Moley's course—given from a perspective to the right of Hofstadter's and thus providing potential friction for him—directly encouraged his political criticism, the coincidence between the change in subject and tone of his letters and enrollment at Columbia in this course is a striking one. While it is possible that the force of his arguments on paper was greater than its impact orally, it also seems quite likely that through his graduate studies at Columbia, Hofstadter began moving beyond and away from Felice's view of the world, which emanated from Buffalo, and toward concentrated development of his own.

Hofstadter's writing career took another turn during this early spring of 1937. In March or April, just as Felice was being disciplined by the Party, Hofstadter published several book reviews. He must have gone to wait in the pool of would-be reviewers at the *Herald Tribune* offices—a pool such as that described by Alfred Kazin which formed outside the book review editor's office at the *New Republic* on a regular basis in those days. Or perhaps he had been introduced to someone on the staff of the *Tribune*. In any case, two signed reviews appeared in the April 18, 1937, issue of the book review section. There were to be three more, through July.[5]

Two of these are of particular interest. One was entitled "A Medieval Spirit in the Modern World" and was a review of Vida Scudder's *On Journey*. Miss Scudder, a Christian Socialist, was a prominent member of the LID and a teacher of forty years at Wellesley. Of her socialism, Hofstadter said:

Later she was impressed by Marx's work but could not accept Marxism in its entirety. It is typical of her intellectual outlook that she rejected it not because of its inconsistency with her Christian beliefs, but because the class-struggle doctrine was morally repugnant to her. Her socialism arose from a deep desire for justice rather than from intellectual analysis; its ultimate source was Christianity and the two became subtly identified in her mind. Like the Fabians she speaks of "revolution by consent," and in her own idiom it is the "Christian revolution."[6]

Hofstadter appears to have appreciated Miss Scudder's liberal-minded eclectic approach, while finding little in common, himself, between Marxism and Christianity. Here, in fact, is an example of the reverse approach to that alleged to characterize Hofstadter's friends. If they approached Socialism as a science and concluded from "pure calculations" that Capitalist society was doomed, Scudder approached it as a *morally* superior system and as a committed activist (or, because of her age, as a "do-gooder"). Hofstadter could, however, meet Scudder on the ground of justice. He concluded his review both sympathetically and critically: "It is because of the author's personality, and almost in spite of her writing, that the book is of interest." Such was the sharply critical Communist face to face with the soft-minded Socialist, and the precocious youth in face of his elder's similar but chastened experience of forty years.[7]

The second review was entitled "The Need of New Values." Here Hofstadter demonstrates why he later told an interviewer, "I was astute enough to see . . . I had no gifts in the field [of philosophy]." He was critical of Georgia Harkness's *The Recovery of Ideals*, which "subscribed to the ancient theory of the duality of human nature" and which argued against the theory of materialism. The discussion was directed "with deadly seriousness" at contemporary young people. Values, for Harkness, had a "cosmic foundation" and, she said, "mystical and moral experience have their place along with scientific evidence." Thus, "to interpret human nature materialistically is to destroy the source of ideals. Hence the need for the spiritualistic metaphysic which the book attempts to establish." Anyone tutored under Marvin Farber would have found such a defense of idealism fallacious. To a Marxist, values developed from the material basis of economic production and were relative to that base. Hofstadter could have directly presented such an opposing philosophical perspective. Instead, not wishing to explicate that point of view— perhaps because he was writing for the *Herald Tribune*, instead of the *Nation* or the *New Masses*—he embroiled himself in a technical aspect of Farberian Phenomenological philosophy that did not truly convey the nature of his objections. Arguing against the equal validity of mystical, moral, and scientific experience, he said: "This line of reasoning embodied the conventional identification of the factual status of an ideal or experience with its logical import that stands at the base of so much of value-centric idealism."[8]

One recalls that the only way to know for the Phenomenologist was to return to the basic mental processes—remembering, perceiving, believing, etc., tie them to the physical, geographical, and social context in which they occurred, and ignore "preconceived" or "ideal" conceptions. Thus, the "identification of the factual status of an ideal or experience with its logical import" would have been severely criticized by Farber, since reality or "fact" would have developed only from a complicated interaction between the knower and his environment. But Hofstadter did not make his criticism or his point of view completely clear, and garbled his syntax in the process.

This was the next to last review he wrote for the *Herald Tribune*, though he described himself as an incipient journalist at the time. A friend, remembering the temporary nature of many of these review assignments, has commented that it was easier to obtain a first review than to continue receiving them. If, after five reviews, Hofstadter was denied others, the weaknesses in the Harkness review may explain the reason. Although his writing was terse and disciplined, his general outlook kept him from being completely clear. He also lacked the command of language— and perhaps the political and social perspective—which would have been necessary and appealing to the Republican readers of the *Herald Tribune*. Knowledgeable and precocious as the twenty-year-old was, his logic outstripped his insights at this point, as it had the year before in his tutorial thesis, and he was left with the tortured syntax that appears above. Also, the guarded and disciplined tone of these reviews contrasted markedly with his correspondence of the period. Factual and logical in both, he never let his imagination function in his reviews as he did in his letters. Whereas logic had served him well in his academic work, imagination characterized his personal writings. In attempting the reviews for public consumption, he had not yet successfully combined the two, as he was later to do in his historical work. Whether this was to some extent due to the involvement in a minority, opposition movement in which one spoke one language in private and another in public cannot be measured. But the readers of the *Herald Tribune* would have had little use for Hofstadter's politics, and because of that, Hofstadter also undoubtedly thought they would have little use for the wit, humor, and innuendo that marked his other writings. The reviews were written with a particular—even a hostile—audience in mind. Self-protection was a natural reaction.

Hofstadter became a full-time graduate student in the fall of 1937. At that time he registered for five history courses, three of which were taken for residency purposes only. These three were "Historical Methods," taught by Professor James T. Shotwell, "Europe in the Middle Ages," taught by Professor Austin P. Evans, and "Europe in the 19th Century, 1815–1875", a course on European Federalism taught by Professor Robert C. Binkley, who was that year visiting professor from Western Reserve University. The other two courses, taken for full credit, were "European Colonial Expansion in the 19th and 20th Centuries," taught by Professor Walter Langsam, and "Economic and Cultural Aspects of American Civilization, 1865–1900," taught by Professor Harry Carman. It was the last of these that was most important to Hofstadter.[9]

Compared with most faculty members at Columbia, Carman had advanced the hard way. He had been born on a farm, had taught grade school, had served as principal of a high school while working for his Master's degree at Syracuse University, and then had taught history and political science at Syracuse. Having completed Ph.D. classwork at Columbia, he was asked to teach there during World War I before he had completed his dissertation. That study, "The Street Surface Railway Franchises of New York City," was completed in 1919, and Carman stayed on at Columbia. He was an open-minded generalist and a popular teacher. His graduate course in American Civilization, as offered in the 1937–38 academic year, emphasized "the relation of economic forces to cultural conditions" and was structured around student reports and group discussions. Hofstadter was one among five students slated to work out his Master's thesis in this format. At an early date Hofstadter entertained the idea of writing on the New York Board of Assessors in the late nineteenth century, in probable close association with Carman. But by the 1930's, Carman had developed an avid interest in agricultural history, and it was this field that came to concern Hofstadter too.[10]

Carman focused on the social problems of agriculture. One of the most pressing needs in this area involved adequate care for those on the lowest rungs of the social ladder: sharecroppers and tenant farmers. By this time, Carman had worked out an introductory history lecture on the subject, setting forth the development of tenant farming from its antecedents in slavery for Black people and in declining real estate land prices for Whites.[11]

This lecture showed Carman's liberal concern for the subject as a challenge to national priorities and concluded with a stirring statement, which was clearly meant for public consumption. Noting the reversed mobility of farmers who had lost their lands in depressed periods and had become renters, he stated that balance was a prime necessity in any governmental policy dealing with this problem: "That such a balance will ever be achieved under a system of laissez-faire is improbable, if not unbelievable. Meanwhile, unless constructive action is soon taken we shall *in all likelihood* witness a further drift in the U. S. toward farm tenancy and a poverty ... strickened [*sic*] landless peasantry." It is very likely that Hofstadter absorbed the concern expressed by these words, for by the end of December 1937 a paper he had written on sharecroppers was, according to Felice, "turning out to be a Big Thing."[12]

The problem in any case had attracted national attention when the Agricultural Adjustment Administration (AAA) was created as one of the cornerstones of the New Deal. And one of the first and most basic elements of the AAA was to limit crop production in the areas of wheat, corn, hogs, and cotton through reducing the proportion of acres cultivated. Between 1933 and 1935, the Agriculture Department had drawn up millions of contracts with farmers, whereby farmers received parity and rental payments in return for withdrawal of their lands from cultivation.

In the South the problem had been complicated by the existence of sharecroppers and tenants who divided with the landlord ownership of the crop, but not ownership of the land or the means to produce the crop. Inequities in the program had attracted widespread attention and condemnation from critics on the Left, especially after an investigatory committee from the LID had published a survey, appended to Norman Thomas' pamphlet on the topic, *The Plight of the Sharecropper*. Thoughts of a new farmer-labor coalition had sprung up. And a purge had been made among AAA personnel when Chester Davis, the top administrator for the program, clashed with Jerome Frank and others who were intent on purifying the original intentions of the program.

This current national program, then, became the subject of Hofstadter's M.A. thesis. The choice tied in with his own ideas on a new farmer-labor coalition, a move in which the Communists had been interested since 1923–24. The project developed from a paper that had attracted Carman's attention and approbation, providing Hofstadter with his first Columbia success. The thesis itself he entitled: "The Southeastern Cotton Tenants Under the AAA, 1933–1935."[13]

This was a technical treatise, weighted with statistics, tables, legal language, and dry, unadorned logic. It remains as the prime example in Hofstadter's corpus of his belief in "the science of society" and "the pure calculation that existing society was finished."[14] Hofstadter had succumbed to the temptation to look at society from the perspective of the social sciences, to use statistical data, and to utilize his Marxist base and methods as an unexplained starting point for interpretation. Behind the calculations, however, lay the same passionate concern for the American situation as had existed in his tutorial thesis. That passion was the cause for the calculations, the cause for the choice of subject, and the cause for the confusions in the study.

The work itself was divided into two main problems in the AAA acreage reduction program. The first treated landlords' confiscations of monetary benefits intended for tenants. The second treated the extent of tenant displacement in several forms—reduced social status, forced removal from the land, and forced removal from employment. Of the two problems, Hofstadter gave the bulk of his attention to displacement—four chapters in comparison with one for the confiscation of benefits.

It was Hofstadter's contention that owing to weaknesses in the contract between the Department of Agriculture and the farmers and to inequities in the social structure of the South, the major provisions of the acreage reduction program remained unfulfilled. The AAA benefit payments for retired land were intended to be prorated, or spread evenly among workers on the land, whether they owned the land or not. Tenants in the South were particularly vulnerable to abuse because of their economic dependence on their landlords. In the past, depending on his status as tenant farmer or sharecropper, the dependent farmer had received three-fourths to one-half of the proceeds of the cotton crop. The "tenant" who could afford to rent the land paid one-fourth of the proceeds from the crop for rent, furnishing his own tools and work stock. The "sharecropper" who could not afford to rent the land paid one-half to three-fourths of the proceeds from the cotton crop, and in addition rented the tools and work stock with which he performed his labor. The interest on these "furnishings" might run as high as 200 percent, Hofstadter reported.[15]

In the original 1933 AAA contract, a signer had been defined as the person who had "legal ownership of the crop." In the legal structure of the South, however, sometimes a landlord held a lien on the crop of a tenant, sometimes he had title to the entire crop. Even if the tenant held the lien on the crop, it was easy to avoid obtaining his signature. In the two-year 1934–35 contract, some oversights had been corrected. Benefits could be made in kind rather than in cash, and the bulk of total payments was made in the form of rental for land plowed under. Many legal loopholes still existed, however. "Rental" money went only to landowners. Hofstadter contended that there was an eight to one benefit ratio in favor of the landlord and that rental money was given those landlords primarily to induce them to reduce acreage in the face of higher actual benefits to wheat and corn hog raisers. Even without the inequities of the Southern social structure or the weaknesses in administration that existed, he said, the law itself contained inherent inequities in favor of the landowners.[16]

But administration of the program also effectively precluded equitable distribution of benefit payments. Because of the extent of the program, administrators were drawn from local areas and were often very closely connected socially to the landowners. Agents for the program appointed county and community committeemen from "leaders in their communities" to local production control boards. Thus, landowners were really policing themselves and effectively kept tenants and "croppers" off committees and production control boards. In a jolting metaphor, Hofstadter referred to these boards as "innumerable small soviets of landlords."[17]

The landlords possessed other means by which they could elude the original intentions of the AAA contracts. They could confiscate benefits to tenants on the basis of alleged or real back debts for "furnishings." They could plow up fields not worked by tenants. They could forego renewal of the annual contracts with their tenants, forcing the tenants into the aforementioned status of wage laborer, a position that was seasonal in extent and even less secure than the sharecropper's. They could force tenants off the land entirely. According to several revealing studies—one prepared by Federal Emergency Relief Administration, (FERA) research workers—the confiscation of benefits, whether through direct or indirect means, was indeed very high.[18]

In a single larger look at the program, Hofstadter attributed failure by the Administration—whether by the Department of Agriculture or by the President—to enforce the provisions of the law directly to political interests. On the one hand, he pointed out that the inequities of the system had produced in one year a union of farm laborers—the Southern Tenant Farmers' Union (STFU)—among people totally unused to labor organization. On the other hand, the inequities went unchallenged by the Administration because of the entrenched nature of the Democratic Party in the South.

A comparison of production costs with cotton prices during the years in question shows quite clearly that the AAA subsidies were the real source of net cash income from cotton production. Perhaps it were more accurate to speak of them as the profits of non-production. The pitifully small share of the tenants in such profits served to increase very sharply the spread between the lowest and highest incomes among cotton producers. This alone seems to be the explanation for the fact that the Southern Tenant Farmers' Union could organize 15,000 people in one year, despite the total absence of union traditions among tenants and the formidable obstacles of race feeling and armed terror. Of all the undertakings of the Roosevelt Administration, the AAA cotton program was farthest from giving a fair distribution of governmental largesse to all classes. It is no accident that this occurred in the least democratic region in the United States, and one upon which the Democratic party is heavily dependent.[19]

To Hofstadter, cynical political considerations had clouded the original purposes of the program and the blame could be laid squarely on the doorstep of the American political system.

The problem of displacement was open to more confusion and lack of clarity than was the problem of benefits. Displacement had been occurring regularly before the advent of the AAA acreage reduction program and at a higher rate.[20] As Hofstadter defined the phenomenon, it was the net quantity of people thrown off the farms or demoted in status because of acreage reduction. But this net amount was subject to variation and replacement or the substitution of new tenants for old, and had to be calculated also to arrive at an accurate net displacement figure.[21]

An attempt to resolve the problem was made in the second 1934–35 AAA contract. This document included a controversial seventh section, stipulating that landlords prorate their acreage reduction, retain a "normal number" of tenants on their lands, allow the tenants the use of some acres for subsistence crops, etc. But, Hofstadter maintained, this section provided only a loose, weak, and ineffective check. Expressions in the language of the contract, such as "endeavor in good faith" and "as nearly ratably as practicable" (referring to prorating the lump benefit), were simply "free and easy expressions" allowing landlords easily to bypass the stated stipulations. In addition, the section provided "two loopholes large enough to fit the necks of thousands of tenants." Landlords could retain the normal number of tenants while no mention of their status or stipulation as to their person was made. They could also change the status of sharecroppers, specifically, to that of day laborers at will. An additional phrase referring to the advisability of dismissing "nuisance-makers" established yet another loophole for landlords.[22]

Legally, then, in the 1934–35 contract, many avenues existed for bypassing the original intent of the program. In a test case in the Arkansas courts, called the Norcross case, Hofstadter reports, twenty-five tenants, evicted from the same plantation and belonging to the STFU hoped to regain their lands. They developed their case based on the idea that the original AAA program had intended to benefit people like themselves. The Court decided that the tenants had not demonstrated that the contract had been made *expressly* for them, that they were basing their argument on an incidental clause, and that thus it would rule against them. A month before this verdict, Secretary Henry Wallace had made a "narrow" interpretation of the disputed clause in Section 7 of the 1935–35 contract. He had said, "Landlords shall in good faith, endeavor to keep the same number of tenants on their farms, but not necessarily the same identical tenants." The Arkansas Court was thus able to cite the Secretary of Agriculture's statement as part of its decision, for the landlord in question had replaced the evicted tenants—with non-STFU members.[23]

Investigative agencies were also biased. In 1934 an Adjustment Committee was formed by the AAA to hear complaints about the alleged abuses within the program. It reported that there existed little evidence for increased displacement under the AAA. Hofstadter's opinion, however, was that its reports could not be trusted because the complaints were reviewed by the administrative structure of the Old South, the local power structure already described. Often the Adjustment Committee representative investigated complaints accompanied by a county committeeman who was a friend of the landlord himself. Sometimes the agent passed the complaint directly to the landlord. The result was reprisal—beatings and/or evictions for those who registered the complaints. Under those circumstances the Adjustment Committee would not find evidence of displacement.[24]

Other studies, however, did show varying degrees of displacement. One such, conducted by William R. Amberson for the LID, indicated that acreage reduction had not been evenly prorated among the various laborers on individual farms. Of all tenants who signed AAA contracts in the area covered in this particular study—parts of Missouri, Arkansas, Tennessee, and Mississippi—37 percent did not plow up *any* of their lands in 1933 and were therefore ineligible for any benefits, while only

5 percent plowed up all their land. Benefits given in these cases were given illegally.

Complicating factors also entered the picture. Even when land was not plowed up, tenants often remained on the land as subsistence farmers or wage laborers, sometimes aided by relief. Sometimes the tenant was pulled into the Works Progress Administration or other work-relief programs. What pattern did seem to emerge, for Hofstadter, was a close association between cotton production and losses in tenancy status between 1933 and 1935. In the counties in Georgia and Alabama most completely devoted to cotton production, the number of tenants invariably declined between 1930 and 1935. Those tenants were slipping back into the share-cropper or wage laborer status, not climbing into a higher one.[25]

Hofstadter, with a surface neutrality, concluded that reduction in cotton acreage had caused a substantial, but not overwhelming, displacement among rural workers. Numerically he fixed the total at just under 100,000 for the Cotton Belt as a whole, disagreeing with those who had set the sum higher. The prospects for the future looked dim, he thought. It appeared that the acreage reduction policy was becoming a permanent governmental policy. This was especially devastating for the Cotton Belt because cotton was a much more profitable crop for the area than any other. Despite the excellent opportunities for diversification in the area, no real innovations along this line had been instituted. Also, with the continuation of the policy, Hofstadter predicted displacement of as many as 500,000 in the future. In light of all these factors, he concluded with a "recommendation for the re-orientation of the national economic life in the direction of abundance rather than scarcity."[26]

This is a confusing study, not well organized and indicative of the adverse effects of the intensive political involvement in which Hofstadter found himself at this time. He tried to present a judicious, unbiased study of the issue by coolly examining a host of statistical surveys, but he ended with an undigested set of data. In referring to pro-Administration studies, he presented arguments against their validity before he summarized the findings. With anti-Administration studies, his approach was the opposite, referring to them several times before fully introducing

them as a piece of evidence, thus confusing the reader and load-
ing the data.

He made little effort truly to assess the pre–1933 rate of displacement, which might have set up a good comparative point,
indicating the operations of a Capitalist economy. Instead, he
avoided acknowledging the similarity—which was very real—
between his own conclusions that displacement was lower than
some studies indicated and the conclusions of pro-Administration studies. What his evidence seems to show is that while abuses
of the AAA acreage reduction program certainly existed, the
rate of displacement had been eased by AAA measures, not
increased. The fact was never squarely faced by Hofstadter. He
was still more partisan than historian.

Another aspect of this study bears scrutiny. For Hofstadter
the AAA acreage reduction program was not operating as had
been intended. It was fomenting problems, on a long-term basis,
which did not need to exist. The main reason for those problems
was the originally incorrect purpose of the program: to raise
prices by decreasing production. In this sort of assumption, one
sees again the tendency in these years to assume that there was
a key that when applied correctly, would operate to set in motion
a chain of correct processes that would then proceed automatically and independently. Critical of the existing program, Hofstadter had not thought enough about an alternative, so although
he may have perceived the root of the problem economically,
the study had little merit as positive social criticism.

In terms of research procedure, this study was also unsound.
Hofstadter has been accused by colleagues of inadequately investigating the primary sources. He has also been accused of
using one pivotal study as basis for his own work, while not giving
it adequate recognition. Here, as has been mentioned, Hofstadter leaned heavily on the Amberson Committee study published
with Norman Thomas' book in 1934. This Hofstadter used as
his first and strongest evidence providing data for displacement
under the AAA. But Amberson had also published an article
entitled "The New Deal for Share Croppers" in the *Nation*, after
publication of the Committee report. This article was also strongly
critical of the Administration, and Hofstadter cited it twice among

his arguments against the validity of those studies in favor of the Administration.[27]

But the article, as well as referring to evidence collected by the Committee, included at least *ten* of Hofstadter's major points. Amberson's discussion of Section 7 of the 1934–35 contract provided exactly the same quotation from the section as Hofstadter had used. Amberson pointed out the loose wording of the clause. He also pointed out the eight-to-one ratio of benefits in favor of the landlords. Amberson quoted the same source—Paul W. Bruton—as critic of the contract, and cited previous work, namely, that of Calvin Hoover, who had been commissioned by Secretary Wallace to investigate tenant displacement. He also indicated doubt about the magnitude of displacement, concluding that one-third of the current rural unemployment resulted directly from the reduction program. He discussed the Adjustment Committee, describing in more comprehensive detail than Hofstadter a particular farm, cleared for thousands of dollars of AAA benefits, but on which an FERA worker had spent $1,400 to clothe and feed the tenants, some of whom owned only the clothes obtained from the worker. The farm, 22 square miles in extent, had been investigated and and cleared of the charged abuses in six hours by a governmental investigator and county committeeman. Amberson discussed the Norcross case in which the twenty-five SFTU members "pennied out" payments week by week for the legal case that decided their fate negatively. And Amberson concluded his article with the remark: "Once the basic error of production restriction has been made, it is no longer within the power of administrators, however humane, to prevent a train of vicious sequelae."[28]

What do all these overlapping points indicate? That Hofstadter was not doing original work? That the literature on this very current and "hot" issue, for such a limited period, could be covered by two researchers with nearly the same point of view in almost exactly the same way? That Hofstadter consciously or unconsciously used the article as a basic outline from which to expand his research? One is left with some unanswered questions and it is impossible to come to definite conclusions, but some tentative observations are in order.

Hofstadter's research did probe further than Amberson's. He interviewed May Conner Myers, acting representative for the Department of Agriculture who was sent to investigate the Norcross case. He also interviewed Gardner Jackson, formerly of the AAA Consumer's Counsel. He looked at the actual briefs for the appellants and the appellees in the Norcross case. And he reviewed a variety of census figures and other secondary literature. However, he did not go beyond the conclusions of Amberson.[29]

It seems that Hofstadter was still caught, here, between external expectations and personal internal commitments. He seems to have been trying to present an "unbiased," "scientific" survey of evidence and to assess the validity of the several studies on the subject. On the surface, he accomplished this goal, almost letting the evidence speak for itself. But Hofstadter also made a polemical statement, much more in accord with his current political opinions and with his passionate concern for human betterment than with Columbia's graduate school requirements.

The issue is one of forthrightness. If Hofstadter did use the Amberson article as a type of guide for his research, he could have made an interesting and coherent essay by presenting it at the beginning of his study. If all the overlapping points were merely coincidental, and Hofstadter simply ended a more extensive survey by agreeing with Amberson, he should have said so. But he did neither of these. What he did do was reminiscent of his reviews for the *Herald Tribune*. He applied his admittedly formidable powers of logic to the studies under consideration, but evidently felt too constrained to let his imagination go. Thus, the hypotheses with which he began—the radically critical framework of his political position—were never questioned or truly tested. And what resulted was a series of brittle, logical deductions without the establishment of the assumptions from which they sprang. One is left with a mass of statistical data, inadequately organized and poorly presented.

What emerges from this project, because of the nature of the subject, is a picture of the thwarted intentions of an American reform administration, intentions gone awry at their very inception, and gone awry because of deep-seated political and social inequities. One of the unintended consequences of the AAA program was a continuation of the inequity of the Southern social structure and of the misery and suffering of those displaced by that structure. Felice's observation of criss-crossing purposes, made in discussion of the social structure in her M.A. thesis, appears thus to have been applied to the acreage reduction program and its historical context.

In his tutorial thesis, Hofstadter had done well in applying Beard's methods to his questions about the "Second American Revolution." Here, two years later, Hofstadter had again attempted to use Beard's techniques. This time, however, because of the current nature of the materials, he had succeeded in writing a kind of sociological tract, which lacked the salient elements of history. He was attempting to make the past bear on the present, but he had not yet found the particular approach that would be effective in that attempt. He had not yet connected the powerful logic of his political analyses and the imaginative side of his personality. That integration would come during the following year.

NOTES

1. "Unofficial Transcript," Columbia University, Record in the Graduate Faculties of Political Science, Philosophy, and Pure Science—Richard Hofstadter; *Columbia University Bulletin of Information*, 36th Series, #39, May 27, 1936, pp. 19, 28.

2. *Columbia Bulletin*, #39, pp. 19, 28.

3. Alfred Kazin, *New York Jew* (New York, Vintage Books, 1979) p. 25; Alfred Kazin, personal interview with the author, November 19, 1980.

4. This was a concern at several points and in various contexts. Felice wrote of Robert Terrall, "I think he's just scared of Dick—too tough." Felice Swados to Harvey Swados, March 8, 1938, Harvey Swados Papers, Courtesy of the Archives of the University of Massachusetts, Amherst, Mass. Hofstadter wrote "I hope you and Harold will not seriously believe that either one of us considers you afraid of me, intellectually or otherwise. " Hofstadter to Swados, April 30, 1938.

5. The three others were "Old Sugar Mills of Georgia," *New York Herald Tribune Books* (April 28, 1937) p. 14, "An American Zionist," (April 25, 1937) p. 19; "Mind and Matter," (July 11, 1937) p. 10. Felice was also reviewing books at this time, a fact that may have produced

some competitive tension between them. Alfred Kazin has made the suggestion that they were intellectually competitive. Kazin, official interview, Columbia Oral History Office, May 1, 1972.

6. Richard Hofstadter, "On Journey," *New York Herald Tribune Books* (April 18, 1937) p. 3.

7. Ibid.

8. Richard Hofstadter, "The Recovery of Ideals, " *New York Herald Tribune Books* (June 6, 1937) p. 13.

9. *Columbia Bulletin,* 1936–37, 37th Series, Announcements 1937–38, # 18–38, pp. 7, 15, 18, 22; "Unofficial Transcript"—Richard Hofstadter.

10. Richard Hofstadter, "The Department of History," in R. Gordon Hoxie et al., eds., *A History of the Faculty of Political Science, Columbia University* (New York, Columbia University Press, 1955) pp. 237–38; *Columbia Bulletin,* 37th Series, p. 22; Hofstadter to Harvey Swados, October 17, 1937, November 26, 1937, Swados Papers.

11. Harry J. Carman, untitled MS, Carman Papers, Rare Book and Manuscript Library, Columbia University, New York, N.Y.

12. Ibid., p. 10 (emphasis in original); Felice Swados to Harvey Swados, December 29, 1937, Swados Papers.

13. Arthur M. Schlesinger, *The Age of Roosevelt, II: The Coming of the New Deal* (New York, Houghton Mifflin, 1965) pp. 74–80; Theodore Draper, *American Communism and Soviet Russia* (New York, Viking Press, 1960) pp. 29–51.

14. See Alfred Kazin quotation at note 5 in text of chapter 4 above.

15. Richard Hofstadter, "The Southeastern Cotton Tenants Under the AAA, 1933–1935" (M.A. Thesis, Columbia University, 1938) pp. 5–8.

16. Ibid., pp. 9–17.

17. Ibid., pp. 18–23. For quotation see p. 22.

18. Ibid., pp. 35–38.

19. Ibid., p. 42.

20. Ibid., pp. 12–13.

21. Ibid., pp. 45–46.

22. Ibid., pp. 49–51.

23. Ibid., pp. 53–59.

24. Ibid., pp. 60–77.

25. Ibid., pp. 78–94.

26. Ibid., pp. 95–99. For quotation see p. 99.

27. Ibid., p. 63 n. 10, 11.

28. William R. Amberson, "The New Deal for Share-Croppers," *Nation,* CXL (February 13, 1935): pp. 185–88.

29. Hofstadter, "Southeastern Cotton Tenants," pp. 53–55, 57, 59.

6

Hammering Out the Ideology of Capitalism

The period between September 1938 and January 1941 marked several major developments for Richard Hofstadter. He made the decision to push beyond his M.A. to work for a Ph.D. in history. He met Merle Curti who inspired and encouraged him. And he added several new elements to his written history.

Originally, Hofstadter had planned to obtain his Master's degree and find a teaching job on the basis of his work at Columbia. As it turned out, completion of the Master's degree marked both an end and a beginning. It was an achievement because he had overcome the hurdle of the thesis. A cartoon drawn at this time pictures an abashed and very small student in front of a desk as large as he, behind which loomed an enormous professor with long nose and small goatee, pointing an equally long, sharp finger at the student, who stands cringing, with paper in hand. The caption for the cartoon: "It may be interesting but it's NOT a master's thesis." Overcoming that hurdle gave him the confidence to continue his studies. That confidence was crucial.[1]

Hofstadter must have been given some extra encouragement, however, because in the fall of 1938 after he returned to Columbia, he planned to submit an article, written in conjunction with Professor Carman, on farm tenancy. His Master's thesis and this projected article had inspired the idea for a trip to the South during the summer of 1938, and Hofstadter and Felice traveled through North Carolina, stopping in Chimney Rock and Memphis, Tennessee, and other places. They went out of curiosity and concern for the hinterland, because of Hofstadter's interest in sharecropping, and because of a tradition established by Northern intellectuals in the 1930's to expose the inequities of Southern backwardness. The trip had become a kind of pilgrimage for these Northern radicals. Felice, for her part, had become interested in writing an article on Negro health in the antebellum South for the *Political Science Quarterly*.[2]

In the fall Hofstadter registered for 21 hours of history courses. As had been the case the year before, his choice of subjects reflected better the international political situation than it did any presumed plans for his academic future. His courses included "The British Empire," "Economic and Political History of France and Italy from the French Revolution," "The History of American Social Thought," "Economic and Social History of the U. S. Since 1865," "History of European Nationalism," "European Thought and Culture in the 19th Century," and "American Life at the Beginning of the Machine Age." He had obviously overloaded himself. He spoke of the "arduous" task of keeping up with course work at the same time as he was trying to write his article with Carman. He ended by dropping two courses in the European field, but the overload suggests a number of things about Hofstadter's attitude at this time. He was hungry for the subject of history. He was confident of his ability to do good work at Columbia. He was in a hurry to complete the requisite requirements.[3]

As time wore on and course work demanded so much of his time, Hofstadter let the idea of an article on farm tenancy slide. The project lost priority status for him because other new interests were crowding in. The focus of his attention was on "The History of American Social Thought." The course, given at Teachers' College but "attended ... by as many students from the Faculty of Political Science ... as from T.C.," was described as emphasizing the "forces molding ideas, conditions modifying ideas, and the relation of social ideas and attitudes to cultural values and achievements."[4]

The instructor, Merle Curti, had come to Columbia the year before after eleven years at Smith College. He had attended Harvard and studied there under Arthur Schlesinger, Sr. Professor Curti was a friend of George Counts, who had traveled to the Soviet Union in the early 1930's, as had many others, and had returned enthusiastic about the social experiment there. After the Commission on Social Studies of the AHA had been formed under the influence of Charles Beard and Counts, Curti was asked to write *The Social Ideas of American Educators* under its auspices. That book was published in 1936. By the fall of 1938, when he first met Hofstadter, Curti may have already started work on his next large volume, *The Growth of American Thought*, to appear in 1943.[5]

Curti's approach appealed to Hofstadter. *The Social Ideas* had been written from a Marxist perspective and was a study of the attempt by established groups in educational instututions to maintain the status quo against the threats of anarchy, rebellion, and insurgency. Curti criticized the nineteenth century philosophy of rugged individualism. He found its reflection in the philosophies of William James and Lynn Thorndike. He viewed Herbert Spencer and Lester Ward as attempting to fit society to the needs of individuals, rather than fitting individuals to the needs of society. Curti saw Dewey as influenced heavily by Hegel through William T. Harris, an earlier educator who was a proponent of environmentalism and social conditioning. In such views Curti anchored himself in the widespread revulsion against individualism of the 1930's. Curti may be interpreted as making an attempt to put the intellectual "superstructure" of Capitalist society into historical perspective.[6]

It was important for Hofstadter that Curti was a Marxist. He viewed the work that Curti was doing as "pioneer work in that line [the history of social thought]." The two first met in class. Curti was impressed with Hofstadter's performances there, and the two began having lunch together. According to Felice, they had formed a regular "mutual admiration society by the middle of the year."[7] It must be concluded that this friendship and the model Merle Curti presented—that of an established, accepted, and successful scholar of Marxist persuasion—wrought in Richard Hofstadter an important liberation. To date, his life had been bifucated. Publicly—outwardly—he had attempted to be "scientific" and "objective" in his scholarly enterprises. His academic work emphasized logic and deductive reasoning. In other writings he had stressed logic and publicly eschewed traditional philosophical theory. Privately he had espoused the philosophy of Marxism, which stood for values diametrically opposed to those of the Capitalist society around him and which dominated the academic establishments within which he was ensconced. In his prior academic work and in his newspaper reviews, he had been constrained to camouflage that political bias. Now, as we shall see in his Ph.D. work, he was able to combine effectively that outward show of detachment and his inward passion for political and philosophical "morality." The result was greatly increased coherence in his work, a new vitality, and more depth.

Through Curti, Hofstadter encountered for the first time the history of social thought. He had, it has been noticed, encountered intellectual history *per se* in Marvin Farber's "History of Philosophy." Curti's approach stressed not only the social and economic background of thought, but the impact of that thought on the intellectual's own environment and social institutions. As for training, Curti came from the study of popular social institutions and their development, in the vein of Arthur Schlesinger's *New Viewpoints in American History*. To that social element, Curti added his own intellectual questions. He was interested not in the thought of the few, but in the effects of ideas, through people's institutions, on the many.

The effect of this new influence on Hofstadter was apparent as early as November 1938, when he reported in cryptic, tongue-in-cheek fashion:

I have just had returned to me an extended paper written by me for the Course in the History of American Social Thought, which the Prof.— who is a Marxist, incidentally—and myself think shows signs of genius. The paper is on Jefferson's Ideas on Class Relations, and probably throws more light on this aspect of Jefferson's thought than anything which has heretofore been written. Among my works I rank it second only to The Problem of the Unmarried Mother, which you need not hurry to return, since it deserves the widest possible audience.[8]

Whether or not the "Unmarried Mother" ranked above or below "Jefferson's Ideas," the latter paper demonstrates a new integration and a new straightforwardness in Hofstadter's writing. It also shows the ahistorical bias of Marxist thinking common in the 1930's. And in it Hofstadter began to develop the type of structure that he would use throughout his career as American historian.

The paper was based on Jefferson's correspondence and offers a good insight into the actual state of Hofstadter's mind, as it stands unrevised. As in his tutorial thesis, Hofstadter was testing a matter of consciousness: this time Jefferson's consciousness of class conflict. The leading quotation, from Charles Beard's *The Economic Basis of Jeffersonian Democracy*, read, "His faith was a class faith and his appeal was a class appeal." The section headings were "The Formation and Solidarity of Classes," "Jefferson and the Small Farmers," "The Economic Relations of Classes," and "The Political Relations of Classes." The purpose of the paper: to determine the "extent to which the class struggles of his day were reflected in the thought of Thomas Jefferson." As in earlier work, Hofstadter had limited his focus well.[9]

He had found, however, that one could not expect from Jefferson any "such sharp, penetrating, and yet comprehensive statement about class relations as may be found in the Federalist Number 10 or in the Communist Manifesto."[10]

Jefferson, Hofstadter found, was aware of the conflict in interests between the groups—or classes—that made up his society. His championship of small farmers and landowners and his aversion to artisans and other city dwellers Hofstadter interpreted as consciousness and acceptance of "the mutual antagonism [of these classes] over the manner in which the social produce is distributed." Since Jefferson was constantly aware of the economic and political interests of the farmers, he "never failed to see the class aspects of domestic legislation." In his constant attempt to protect those interests against the intrusions of merchants, sea traders, and speculators, Jefferson appeared to Hofstadter to be particularly aware of "the *use of political means to carry out economic exploitation*." Furthermore, since Jefferson never mentioned any intra-class conflict, Hofstadter concluded that he accepted the "solidarity" of class interests without question.[11]

But this was as far as Jefferson's awareness went. Hofstadter was critical of Jefferson's tendency to confuse economic, political, and "psychological" categories. When Jefferson lumped together

"British merchants ... speculators, most officers of the federal government," and "nervous persons afraid of change" as anti-Republicans, for example, Hofstadter wondered at his acceptance of such "innate" qualities. He observed, "he did not see, as Marx would have seen or as John Taylor of Caroline *did* see, that the non-economic groups were simply servitors of sub classifications of the fundamental economic classes."[12]

Jefferson's inconsistency in terminology and failure to recognize the causative nature of economic factors could be attributed, in Hofstadter's mind, to Jefferson's "own peculiar personal status." Having chosen "to advocate the cause of the little man out of a mixture of humanitarianism, distrust for the ways of city men, and certain highly intellectual convictions about the nature of desirable government," Jefferson attributed these motives to other men "in an unwarranted degree." In other words, he *projected* the qualities of his own mind—and his intellectually based convictions—onto others and made "the political universe ... mirror Jefferson's own mind."[13]

Jefferson's "anomalous class position" also explained the gap between his theory and his practice, according to Hofstadter. In theory a radical democratic fire-eater, in practice Jefferson amounted to a "mild agrarian reformer." Although Jefferson saw class struggles as effectively marking the politics of his own day, he failed to make them "an integral part of his social theory." He did not see that they would extend into the future. This was so, Hofstadter thought, because he expected "the enduring victory of the agrarian democracy." Settlement of the lands to the west would ensure "a rapid expansion of the agricultural class."[14]

In a word, Jefferson was not consistent. As a political philosopher," Jefferson projected or mirrored his own mind, projecting his wishes for peaceful, harmonious society into the future. As a "historian of his own time," Jefferson understood the process of economic causation.

If he had belonged to a different class himself, Jefferson would have been different, Hofstadter thought.

Had Jefferson himself been drawn from their ranks, his championship of the small farmers might have been less philosophical [psychological] and more militant [economic and class conscious]. Perhaps then his theory would have been more rigorous and consistent, his endorsement of agrarian rebellion more pregnant with practical significance. However that may be, the farmers paid a heavy price for having as their leader this magnanimous aristocrat, who could erect in his hall at Monticello a marble bust of his greatest foe.[15]

Jefferson simply possessed too much equanimity, too much tolerance, and not enough militance for theory and practice to coalesce. He should have led the farmers in class warfare. Instead, he open-mindedly succumbed to the policies of tolerance and "psychological" magnanimity. Jefferson represented for Hofstadter the unconnected, liberal, and middle-class mind, too relativistic and tolerant to come down clearly on a definite, critical position.

Hofstadter concluded his paper by observing how time had effected the Jeffersonian ideal: "History, with characteristic brutality, chose to strangle the Jeffersonian ideal in the slow course of a century." And now, "the vital substance of Jeffersonian democracy, its peculiarly Jeffersonian aspect has little relation to current political and economic realities."

The small farmers have been outnumbered and crushed; the landed Southerners have become servitors rather than opponents of the great capitalists, into whose hand control has fallen; and the city "mobs"—those "panders [sic] of vice and the instruments by which the liberties of a country are generally overturned"—have become "the people," upon whom the preservation of democracy depends.[16]

The social make-up of the American nation had become realigned and the balance in numbers reversed.

Several observations are in order here. First, this is Hofstadter's most explicitly Marxist statement. It was written at the same time as he was a committed party member and was attending Columbia graduate unit meetings. His terminology and approach show that influence. It affected his presentation of Jefferson's ideas. It intruded on his interpretation of those ideas. The terminology of Marxism—phrases such as "social produce" and the "functional interdependence of economic classes"—did little to clarify Jefferson's actual ideas.

His political philosophy also affected his interpretation of the

Jeffersonian legacy. Because Jefferson was *not* a member of the
class of small farmers that he supported—because he was not a
working person—his vision and understanding of social developments over time were limited. He thought that class conflict
would come to an end. The truth, for Hofstadter was that it
simply changed in social make-up.

Hofstadter's political philosophy also affected how he saw the
long view of history. The Jeffersonian ideal had become outmoded by 1938 because the urban proletariat had replaced the
small farmers in the strength of numbers. Hofstadter's observation of this inversion was the key to his interpretation of Jefferson. This type of observation recalls his tutorial thesis, in
which he noted that the German immigrants were a "living contradiction" as members of the Democratic Party. Their switch in
allegiance—their inverted Party affiliation—caused earthshaking
consequences for the future of the Union. Here, the "slow course
of a century" brought a similar inversion in numbers on the
farm and in the city and proportionate changes in their balance
of interests. The preponderance of the urban proletariat now
seemed as if it too would bring earthshaking consequences for
the political and economic systems of the United States.

Hofstadter was working in the field of intellectual history for
the first time in this essay. His orientation to that field was colored
by Merle Curti, as well as by his political philosophy. As Curti
had attempted in *The Social Ideas*, Hofstadter also treated Jefferson's ideas on classes in terms of the socioeconomic milieu
from which they had sprung, finding the cause for Jefferson's
limitations in outlook in his own social position. This type of
relationship between ideas and their context, still germinal here
but evident nonetheless, shows Hofstadter's own effort to clarify
the intellectual superstructure of a Capitalist economy.

One is impressed with the new flow to Hofstadter's writing
here. He appears to have found his real medium. No longer
locked into the subject of current economic issues, as he had
been with his M.A. thesis, he was free to deal directly with ideas
and treat socioeconomic factors as background. Gone are the
jerky, tense summaries of his M.A. thesis and the awkward logic
of his tutorial thesis. The new medium gave him the opportunity
to combine both his imagination—the imagination that had pro-

duced the character of Jeeves in his high school play—*and* his penchant for logical analysis and tough-minded political realism. Without abandoning the institutional history he had dealt with in the past, with the warm support of a new mentor, Hofstadter had added the social and individual aspects that were to make of his history so variegated and "luminous" a product later on. In this process, Curti was the catalyst but Marx the source.

In the same letter of November 1938 to Harvey Swados in which he had mentioned his paper on Jefferson's ideas on class relations, Hofstadter also referred to another paper he had begun, called "Physiocratic Elements in the Thought of Jefferson and Franklin." He thought it would give him "an excellent chance of publication" when he finished it. Although the early forms of this paper are not available, it is quite clear that this paper, again written for Curti's class, was the forerunner of a final version, published in the *Journal of the History of Ideas* for October 1941, entitled "Parrington and the Jeffersonian Tradition."[17]

The journal article marked the first place in which Hofstadter had come to grips with Vernon L. Parrington, whom he was then reading for the first time.[18] Hofstadter took issue with Parrington on the essence of Jefferson's economic views. Parrington had argued that Jefferson's theory was essentially similar to that of the Physiocrats of France. This was not the case, thought Hofstadter, because "the gulf between the French estate and the American frontier" was too great. The Physiocratic doctrine of the single tax on heretofore exempted landed wealth contradicted the teachings put forward by Jefferson and his follower John Taylor. Their goal had been to *limit* the taxes on landed wealth, thus protecting the freehold tenure system of small farmers. They did not wish to make land the sole source of revenue, Hofstadter argued. However, the Physiocrats had incorporated anti-monopoly and anti-protectionistic policies into their approach, and thus they were also proposing an early form of laissez-faire. In this way, and only in this way, could Jefferson be considered a Physiocrat. He was a Physiocrat only insofar as the Physiocrats were also advocates of laissez-faire.[19]

Parrington had argued that others had also adopted the Physiocratic arguments: Benjamin Franklin, John Taylor, Andrew

Jackson. Not so, wrote Hofstadter. All four figures in question
espoused the general tenets of laissez-faire. There had been no
general "conflict between the rival principles of Quesnay and
Adam Smith, between an agrarian and a capitalistic economy"
in this country. The orientation represented by these four "accepted the capitalist order, without desire or ability to propose
an alternative society." They simply proposed innocuous "reforms which interfered with its smooth functioning." Besides,
Hofstadter added, none of the devices of these reformers could
ultimately make a difference because "the ultimate triumph of
the capitalist order was inevitable." The very strength of Capitalism in America was the cause for the relative weakness of
other theories in this country.[20]

Hofstadter concluded:

Visitor's at Monticello in Jefferson's later years were surprised to find
there a marble bust of Hamilton. With the perspective of the twentieth
century, they would not have been surprised: within the mansions of
Jeffersonian Democracy there were busts of Hamilton everywhere.[21]

Jefferson's tolerance pushed him closer to Hamilton than Parrington would have been ready or willing to admit.

Hofstadter had argued that "the principal tenets of the Physiocrats were quickly rejected or forgotten because they were
fundamentally unadaptable to the American economic milieu."[22]
Given the economic base in the United States, no theory would
be competitive with Capitalism. This was so because, according
to Hofstadter's Marxist assumptions, all ideas were conditioned
and subject to the more basic aspects of life, which were economic. Hofstadter had outlined an argument that would become
the hallmark of a later school of American historians. Seen in
the light of its original context, that consensus theory takes on
its true significance.

Hofstadter had originally believed that he would be able to
find Physiocratic elements in Jefferson's thought. The discovery
that he could not, then, was a historical insight of some importance to him during this year of intellectual growth. From the
first indication that he was working on the idea in November

1938 until he gave it up in the spring of 1939, he had kept the project in the front of his mind.[23] Probably, as he searched for signs of class consciousness in Jefferson's writings and correspondence, he also kept his eyes open for Physiocratic ideas. At the same time, he was also reading Parrington. Perhaps the latter reading even inspired the former. At any rate, the project was of primary importance in the Hofstadter/Swados household, and Felice also became involved.

Since the couple at this time were extremely close, both emotionally and intellectually, one is justified in accepting Felice's statements as adaptations of Hofstadter's own and in using them to evaluate Hofstadter's mind and positions at the time. Felice's brother, Harvey Swados, then an undergraduate at the University of Michigan, was at that point planning a book on literary criticism. Harvey had sent a preliminary outline of his idea to his sister and brother-in-law for their comments and criticism.

For Harvey, Parrington appeared to be one of those "sociological critics who . . . had no philosophical standards." That is, Harvey could not easily fit Parrington into the categories he had devised. Felice, in responding to Harvey's judgment of Parrington, was critical. She believed that Parrington, "had he lived a little longer, would have also been a Marxist" and therefore would have come to possess "philosophical" standards. Parrington's "biggest mistake," she said, alluding to her husband's academic work, had been his interpretation of Jefferson. The tension in Jefferson's life, her husband was finding, was due to the pull between his emotional attachments to the land and the lack of systematic economic theory to support that attachment.[24]

In struggling with the question of how Parrington went wrong, Hofstadter's own historical orientation was emerging. While both he and Felice read and appreciated Parrington, in contrast to Harvey, for his "philosophical standards," they found those standards conspicuously absent from the thought of the figures Parrington was treating. By process of elimination, then, they concluded that capitalistic thought in early America dominated the thinking of people in a variety of political positions. Parrington, on the other hand, by reading history backward, had found radical thought akin to his own. Hofstadter, feeling more alien to the American past than had Parrington, inverted Parrington's findings and discovered only the beliefs in a Capitalism that appeared outmoded by 1938.

There had been growth between Hofstadter's first paper on Jefferson, with its single-minded search for class consciousness, and this second paper, which noted the tension between Jefferson's love of the land and his lack of economic theory to support it. The two papers were clearly taken from the same basic research. They overlapped on many points, the most marked of which was the observation of Alexander Hamilton's bust at Monticello and the speculation about the significance of this fact. In both papers Hofstadter had focused on the economic elements of Jefferson's thought. But whereas he had derided Jefferson in his early paper for not conforming completely to Marx's dicta, in the later one Hofstadter applied the larger Marxian historical assumptions to Jefferson's economic theories. Instead of displacing bits of Marxist economics onto the past, he now saw the past in the greater terms of the Marxist long view. In the published paper on Parrington, Hofstadter found a hidden and "inevitable" Capitalism growing up in America during the same period in which Marx had first taken to writing down his thoughts. This American Capitalism grew up, furthermore, in a new, clear environment, freed of the fetters and contradictions of feudalism. That it did so was due to the fact that the economic system was part of a larger, "inevitable" unfolding of history—by definition dialectical in nature—and *not* because it was correct, good, or morally preferable.

Again, as Curti had attempted in *The Social Ideas*, Hofstadter jumped on the opportunity to picture the development of what would have been to him the "ideological superstructure" of the early Capitalist economy, as it grew into maturity during the early national years. Parrington had been wrong on Jefferson and Physiocratic ideas in America precisely because he had not understood the growth of ideas in relation to their economic base. Parrington understood ideas only in relation to each other. The conflict in America was not, as Parrington had maintained, between Physiocratic agrarianism and Capitalism. It was between laissez-faire and economic nationalism. The latter consisted of the American form of a dying mercantilistic, postfeudal order, more marked in Europe but still dimly reflected on the western shores of the Atlantic as well. On these shores, in actuality, occurred the birthpangs of the purest version of Capitalist economy yet to appear. From this perspective, a person like Alexander Hamilton appeared to express a system of economic thought that harked back to the pre-Capitalist days of mercantilism. It was he, not Jefferson, for example, who "could not incorporate laissez-faire into his philosophy." It was he who served as "the predecessor of modern economic nationalism" and who inspired the "theoretical father of nationalist economics," Freidrich List. "The ideological side of the Jefferson-Hamilton struggle," Hofstadter concluded, "may therefore be approached as a part of the world-wide struggle between laissez-faire and economic nationalism." With this point Hofstadter clinched his argument against Parrington by invoking some points from Marxist theory about the history of the Capitalist revolution.[25]

The third paper Hofstadter wrote during this intensive year was also produced for Merle Curti. It appeared in the second semester of the academic year. The subject was Wendell Phillips, and the paper dealt with Phillips as an American alternative to Marxian radicalism. Just as Jefferson had been allergic to the "systematic and 'metaphysical' character of Physiocratic doctrine," so Phillips also eschewed system, ideology, rigor, and speculation. But Phillips represented for Hofstadter the indigenous radical who joined, through the growth of his own vision, the two essential arms of the social movement: Abolitionism and labor. In treating Phillips, Hofstadter was also joining his own formerly disparate interests. He was combining his focus on the causes for Lincoln's election, which he had treated in his tutorial thesis at the University of Buffalo, and his interest in the consequences of the slave system, as suggested by his M.A. thesis. Phillips, with his nonideological, anti-intellectual approach, represented more directly than anyone Hofstadter had yet treated an American hero—a lonely agitator, "hovering on the extreme left border of the reform movements which he found in America." He exemplified for Hofstadter "the unique development of American radicalism."[26]

The paper shows a marked difference from Hofstadter's previous academic work. For the first time, he was dealing with biographical materials. In this genre he was able to give expressive leeway to those nonscientific aspects of the historical past that he had avoided before, the aspects of personality and the personal transcendence of economic or social "forces." It is significant in this light that Hofstadter began his paper with the statement, "By all the lights that govern the careers of ordinary men, Wendell Phillips should never have become a radical agitator."[27] People with Phillips's background, evidently, had roots in the American system too strong and deep to allow them to oppose it. Radical agitators, in Hofstadter's lexicon, were immigrants like Louis Fraina or Jay Lovestone, first or second generation, too recently arrived to be on more than the fringes of American wealth or prestige. Phillips in fact had quite a different background.

The first Phillips had come to this country in 1630, and the family had prospered. Wendell's father, a wealthy lawyer with fine mercantile connections, became the first mayor of Boston. Wendell had everything that a Boston boy could want—a family, a good name, good looks, money, connections, brains, and an education at the Boston Latin School and Harvard.[28]

He was, in a word, purebred Anglo-Saxon.

But Phillips was an anomaly for his class, and this is what fascinated Hofstadter. Phillips's life represented the unintended consequences of dramatic irony. The irony here—the first of its kind in Hofstadter's academic work—arose from the Marxist assumption Hofstadter was making about social causation. He assumed that specific social and economic spheres produce only specific, limited ideas and/or occupational types. At the same time, he was faced with the fact that Phillips's career lay in a direction other than that to be expected. Unlike in his M.A. thesis, Hofstadter did not shirk from this new truth here. His efforts to describe and explain the anomaly adequately took him much further in his development as a historian than had his thesis.

There are reasons to think that Hofstadter identified personally with this champion of Abolitionism and the working man.

Aspects of Phillips's early career paralleled Hofstadter's own. He wrote: "His studies [of the English and American revolutions] made a deep impression, *but* did not keep him from becoming a lawyer or from studying under the conservative [Joseph] Story." Hofstadter, too, had studied revolutions, worked under conservative mentors, and attempted to combine radical agitation with the law. Also, "for a short time the young man played but a minor role in the abolition movement—although this wanton risk of his budding law practice was enough cause for his family to think him insane." Hofstadter too had experienced family problems over the choice and establishment of a career and tension between his political orientation and his original, intended profession. Hofstadter too had operated on the fringes of a movement. Phillips was also likely to use "sharp irony" and "had a great genius for invective." And Phillips married a woman originally more devoted to his cause than he—"Ann Terry Greene, an abolitionist extraordinary and a stern, militant spirit." At that point, however, the two parted company, for Phillips "really found himself" in 1837 when he "leapt to the platform" to protest the killing of Elijah Lovejoy by anti-Abolitionist fanatics. Hofstadter was a writer who realized himself most fully by committing words to the page. But these similarities and Phillips's lonely stand would have endeared this revolutionary to Hofstadter and made what he observed in Phillips especially pertinent to his own intellectual development.[29]

The influence of his ideological and academic background made Hofstadter guilty of curious anachronisms in his reading of Phillips's mind and life. He assigned, for example, many of the familiar revolutionary labels to the discussion of Abolitionism, again indicating the ahistorical tendency of this period. He wrote:

The abolitionist movement was not based upon *self-conscious* economic discontent. Its immediate impulse, whatever socio-economic factors lurked in the background, was religious. It should not be surprising, therefore, that it never developed a serious philosophically grounded body of social criticism, and that programmatically it was underdeveloped and adolescent.[30]

The yardstick of current Marxism dictated that any social movement be both "self-conscious" and scientifically thought out, as
well as economic in its goals. By these criteria Abolitionism could
not measure up.

Hofstadter continued the above discussion with the following:

> Hence, its futile wrestling with the problems raised by the slogan of
> immediatism. However revolutionary some of its partisans became in
> the technical and legal sense.... it could not conceive a social program
> which would give skeletal structure to its moral substance.... The move-
> ment never worked out a clear program by which the Negro might be
> freed and securely established in the new social and economic relation-
> ships that freedom would entail.... It had neither a fully rounded phi-
> losophy nor a program. It hoped to free the slave by faith.[31]

While it is true that the Garrisonian faction of Abolitionists with
which Phillips identified urged freedom for the slaves immediately, Hofstadter had learned the tactics of immediatism from
Communist Party policies. In long discussions with his friends,
Hofstadter had argued against immediatism. Now he criticized
the same approach as wielded by the Abolitionists. His understanding of the historical movement originated in his experience
with the current one.

It is also pertinent here to observe that Hofstadter was noting
the theoretical bankruptcy of the Abolitionist movement. The
moral fervor of that movement appeared to have hindered the
hard-headed thinking and orientation toward the future that
characterized the left-wing movement of the 1930's. As with
Jefferson, the limitations of the Abolitionists were based on their
lack of awareness of economic causation and the essential nature
of economic relationships to reform. It is the burden of Hofstadter's paper on Phillips to demonstrate Phillips's response to
those limitations.

Hofstadter found that Phillips grew over the course of his
reform-minded activities. Phillips developed from a "Romantic"
before the Civil War to a "Realist" after the Civil War. The switch
paralleled Phillips's change of focus from race to labor. In this
original paper for Curti, there remains the evidence of the dialogue between teacher and student on an aspect of this change.
Hofstadter had written:

During the long abolition struggle, and especially during the crisis and reconstruction, his attention had become focused upon economics. The problem of securing justice and equality for the Negro had shed new light upon the *real forces* which underlay the formal and legal relation of social classes.[32]

Curti asked in the margin: "Is there documentation for this?" Further on in the text Hofstadter inadvertently answered Curti's question.

The inadequacy of the pre-war abolitionist creed, with its simple-minded faith in the efficacy of mere moral exhortation had been only too well demonstrated. The possibility that men's material interests might serve the uses of social progress had impressed itself upon Phillips's mind.[33]

In a footnote to this point, Hofstadter added:

It is significant that during the days between secession and Civil War, when Phillips rested his hopes upon economic factors to bring freedom, he reached back into our history for an economic interpretation of the Revolution and discovered that it was fought because our merchants wanted direct trade with the West Indies and planters wanted "to cheat their creditors." Thus economic interest, as moral principles, could push the world forward.[34]

Hofstadter had discovered this insight in Phillips's *Speeches, Lectures, and Letters*. Curti thought it "too important as a key" to be "tucked into a footnote." Hofstadter had found in Phillips an unsystematic precursor to Beard, and he felt at home. Phillips, as more mature "Realist," was turning to the Marxist truth of economic causation and Hofstadter approved.

Phillips did develop the "skeletal structure" for his moral principles in the latter part of his life. His championship of labor and his opposition to capital took the practical forms of an attempt to establish a cohesive labor party, to use the vote as a class tool, and to equalize property. The program amounted to a Socialistic one and grew directly out of Phillips's Abolitionist experience.[35] Hofstadter's evaluation of Phillips at this point hinged on Phillips's expanding definition of ownership. He quoted Phillips's reflection in 1865:

The labor of these twenty-nine years has been in behalf of a race bought and sold. The South did not rest their system wholly on this claim to own their labours but ... asserted that the laborer must necessarily be owned by capitalists or individuals. That struggle for the ownership of labor is now somewhat near its end and we fitly commence a struggle to define and to arrange the true relations of capital and labor.[36]

Hofstadter's comment on this speech: "It was a strange course, then, that the brilliantly formulated ideas of the best pro-slavery theorists had taken—to be transmuted by an abolitionist into an argument for the use of the radical labor movement!"[37]

This is yet another example of what we have seen in Hofstadter's tutorial thesis and in his first paper of 1938 on Jefferson. This type of observation, the notation of an inversion whereby an idea or a situation became transformed into its opposition, would become central to Hofstadter's particular view of the way in which history—and human social life as a whole—developed. Here, Phillips had taken Southern arguments and applied them to the new relations existing in postbellum America in an attempt at establishing equity for the working classes, as equity had legally been established for the Black race. There is more than a hint of the Marxist dialectic to this "transmutation."

It is not surprising, then, that one should find handwritten notes accompanying this paper in which Hofstadter had written to himself:

Dialectics of slavery-labor. Southerners said *all* labor should be owned by capital. Focussed attention on that. Negro not free in fact, tho formally so: Why: Because he did not own land, which was essential to his human independence and political independence. Northern workers in a similar position. When the Negro became a free laborer Phillips began to see with clarity the problems of the free laborer.[38]

Hofstadter had chosen to depict Phillips's memory of 29 years of work in order to show him working out the transformation of one set of ideas into a new, more inclusive whole. When legal ownership was no longer a problem, economic ownership—exploitation or control—became the central issue. White Southern landlords had appropriated Northern Capitalist rationalizations to legitimize their continued control, thus sparking the idea, for

Phillips, of the *economic* aspect of ownership, an aspect which had eluded him as long as the legal aspect had claimed his attention. Phillips, through brilliant insight, linked the justification for slavery to the ideology of Capitalism as expressed by Southern overlords and came out a Socialist, arriving at the insights of Marx by an independent route. Hofstadter's depiction of Phillips's life expressed the dialectical configuration of history that Hofstadter had absorbed from his own time and friends. This configuration would remain a basic and essential part of his later work in history.

Phillips was not Marx, of course, and in contrast to his earlier attempt to find in Jefferson Marx's notions, Hofstadter did not disparage the fact. In fact, he closed his essay by again taking Vernon Parrington to task for finding in Phillips "pretty much all of Marxism." Phillips was simply not systematic or metaphysical, as Marx had been, Hofstadter argued. "Phillips was a homespun Yankee product ... less academic, speculative, and rigorous in temper." He was inhibited by "New England provincialism, his religious background, and organizational isolation." Furthermore, "it is not his theoretical accomplishments, but his great-hearted fraternity and profound democracy, his willingness to champion any underdog and his eagerness to protest every injustice, that constitutes Wendell Phillips' supreme bequest to American radicalism."[39]

In contrast to Jefferson, who had been limited by his landed aristocratic heritage, Phillips's personal qualities dominated and overpowered the legacies of his background. In theory Phillips produced little, in practice much. In theory Jefferson produced much, in practice little. It was just the pragmatic and even *anti-intellectual* approach of Phillips that made him a particularly American radical, in contrast to both Jefferson and his European counterparts.

This had been a year of enormous intellectual growth for Richard Hofstadter. Between "Jefferson's Ideas on Class Relations" and this paper, he had gained tremendously in perspective. In looking so closely at Phillips, he himself had become less disposed to displace Marxian thought on alien minds and more sensitive to the particular circumstances and intellectual currents of American life that contrasted to Marx's categories and terminology. The formative influences on Phillips, Hofstadter had come to see, were not derived from his economic background but existed despite it. They were "religious fervor, the revolutionary heritage, the natural rights philosophy, and a typical nineteenth century optimism: boundless faith in the power of agitation, education, and the sweep of moral progress."[40]

Parrington appeared wrong to Hofstadter because Parrington had attempted and accomplished just what Hofstadter himself had set out to do in his first paper on Jefferson. Hofstadter had tried there to interpret the past in terms dictated by his own experiences, and in fact moved away from that mistaken type of effort only slowly. Parrington had operated along similar lines but never came to the more comprehensive view Hofstadter was developing. In attempting to set Parrington straight on the historical points, Hofstadter had developed the analytical tools of the Marxian interpretation of history with more depth, subtlety, and finesse than had Parrington. Those tools were the importance of class and ethnic background as formative influences, the tension between conscious purpose and the force of economic factors, the teleology of historical materialism, the moral outrage against Capitalist inequities, and the attention to ideological superstructure.

Hofstadter's quarrel with Parrington was an in-house quarrel. Instead of "all of Marx," he found in Phillips the fashioning of an American Socialist who combined both Abolitionism and labor in a strange dialectic made up of purely American ingredients. He found an anomalous figure, who reached Socialism *despite* the forces of his background and *because of* the brilliance of his untutored insight into the Capitalist ideology that dominated his society. Hofstadter's was a less systematic, more open and flexible, more varied use of Marxist tenets than was Parrington's. Hofstadter emphasized the social context of this American radical, rather than the purely intellectual one. Yet that social context remained firmly rooted in its (ostensible) economic base. It is, indeed, that rootedness and those assumptions that give to Hofstadter's history, even at this early stage, its depth and luminosity.

Having set out in this academic year of 1938–39 to "raid the past" for "usable" materials—i.e., those that were similar and parallel to current concerns—Hofstadter had been compelled to admit that the past did *not* yield those materials in the simplistic way in which he had first set out to find them. But in the process of searching, he found that the past did yield a larger truth, which corresponded to his current views: Capitalism as an epoch in history developed and held free sway on the shores of the new American nation. As an epoch it was necessary and inevitable—and "quintessential" in form. Those individuals who came to socialist insights in the midst of nineteenth-century Capitalist growth were anomalous critics who operated against the grain like so many poppies in a field of dandelions. The American experience fit the categories of Marxist thought, not in the smaller sense of displaced class conflict, but in the much more significant sense of a dialectical pattern of development. It was during this year of intensive Ph.D. study that Hofstadter came to hammer out the ideology of Capitalism as it existed unfettered on the American scene—a Capitalism contrasting with the more class-conscious, splintered, and theoretical European system, but a Capitalism whose idiosyncracies affected every aspect of American life nonetheless.

Here, it is important to add, Hofstadter, through working with Curti, was first introduced to an acceptable form of biographical writing, one that skirted the 1930's heresy of individualism and "subjectivity" and presented individuals as evidence of forces larger than themselves. Through this medium Hofstadter had been able to recover something of the character of Jeeves in his high school play—the importance of personal qualities of individuals and the drama of their development. We have never before seen in his academic efforts, for instance, a character "slide out of back exits" as Phillips did, or anyone who "leapt to the platform." He caught again in history the elements of drama and action that he had worked with in imaginative, fictional pieces but that he had felt compelled to abandon when institutional and economic factors appeared to be the dominant aspects of the past.

It was the inherent potential of intellectual biography, tied to the social forces from which it sprang, that freed Hofstadter from the stultifying aspects of Marxist scientism that had constricted his work to date. If, as Alfred Kazin has written, "he was certainly not to emerge as a historian until he had doggedly looked after [his wife] in her ... fatal illness [in 1945]," the seeds for that emergence had been sown much earlier.[41] Here, in his year of Ph.D. classwork, two of those seeds that later blossomed in published form were planted. But these seeds, even this early, were hardly the undifferentiated forms of primitive plant life. They had been nurtured in the garden of Marxist horticulture. In the biographical approach, Hofstadter had found his answer to the unsatisfactory reductionism he had at first thought was demanded by that Marxist discipline. He had gone beyond the "science of society" into the ideology of Capitalism and the dialectics of change.

NOTES

1. For his plans to teach after the M.A., see Felice Swados to Harvey Swados, December 29, 1937, Harvey Swados Papers, Courtesy of the Archives of the University of Massachusetts, Amherst, Mass. Cartoon accompanies correspondence of May 29, 1938.

2. Felice Swados to Harvey Swados, December 29, 1937, June 28, 1938, February 6, 1939; Hofstadter to Harvey Swados, October 1938, all in Swados Papers.

3. Hofstadter to Harvey Swados, October 1938, November 10, 1938, Swados Papers; "Official Transcript", Columbia University, Record in the Graduate, Faculties of Political Science, Philosophy, and Pure Science—Richard Hofstadter.

4. Merle Curti to the author, February 24, 1980; *Columbia University Bulletin of Information*, 38th Series, Announcements 1938–39, # 32, p. 20.

5. David Van Tassell, Personal interview with the author, n.d.

6. Merle Curti, *The Social Ideas of American Educators* (New York, Scribner's Sons, 1935) especially pp. 257–60 and Chapters XII, XIV, XV.

7. Hofstadter mentioned Curti's Marxism at least twice to Harvey Swados—Hofstadter to Swados, November 10, 1938, February 16, 1939; Curti to the author, February 24, 1980; Felice Swados to Harvey Swados, February 6, 1939.

8. Hofstadter to Harvey Swados, November 10, 1938.

9. Richard Hofstadter, "Jefferson's Ideas on Class Relations," unpublished MS, Richard Hofstadter Papers, Columbia University, New York, N.Y. The placement of the paper with notes from Beard's *Eco-*

nomic Origins of Jeffersonian Democracy and from the P.S. Ford edition of Jefferson's writings as well as the age of the paper and the carbon copy all indicate that it is the original paper. For quotations, see pp. 1, 3.

10. Ibid., p. 3.

11. Ibid., pp. 3, 4, 5, 6 (emphasis in original).

12. Ibid., pp. 9, 10 (emphasis in original).

13. Ibid., p. 11.

14. Ibid., pp. 11–12.

15. Ibid., p. 12.

16. Ibid.

17. Hofstadter to Harvey Swados, November 10, 1938; Richard Hofstadter, "Parrington and the Jeffersonian Tradition," *Journal of the History of Ideas* II (October 1941): pp. 391–400.

18. Hofstadter to Vernon Parrington, Jr., September 22, 1967.

19. Hofstadter, "Jeffersonian Tradition," especially pp. 394, 396.

20. Ibid., p. 392.

21. Ibid., p. 400.

22. Ibid., p. 393 (emphasis added).

23. References to the project were made in Hofstadter to Swados, November 10, 1938; April 15, 1939; Felice Swados to Harvey Swados, February 6, 1939. Hofstadter indicated dismay with the project on April 15.

24. Felice Swados to Harvey Swados, April 17, 1937, Swados Papers. Felice wrote: "Jefferson, although he was afraid of the growing power of capitalism, and although he thought that the basis of national prosperity lay in the land, nevertheless entertained no technical economic systematic ideas on the subject. That is, he was *emotionally* attached to the land, but he had no physiocratic *economic program* based on this belief. If I am not mistaken, he belonged to the Manchester school" (emphasis in the original).

25. Hofstadter, "Jeffersonian Tradition," pp. 398, 399.

26. Richard Hofstadter, "Wendell Phillips 1860–1884," Unpublished MS, Hofstadter Papers. For quotations see pp. 35, 36.

27. Ibid., p. 1.

28. Ibid.

29. Ibid., pp. 1–4 (emphasis added).

30. Ibid., pp. 7–8 (emphasis added).

31. Ibid.

32. Ibid., p. 22.(emphasis added).

33. Ibid., pp. 22–23.

34. Ibid., p. 23, n. 41.

35. Ibid., pp. 28–30.

36. Ibid., p. 26.

37. Ibid.

38. Notes accompanying Hofstadter, "Wendell Phillips," (emphasis in original).

39. Hofstadter, "Wendell Phillips." All quotations are on pp. 35-36.

40. Ibid., p. 13.

41. Alfred Kazin, *New York Jew* (New York, Vintage Books, 1979) p. 25.

7

Disaffection and Betrayal

As a history Ph.D. candidate in the world of the New York Left in the 1930's, Hofstadter went through several experiences that are appropriately labeled as an identity crisis. The first of these was his exit from the Communist Party. The second was an intensely personal crisis connected to his family. The third was the necessity for coping with the meaning of the Nazi-Soviet Pact of 1939. Having undergone these crises, Hofstadter brought parts of them to the writing of his Ph.D. dissertation and first full-length historical study, *Social Darwinism in American Life*.

Because he had been pursuing such intensive academic work, Hofstadter found less time during the academic year of 1938–39 to be involved with politics. Only once during the fall did he write his brother-in-law the kind of full-blown analysis that he had written so often in the spring. This was after the Munich crisis had given guilty consciences to many in the West. Hofstadter's response to that crisis was couched in the old defense of collective security, a line he had been arguing since February when he joined the Party. Speculating that collective security and appeasement both ultimately led to war, he argued that appeasement was the greater of the two evils, because through it the balance of powers grew more forbidding. Of the Munich crisis itself he said, "Frankly, I was very disappointed when this recent crisis did not result in war." Realistically assessing the situation, he went on:

Now with the Czech fortifications gone, it will be easier than ever for Hitler to attack. The new guarantees will mean nothing to him, and it is very doubtful that [Britian] and [France] will back them up if Czechoslovakia is going to be so weak that she can't be saved anyway and will be a poor ally. Besides central Europe will have to go with Hitler, since Fr. commitments now aren't worth a continental. With the passage of time, God knows what will happen in Fr., so that if Hitler can wait long enough he is likely to get benevolent neutrality from Br. and Fr. in an attack on the Soviet Union. To prevent such a lineup I would be glad to see a war now, and if the adoption of cs by the US could have prevented such a lineup, even at a high risk of dragging us in, I would have been in favor of it.[1]

Quite clear on Adolph Hitler's cynicism, Hofstadter foresaw in October 1938 the takeover of further portions of Czechoslovakia in March 1939, which seemingly took the leaders of England and France by surprise.

But Hofstadter feared primarily for the continued and extended isolation of the Soviet Union by the "democracies." With others who were commenting on the European situation at the time, Hofstadter felt that the Soviet Union provided the only real deterrent to Fascism in Europe. The democracies had babied Hitler. Since the beginning of the Popular Front, the Soviet Union had followed an aggressive policy of collective security. In the Munich crisis, England and France had acted in concert with Hitler and Mussolini, ignoring the interests of Russia and the French alliance with Czechoslovakia. (Hofstadter's earlier coupling of England with Germany and Italy hardly appears surprising in this context.[2]) The Soviet Union had stood ready to defend Czechoslovakia if France honored her agreement. So, in a very real sense, the agreement at Munich was a betrayal of the Soviet Union, the effect of which was to isolate her almost completely from defensive alliances, which she had been seeking through the policy of collective security. It was with sympathy for this situation and a realistic analysis that Hofstadter viewed the situation.[3]

What could the United States do? Hofstadter was very pessimistic. As he had argued in April, collective security from the viewpoint of the Left was the morally right decision. But it was *very* unpopular in the United States, isolationism being overwhelming "among the masses" and the influence of the political Left almost nonexistent. "All the time that we have been debating cs pro and con, the highly practical realization has eluded us that our stand on it one way or the other makes little difference in practice, i.e. has no effect on what the US does." Hofstadter may have been growing tired of the ineffectuality of his morality. He appears, indeed, to have been making good the statement with which he opened this single letter on politics—that he was "sick" of politics—"tho there is nothing quite so important."[4]

His original disaffection with Party membership was also growing on him. "Having joined," he said, "I find that my disgust with the rigamarole of the faithful plus my doubts about matters of policy immobilize me. I lack enthusiasm, to put it mildly." He was sure there was a place for Party hacks who could not or would not see the complex realities before their eyes. It was these people, on the other hand, he pointed out, who kept the machine running. He knew politics needed men of action—even "lame-brained idiots"—and he felt that someday those people would "do the job," but he simply did not feel that he himself was one of them. Doubts such as those haunting him, no matter how honest or intelligent, were *not* productive. Speaking of people like himself, he wrote: "As Lenin said—quoting Lenin naturally proves anything—only those who do nothing make no mistakes. We may not make mistakes, but we wont [*sic*] make any revolutions either." He was—or felt himself to be—a thinker rather than an activist, a position in contrast to that of his wife, with her Maritime and Newspaper Guild activism.[5]

In the context of this negative outlook and his intense academic involvement, it is not surprising to find that by February 1939, the end of his first semester of Ph.D. work, Hofstadter had abandoned the Columbia unit, quietly and inconspicuously but most decidedly. His rationale:

I cannot swallow arms and a lot of other things, chiefly the whole set of mental attitudes which go with the average party member and so have quietly eased myself out of the Columbia graduate unit, and will stay out. Not to burn any bridges behind me, I have done nothing formal, and will not come out openly with any political reason for leaving.[6]

He knew, as did others, how difficult personally, as well as politically, withdrawing from the movement could be. Many of those who had left earlier—and those who would do so in the fall of 1939 after the Nazi-Soviet Pact—underwent vilification, ridicule, even physical abuse upon breaking from the Stalinist nest. In spite of Hofstadter's hardihood and taste for political dispute among intimates, a public display was none to his liking, nor would it ever be.

As with the timing of his entrance to the Party, so with the timing of his exit. There was an inverse relationship in both cases. Hofstadter's entrance was made in spite of his growing sense of perfidy on the part of Stalin and his henchmen regarding the trials. Thus, some internal tension existed in association with the move. His exit was taken in spite of his sympathy for the isolated position of the Soviet Union vis-à-vis the growth of Fascism in Europe. This tension—or the contradictions between his political commitments and the intellectual convictions that accompanied them—may have made similar tensions and contradictions in the past more evident to Hofstadter than to other historians.

There also appears to have been a curious parallel between the quality of Hofstadter's academic pursuits and the dynamics of his Party membership. In the early period of his membership in the Communist Party, when he was most committed to defending the Party line—particularly on collective security but often on other topics as well—he was also writing his statistically based report on the AAA. The logical gymnastics of the two activities paralleled each other.

In the later months of Party membership, when Hofstadter's aggravation with the hacks began to outweigh his need to commit himself morally, he was writing on or researching Jefferson and Phillips and reading Vernon Parrington on both. Interest in other literary critics, with their personalized, "interior" approach, was also surfacing at this time and one must not forget that Hofstadter had always been interested in creative writing and later in journalism. The self-assessment attached to his doubts as a Party member and his identity as an observer, which were at the base of his decision to withdraw from the Columbia unit, may also have served as the base for his new interest in biography and the personal, dramatic, education.., and social factors of historical analysis.[7]

One further part of the Phillips paper may give additional insight into the internal changes taking place in Hofstadter's attitude at this time. In analyzing the importance of Phillips's contributions to the Abolitionist movement, he said Phillips, "was extremely useful to the abolitionists. . . . He brought to the movement a good name, an ingratiating personality, a considerable fund of money, and a great talent for handling mobs and hecklers. Above all he was useful because he was eloquent."[8] This assessment is proof, if nothing else is, that Hofstadter had not lost touch with his earlier group and institutional interests, but that he was now concentrating on the group-individual nexus. Phillips fit into Abolitionism, both giving the movement his personal talents and qualities and receiving from it a raison d'être. Now, Hofstadter felt himself *not* to fit into the goals of his movement, doubts about policy and disaffection for the mentality being too strong for him to contribute productively.

Hofstadter was just at this time finding himself, as Phillips had, but Hofstadter's self-discovery was bound up in writing, not in speaking, as it had been for Phillips. He withdrew because of personal factors—personal development—not primarily because of a change of heart or mind politically. He "could not stomach arms," but he also could not restrict his thinking to the strict economic determinism or class conflict models of his earlier days. And the catalyst for the change was his new relationship with Merle Curti. With a kindred Marxist soul, who was also a successful academic historian, Hofstadter entered a newly sophisticated phase of Marxism. No longer did he have to behave as a committed Party hack to express his embrace of Marxist tenets. Now he could apply them in the more subtle pursuit of the reinterpretation of the American past. This in itself was a dialectical process, in which the contradiction between his internal interests in drama and individual personality traits and his external commitment to a political movement that demanded an activism for which he did not feel equipped was resolved into a new, more complex synthesis of integrity and wholeness as a professional historian.

It is also important to reiterate that Hofstadter's official po-

sition vis-à-vis Party membership made no difference to his political thought. His sympathies and his principles did not change
no matter what the state of his active commitment might have
been. He remained the tough-minded realist, the proponent of
labor organization, and a Russian sympathizer until the Nazi-
Soviet Pact.

Another episode in the series of steps in his identity formation
took place for Hofstadter in the spring of 1939. A misunder-
standing developed between Hofstadter and Felice's parents.
Hofstadter's feelings about his father-in-law spilled out bitterly.
Aaron Swados had misconstrued a small quarrel between Hofstadter and Felice—a quarrel reported to him by his wife, Rivi,
who had recently made a visit to New York. Aaron proceeded
to write to his daughter privately at her office to beg her "to
consider her future and leave Dick." He thought that Hofstadter
was subjecting Felice to "indignities" and "dominating her," that
she was living in "human bondage." Moreover, as the "bread-
winner" she would only be subject to more and worse treatment
when Hofstadter began to earn money. Hofstadter was, furthermore, according to Aaron, "grandiose"; rather than working
for his Ph.D., he should have been obtaining a humble position
somewhere and working his way up.[9]
These accusations and the spirit and method by which they
were made angered Hofstadter deeply. Although it is difficult,
if not impossible, to sort out truth from fantasy in the accusations
and Hofstadter's retorts to them, what does appear to have been
a real concern on Aaron's part was Hofstadter's continued dependence on Felice, his studies, and the prolonged interim period before he found himself a suitable—remunerative—
professional position. Hofstadter responded by a healthy self-
defense, which indicated more directly than anything yet written
the nature of his plans for the future.

Maybe I'm grandiose because I think that if I work hard at my field
and get a Columbia degree and get to know the right people, there, I
might wangle myself a teaching job somewhere with salary enough to
live decently and keep my wife happy . . . I've started out, I just picked
my profession two yrs ago, and he's already got me marked for a hope-
less mediocrity.[10]

The sting in these unfair accusations from Aaron had originated in a real desire on Hofstadter's part to please Aaron.

> I have always been pathetically eager to please and impress yr pop for some obscure reason not understood even by myself. Maybe precisely because I valued his judgement. I now kick myself for having imagined that he could be impressed by anything less than $5000 a yr.[11]

The sore point was clearly Hofstadter's not making money, and although he had successfully completed his M.A. as he had said he would, Aaron's patience and trust were running thin. The matter blew over but not without a scar left by Aaron's lack of confidence in Hofstadter. This was the family he had adopted, after all, to supplement his own.

That summer, because of the quarrel, the couple did not go to Buffalo but rented a cabin in New England, where Rivi at least visited them. There Hofstadter studied for his orals and Felice relaxed. There, also, they probably heard the first rumors of a new agreement between Germany and the Soviet Union.

The Soviet Union, which had been isolated before and during the Munich crisis, became the target of concern for both Germany and England after Germany's takeover of Bohemia and Moravia. Britain's new position was a firm stance against further German aggression. Part of this new attitude entailed a rapprochement between Britain and the Soviet Union for the security of both. But it was followed only unenthusiastically. During the summer of 1939, direct but slow negotiations were conducted. Hitler, on the other hand, was in a hurry since his schedule incorporated a planned attack on Poland by the end of August. To ensure his own safety he bought an agreement with Stalin, dropping threatening language and behavior toward the Ukraine and offering the opportunity of territorial aggrandizement to Russia. On the surface, the Nazi-Soviet Pact of August 23, 1939, was a simple nonaggression and trade treaty. In the context of the Popular Front policy of collective security, painstakingly developed over the preceding five years, it was perfidy.

A significant public controversy among intellectuals of the Left in the United States had preceded the announcement of the pact. In May the Committee for Cultural Freedom published a letter in the *Nation* grouping the Soviet Union with Germany and Italy and labeling all three "totalitarian." The citizens of all three countries were described as having been "silenced, imprisoned, tortured, or hounded into exile." For Fellow Travelers, Socialists, and Communists, this identification of Russia with the Fascist countries was too much. A group of them wrote an "Open Letter" in response, restating the familiar thesis that unity on the Left was essential, that primitive Fascist tactics abroad and in the United States attempted to divide the Left coalition under the Popular Front, and that the Soviet Union, in its implementation of Socialism, was "diametrically opposed" to Fascist policies. Although the differences expressed in this controversy focused on internal freedoms rather than on foreign policy, the effect of the Pact was, at least temporarily, to prove one group right and the other wrong.[12]

That Hofstadter felt himself more closely allied with the second group, despite his current disaffection, there can be little doubt. Some of his favorite figures signed the Open Letter, among them William Gropper, Granville Hicks, Matthew Josephson, Corliss Lamont, and Max Lerner. Hofstadter had argued for unity among the factionalized Left for years. He had admired true Socialism as he had believed it to be implemented in the Soviet Union. He had stood with those who had looked to Russia as the last bulwark against Fascism in Europe. His exit from the Party had not entailed a rejection of his political beliefs. He had moved from the position of Party member to the position of Fellow Traveler. In this light, then, it is understandable that after August 24, he also found himself among those who were immediately and bitterly disillusioned by the move. In this mood, deeply depressed, he wrote on September 2:

No mood to write abt pact, just like you. One thing I think judgement need not be reserved: American radicals got to cut away from Sov. Union, not insist on defending its every act. No party on Stalin apron strings can be good, honest, convincing, effective over long time. CP very silly now[13]

Furthermore, he displaced this new insight onto the past: "One thing the world proletariat is sold out. Aint this a continuation of an old policy: selling oil to Italy in 1935, pussyfoot policy in Spain, etc?"[14] The abandonment of collective security, he was saying, had begun long ago by the United States, England, and France which all refused to take a strong stand against Italian aggression in Ethiopia by continuing to sell Italy the essential commodity for waging war. These countries had refused, by a collective policy, to equalize conditions within Spain by aiding the Republicans. In a nutshell, then, Russia too had joined the appeasers and sold out its own revolution. His bitterness knew no bounds.

Only from the perspective of Russian national interest was the Pact at all defensible, and that only if the surface appearances were correct and the Pact was truly a nonaggression agreement and not in fact a military alliance—"for which of course there is absolutely no excuse." He was willing from that perspective to take a wait-and-see approach—for a while.

The next few months shd show what the pact is about. Let us see what the Soviet military mission to Berlin is going to do. Let us hope they aint there to sign the anti-comintern pact, ha ha. Let us see how they follow this up apropos of Japan, etc.[15]

The ludicrousness of the shift was uppermost in Hofstadter's mind. He never shrank from the full realization of the impact of the new policy. Equally clairvoyant about England and France, he blamed them for sending an ultimatum to Germany without a time limit, for allowing Hitler to take the lead, for letting themselves be put on the defensive once again.[16]

As far as the preferable U. S. policy went, cash-and-carry was "intelligent." This policy would keep Americans out for awhile but not forever. He did not trust Roosevelt, thought he was not honest or intelligent, but had some hopes for the period after 1940: "Election in 1940 may help [stay out] however; winner must promise to stay out, cant break promise right away."[17] The lessons of World War I were in his mind, as they were in many Americans' minds at this point. On this he was even more specific and made his sources clear:

Very important policy is keeping Ams. off foreign ships & refusing to clear armed merchant ships from our ports. Absolutely. Very seriously

recommend you read Mr. Tansill now, also certain chapters in Hall-
gren's *The Tragic Fallacy*. Latter very informative on possibility of keeping out.[18]

   As the situation evolved, Russia invaded Poland, and it became
clear that the nonaggression pact had indeed become the military
agreement that Hofstadter had feared, his disillusionment with
the American Party grew. At the end of September, he was
remarking the *Daily Worker*'s new attitude toward the repeal of
the arms embargo—a position some had been advocating for
years in light of its hindrance to those who wished to help the
Spanish Republicans. The Communist Party had advocated it.
Hofstadter predicted now a reversal of that policy.

If you have been reading the Daily as faithfully as I have, you will notice
that it has completely straddled the issue of repealing the arms embargo
and has reserved its juiciest billingsgate for the imperialist aims of Britain and France. It is my prediction that this straddle is a prelude to a
reversal of the party position and a stand in favor of the embargo. And
even if it aint, the straddle itself is a subtle form of sabotage.[19]

The straddle was a "subtle form of sabotage" in the sense that
it obstructed the old effort at collective security, of which the
arms embargo had been an integral part. Having recently been
very close to it, Hofstadter's disillusionment and bitterness toward Party members grew and he could hardly contain his anger.

There is nothing so crude as the Stalinist mentality. Once they wanted
Britain and France to stand up against Hitler because they said he would
back down and there would be no war. They wanted us to encourage
them to fight by putting an embargo vs the aggressors on the statute
books. . . . Finally the Br. & F decided they shd stand up vs. H. So they
shd be happy and support them. But instead, they decide it's an imperialist war, that Br & F are responsible for it, that we shouldn't help
them, that they aint democracies.[20]

Forgetting that he too had wondered if they were democracies,
Hofstadter's mind was in the process of changing, through and
because of his anger. He could no longer countenance the changing policies of the Party, based as they now appeared to be on

pure power rather than on consistent principles. In attempting to understand this anger and disillusionment, there is need to reiterate the thought that despite the realities of the international situation and the menace of Hitlerian Germany, a second complete shift in tactics and in priorities was simply too much for the Communist Party to ask of its active and intelligent followers. If those followers had been able slowly to absorb the switch in policy from the doctrine of Social Fascism to the Popular Front doctrines of 1935, those for whom the Party was really taken in good faith would have found this second demand on their emotional and intellectual energies simply too much to handle. Although the demands for discipline and thought control were understandable to a certain extent, when asked to go beyond the realm of Western consistency and rationality, the Party lost many good and leading intellectuals for its cause.

One of those intellectuals, lost early in the fall of 1939, was Granville Hicks, literary editor of the *New Masses*. Hicks wrote a "reasoned and even-tempered explanation" for his resignation from the *New Masses* editorial staff and from the Party, in which he found greater fault with the American Communist Party than he did with Russian behavior.[21] He contended that American Party members had not known what was happening in Russia and were therefore unprepared for the move, but would not or could not admit their ignorance of the situation even by silence, and so were determined to "appear omniscient" and defend the pact blindly "with apologetics completely devoid of clarity and logic."[22] Hofstadter agreed thoroughly.

Granville Hicks' letter said at least as much as any honest person's got to say. Even if you got enough "faith in the Soviet Union," as the DW [*Daily Worker*] puts it, to think that their aims are sound you dont want to be identified with people who made such asses out of themselves in defending the SU.[23]

But whereas Hicks had remained cool and detached in his public letter, even when describing the ridiculous antics of Party functionaries immediately after the announcement of the Pact ("They have clutched at straws, juggled sophistries, shut their eyes to fact. These predictions have almost uniformly been proved

wrong within twenty-four hours. They have shown that they are
strong in faith . . . and weak in intelligence."[24]), Hofstadter mo-
mentarily lost his rationality—his cool.

Personally, I got no faith. I dont believe in faith, not in anything. If I
did, I wd be a Catholic. I used to sneer when I read that Communism
was a substitute religion, but I dont anymore. It is. Not only adherence
to the CI [Communist International] but to the 4th I or any other I.
Marxism itself is pervaded with a quasi-religious teleology. If you dont
understand or believe this, I'll prove it to you some day.[25]

For Hofstadter, the repudiation of the Party was a final conscious realization of the quarrel he had carried on all along with
the behavior and mentality of Party members. One recalls vividly
his first observations of that mentality: "If I doubt the correctness
of the party line . . . therefore my education is deficient and I
have to go down to the section and . . . straighten this out."[26] He
had tolerated that total acceptance of authority. It was, for him,
a means to the superior end of realizing a more equitable social
system. Now with the perfidy of Soviet foreign policy, the obvious
shunting aside of Comintern policy, the mentality of local leaders
came into clear focus and he repudiated it with venom.

He was lashing out at the deductive reasoning that Marxism
shared with revealed religions and that Hofstadter himself had
used with such disadvantage in his tutorial and M.A. theses. It
is therefore of utmost significance that from this point on, the
deductive reasoning and tortured logic that accompanied it dis-
appear from Richard Hofstadter's academic historical work.

As time wore on, the crisis became for him a moment of epi-
phany. In October he wrote:

Now I come to the main reason I am writing this letter. My main
point is that recent events, particularly the behavior of the CP in this
recent crisis, have underlined the importance of a problem that has
been torturing me for some time. I dont know what the relation of
people like us can possibly be toward the changes that are likely to take
place in the world when this war is over. Your mention of a Soviet
Europe drives it home. I don't want to live under any system governed
by glorified clerks like Earl Browder or his equivalents in the 4th Int.,
who, as I have often said, are just as bad. The problem is the very

fundamental one of ends. I hate capitalism and everything that goes with it. But I also hate the simpering dogmatic religious-minded Janizaries that make up the CP. I hate their regimented thinking. I rather doubt that I wd be permitted to live under any system they cd set up, and I am quite sure that if I were I wdnt enjoy it. People like us grow up to believe in a certain set of values—freedom of individual intellectual inquiry, scientific attitude of mind, respect for facts, a certain cultural latitude—which the Stalins, Browders, Cannons and Schactmans dislike and will, if given a chance, stamp out. . . . Ours are not any more valid values than those of the people who follow these guys because they expect better food and clothing. But they are the only values we know and the only ones we can live with. We cant change them any more than we can stop breathing. We can, of course, shut up abt them and outwardly conform—which is the futile course F and I were following in sticking to the party so long—but we wont be very happy that way.

We are not the beneficiaries of capitalism, but we will not be the beneficiaries of the socialism of the 20th century—if any—any more than Kamenenv & Zinoviev & Rykov & Bucharin were. We have probably been kidding ourselves on that score. We are the people with no place to go. . . . Comes the Revolution—which we both agree is far off, thank God—and then what? So where are we and what do we stand for.?[27]

Although he would remain politically conscious and astute at analyzing the political situation both in America and in Europe, Hofstadter would not again be politically committed until Adlai Stevenson's campaign in 1952. What is striking about these words is the bitter futility he was feeling. Because Communism and the leftward movement had taken the place of religion for those growing up in the 1930's, those who had been committed and had become disillusioned appear to have had nothing of faith to fall back upon. They had repudiated God, they had repudiated the Anglo-Saxon tradition, they had repudiated the Jewish religious heritage.

Hofstadter and Felice had espoused much more than the surface elements of Marxism. From their Buffalo days, they had adopted the philosophical materialism that fit their political activities. That materialism when coupled with a Marxist teleology—and when it appeared morally correct—seemed satisfying. It offered some ideal ends as well as a coherent social philosophy that spelled out means to attain those ends. When the ideal ends and material means fell apart, as had happened in the Nazi-Soviet Pact, it appeared that only crude self-interest remained. The only answer was a kind of nihilism. To avoid the full implications of that, Hofstadter retained vestiges of the philosophy of materialism. It had, after all, been the very intellectual substance of the years of his identity formation.

The fact that he believed people like himself and his wife and brother-in-law had "nowhere to go" indicates his consciousness of an existential void, of having pitted his hopes on a movement by which he had been betrayed, and of having now no resting place. Before this, Hofstadter had fit, or almost fit, the Communist movement, as Phillips had fit the Abolitionist movement. Hofstadter would fit again, in a less complete way, the Columbia faculty and academic community of full-fledged thinkers. But this would not be for several long years.

Hofstadter's closest friends had taken part in and endured this experience of belief, commitment, betrayal and disillusionment. Now, for the moment, in company with those friends, there was a time of existential wandering. The subject would arise again in dialogue. But for the moment, Hofstadter was a man without a belief and also without an established career. With willpower and a newly sobered outlook, he pushed on through the obstacle course that lay ahead.

NOTES

1. Richard Hofstadter to Harvey Swados, October 1938, Harvey Swados Papers, Courtesy of the Archives of the University of Massachusetts Amherst, Mass.
2. See Chapter 4, text at note 18.
3. For the background and consequences of the Munich crisis, see Donald W. Treadgold, *Twentieth Century Russia* (Chicago, Rand McNally, 1959) pp. 332–36; Frank Warren, *Liberals and Communism: The Red Decade Revisited* (Bloomington, Indiana University Press, 1966) pp. 198–99. The former is especially informative on Munich as a cause for the Nazi-Soviet Pact.
4. Hofstadter to Harvey Swados, October 1938.
5. Ibid.
6. Ibid., February 16, 1939.

7. Robert Cantwell, for instance, was a collegue of Felice's at *Time*. He was at this point writing a critical article on Faulkner, in which Harvey Swados had some interest. Harvey himself was writing criticsm. All were friends of Alfred Kazin, who was beginning *On Native Grounds* (1942) at this time. See Felice Swados to Harvey Swados, January 16, 1939, February 6, 1939, Swados Papers.

8. Richard Hofstadter, "Wendell Phillips 1860–1884," Unpublished MS, Hofstadter Papers, p. 3.

9. Hofstadter to Harvey Swados, April 25, 1939, May 2, 1939, Swados Papers.

10. Ibid., May 2, 1939.

11. Ibid.

12. Louis Adamic et al., "Manifesto," *Nation* CXLVIII (May 27, 1939) p. 626; Jay Allen et al., "To the Active Supporters of Democracy and Peace," *Nation* CXLVIII (August 26, 1939) p. 228.

13. Hofstadter to Harvey Swados, September 2, 1939, Swados Papers.

14. Ibid.

15. Ibid.

16. Ibid.

17. Ibid.

18. Ibid. This is Charles C. Tansill's *America Goes to War*.

19. Hofstadter to Harvey Swados, September 30, 1939, Swados Papers.

20. Ibid.

21. Daniel Aaron, *Writers on the Left* (New York, Avon Books, 1965) p. 375.

22. Granville Hicks, "On Leaving the Communist Party," *The New Republic* C (October 7, 1939) pp. 244–45.

23. Hofstadter to Swados, September 30, 1939, Swados Papers.

24. Hicks, "On Leaving," p. 244.

25. Hofstadter to Harvey Swados, September 30, 1939.

26. Ibid., n.d. [placed with Felice Swados to Harvey Swados, March 8, 1938].

27. Ibid., October 10, 1939.

8

No Place to Go

Between January 1940 and May 1942 Hofstadter's Marxism continued to be tested and modified in the face of professional and political exigencies. Even though the world around him seemed to be crumbling, he pushed on in his attempt to finish the job he had started and prove himself as a scholar. In this effort there existed the same sort of tension between his own aptitudes and their ideal, peacetime realization and the upsetting nature of the outside world, which called for involvement and action on the part of young people just finding their places in that world. Hofstadter's decisions, given this tension, serve to demonstrate his increasing sense that he himself was better fitted for the contemplative world rather than for the world of action.

The obstacles to finishing the job he had set out to do were essentially three: passing his comprehensives, adjusting to a teaching career, and writing his Ph.D. dissertation. The first of these he had prepared for all fall, not only by reading but by auditing Professor Joseph Dorfman's course "The History of Economic Thought." In addition to the other changes occurring at this time, it is probable that the experience of this course, which was the only one—after his first course in the Political Science Department—that he took or audited outside of the History Department, would have given a new perspective to his Marxist economic view, even without the disillusionments of the Nazi-Soviet Pact. Through this course and Professor Dorfman's

The Economic Mind in American Civilization, Hofstadter was introduced to a systematic, sophisticated history of economic thought,
thorough, erudite, and developmental. Such an introduction may
have helped mute his original tendency to displace Marxist assumptions onto the past and to consider historical actors in the
ahistorical terms of Marxist tenets. Such a modified point of
view, for example, is evident in his Parrington paper published
in 1941.[1]

Even as he played down economics as the major causative
factor, however, and added the perspective of a developmental
line of economic thought, he also retained some key aspects of
Marxist ideology. This is shown in a final paper Hofstadter wrote
for one of his classes, dated February 1940 and entitled "Some
Psychological Aspects of the Slavery Issue." Here the connection
between his interest in sharecroppers and the Southern oligarchy's ideology was explicated to a fuller extent than it had been
in his paper on Wendell Phillips. Here also he acknowledged
economic causation as a primary and original consideration, but
focused on the ideas to which economic circumstances had given
rise. For the first time, he was quite explicit about his assumptions. Speaking of a new book that argued against economics as
a cause of the slavery controversy, Hofstadter commented: "Although this analysis involves an unreal dichotomy between the
psychological or ideological branches of slavery and its roots in
economic life, it is probably true that the psychological side of
the slavery argument has not been adequately appreciated."[2]

The roots of slavery were still economic, while the branches
were ideological or "psychological," exactly as Marx had pointed
out. Also, one notes here the equation—strange to later ears—
of the terms "psychological and "ideological." The term "psychological" for Hofstadter at this point referred to the Marxian
sphere of ideas that grew up to rationalize any given economic
order and was in no way Freudian.

Hofstadter saw the psychological sphere as furthering the force
of the economic order over a long period of time. The connection between his interest in 1930's sharecropping and nineteenth-century ideology was made clear in this later paper. He
said:

The stubborn persistence of caste psychology among southern whites should be sufficient proof that the character of the old slave relationship is not exhaustively explained by reference to its economic aspects. We may well believe that the origins of race prejudice lay in the subordinate economic position of the southern Negro, but it is only too obvious that when such a prejudice is given an initial push by economic events it generates power enough to persist on its own.[3]

Original economic activities spin out ideas, which then take on an impetus of their own, according to this newly revamped theory that Hofstadter was developing.

Thus, little had changed in the South despite war over the issue:

> The Civil War did little in a direct way to uproot the southern economy, to improve the living standards of the plantation Negro, to change the fundamental role of the cotton states in our American polity, or to alter the southern mentality. The psychology of caste has become more deeply rooted in the southern soul. The South is still, although for different reasons a one-crop economy operating with inefficient labor upon exhausted soil. The plantation Negro, as tenant or share-cropper lives at substantially the same physical level as he did in antebellum days. Except in a few rare localities in the border states, he still goes without the rights of man, political or social.[4]

Hofstadter was developing a more sophisticated approach to history in this paper. He was focusing on the Southern system of ideas, as it came to be fashioned in reaction to Abolitionist attacks. The severe Marxist focus on economic causation had been shoved to the background and a new more complex set of assumptions had taken its place. That vision put forward a picture of society with economic *roots* but ideological *branches*. Moreover, the branches had some power of their own, for it was Hofstadter's major point that the entrenched nature of Southern prejudice caused the retention of the economic relationships, despite the upheaval of war over the issue. So, ideology, sprung from the particular relationship between slave and master, became hardened over time and *retarded* the changes that could have taken place with legal emancipation. The threat of Northern Abolitionist sentiments had stimulated the articulation of the Southern rationale for slavery. Tortured by their guilt, Hofstadter wrote, "Those who remained [in the South] were pricked by the criticism of the world and by their own sense of wrong."[5] Conflict had moved for Hofstadter from the area of economics and politics to the recesses of the human mind and heart. And ideas could also change the course of history, not alone, but as offshoots of a fundamental economic system.

Hofstadter passed his orals, after much anxiety and several delays, with flying colors: "They asked me many abstract philosophical question [sic], in which I showed up to best advantage. Have got self very good reputation in the whole dept for them." This was the young man who had started off as a part-time, night-school student, unknown and unconnected. His progress had been marked.[6]

Immediately following his orals, Hofstadter obtained a teaching position at Brooklyn College. He taught that spring of 1940 six hours in the evening session, in a position created by an emergency vacancy. His pay—$2.50 per hour. He was pleased with the job, thinking it "valuable for teaching experience and as entre to city system." Although he had an offer in the fall of 1940 from CCNY which was closer to where they then lived, it came too late, and Hofstadter taught at Brooklyn again the next fall. In the spring of 1941, however, he did accept a position at CCNY. He found for the most part that it was a "lark" to teach undergraduates, although he felt sorry for them, tired after working all day and having trouble learning the facts of Western Civilization.[7]

By the second half of the academic year of 1939–40, as the winter lull in German and Russian aggression set in, there had been enough of a shakedown in events for those on the Left in the United States to attempt a reexamination of their original responses to the Nazi-Soviet Pact. So, just as Hofstadter was beginning to teach, he also found himself taking part in a widespread attempt to devise a new social philosophy from remnants of the old. One way in which he did this was through a tense dialogue with his brother-in-law with whom he disagreed and in contrast to whom he felt compelled to spell out his thought.

One of the reference points for this dialogue was a three-part article, "Marxism Reconsidered," written by Lewis Corey in February 1940 for the *Nation*. The article clearly and straightforwardly accepted the implications of the term "totalitarianism" as applied to Russian Socialism and attempted to elicit some lessons for the American situation from the failures of Socialism in another country. The Marxist-Leninist tradition had always held the *seeds* of dictatorship in it, Corey argued. Its recent turn toward complete authority and away from its initial thrust toward democracy resulted from two mistaken notions of *how* Capitalism would turn into socialism. The views that change would come either through the "catastrophe" of revolution or through the proletariat as "carrier" had both been proven wrong. But neither Socialism nor Capitalism had any monopoly on democracy, Corey said. Capitalism had originally been democratic in the years of small enterprise. Socialists had intended their regime to be socially democratic. Both had succumbed to different forms of collectivization neither of which incorporated democracy. Socialism had succumbed to labor unionism, leaving out the farmers. Capitalism had succumbed to monopoly, which left out labor, farmers, and small businessmen. In order to avoid the ultimate, "inevitable," Fascist outcome inherent in monopoly Capitalism, Corey pressed for "the progressive transformation of capitalism toward democratic socialism." Collectivism could be democratic but only by solving the continuous economic crisis brought about by Capitalism, releasing the "forces of abundance," and raising the standard of living for all functional groups in the society.[8]

Hofstadter saw just as clearly as Corey the lack of democracy in the Soviet Union: "There is no dictatorship of the proletariat. There is no withering away of the state; there is no liberty; there is no economic equality; there is no outstanding cultivation of the whole set of human values that socialism was supposed to bring." Political leadership in Russia had abandoned the ideals that had evoked the Great Experiment in Russia. Why? Either, thought Hofstadter, because the tactics were unscrupulous to begin with—that is, Leninism "was based upon an essentially undemocratic *minority* putchism" and thus "there is a funda-

mental weakness in the Marxist-Leninist political methodol-
ogy"—or, as Trotsky would have it, the wrong clique obtained
control and was now having to guide Russia through a period
of "state capitalism." Hofstadter leaned toward the first of these
as an explanation but was sure of nothing except that Socialism
did not necessarily solve "the problems of democracy or economic exploitation." This alone, he thought, was "a tremendous
blow to traditional Marxism, at a vital point."[9]

The major problem, Hofstadter thought, was not being treated
in the current chaotic situation. He found little of practical value
for that problem from Corey's writing and came out again with
nothing.

But it is no answer to the mistakes of the past that a realization of them
leaves you uncertain as to what to do in the future. That is inevitable
in any period of intellectual transition. Of course Marxism still has more
answers than Wellsism, but to submit that as a solution of these difficulties is silly.[10]

In contrast to his brother-in-law who, evidently, was continuing
to defend "orthodox" Marxism, Hofstadter was concerned with
the realities of an unsolved economic crisis at home and military
warfare abroad. He was attempting to grapple both with long-
term economic and social problems and with the philosophical
underpinnings for those problems, both of which had seemed
soluble under the tenets of Marxism. He had evidently forgotten—if he had ever really swallowed it—the conclusion that Felice had reached in her M.A. thesis and that they had both learned
from Marvin Farber: that "the day of comprehensive world systems is over." In the void left by the treachery of the Soviet
Union, the one nation that embodied the worldview they believed in, people like Corey and Hofstadter were struggling to
understand in a new way how the ideals of Marxian Socialism
could be made to work.

One approach that seemed attractive and coherent at this point
was Leon Trotsky's. Although he did not agree with all Trotsky
said on the current regime in the Soviet Union Hofstadter read
at this time Trotsky's *Revolution Betrayed* and thought it a brilliant

performance. But he did not like the logic-splitting arguments of the Trotskyists either, especially in their attempts to answer Corey's articles. With two such imperfect alternatives, he still tended to be very pessimistic: "It looks to me like T'ism or no Marxism, and to me the latter."[11]

But Hofstadter could not break away from six years of involvement quite so easily as this, no matter what he said. In face of his brother-in-law's doctrinaire and hot-headed arguments, he offered Max Eastman's *Stalin's Russia and the Crisis in Socialism*. These affirmations indicate that although the Nazi-Soviet Pact had presented an enormous crisis for Hofstadter, after a while— and he refers to himself as "cooling off" by December 1940— the ideas that were emerging as most significant and sensible to him were those of the independent, non-Stalinist Left, which did not repudiate many of the basic philosophical and social tenets of Marxism but did question Lenin's tactics and the current regime in Russia. Hofstadter had been actively involved in "minority putchism." Rejecting that did not necessarily mean rejecting all of Marxism as a social philosophy.

But even as far as the latter went, Hofstadter by October 1940 was quite pessimistic. He found no use for an intellectual class in the new, bureaucratic regime, the outlines of which Corey had put forward in his description of Soviet collectivism. To his brother-in-law who was putting his faith in colonial revolutions in the third world—a hard-line Trotskyist approach—and who thought the war made little difference to world revolution in the long run, he wrote:

For people like us, who have become permanently alienated from the spirit of revolutionary movements, its perfectly obvious why we feel we have some stake in this war. We don't like the status quo and we don't mind admitting that it's doomed, but we're more concerned to keep it from getting completely unbearable than in revolutionizing it.[12]

His had become the humbler approach, intent and focused upon immediate policies and their discernible outcome, not upon farfetched, "ultimate" goals. This did not mean that he did not share the outlines of a social philosophy with his brother-in-law. It merely meant he was now reality oriented rather than goal oriented, that he saw many evils in the world and preferred the lesser evil, a more immediate end, to the greater. He wished to lessen the stakes. Continuing the discussion, Hofstadter added:

I know what that [the more limited approach] means too. It means playing into Roosevelt's hand and his conscription fraud and all that goes with it. . . . Admitting that we are heading in the direction of fascism . . . a Hitler victory [over England during the winter] wd precipitate us into it overnight. And then I can see a long period of preparation for war—tremendously costly because of the magnitude of it. And a long, bloody struggle. . . . So you won't think we're softminded then if people with our outlook hope every day that the British are turning back the German raiders and that Churchill and Bevin and Morison dont get pneumonia. We don't have a very rich choice, and we can't bring ourselves to your complete negativism. We just didn't pick a very good time to be born.[13]

If there was some self-interest or self-pity at this point in Hofstadter's outlook, it was due to the fact that he was facing the personal prospects of war now. His own career was just beginning. He had worked long and hard against the approach of this war and now it seemed that he might have to go to fight for a social philosophy he had pitted himself against. As he said at the end of this letter, "I'd like to finish my thesis before I'm in the army."[14]

The realistic gradualism of his earlier days was also reiterated here in contrast to his brother-in-law's fixation on the idea of revolution. Hofstadter's general approach, therefore, was not a new one, but simply a restatement in the terms of new circumstances of a continuing outlook. Now, as with the issue of Spain in 1937, military victory took priority over an elusive worker uprising. The reason was the same as it had been in 1937. A worker uprising unplanned and unprepared for would be quashed immediately and hasten a surge of Fascism wherever it was tried. Then, "revolutionary leadership might just possibly be dead for a generation." Likewise, any policy of agitation within the military would only defeat those fighting against the Axis powers and increase the likelihood of their success. After the war, perhaps, national liberation uprisings would occur. Just as possible, however, was Fascism "in all the advanced countries of the world" for as long as they both would live.[15]

These discussions, the growing distance Hofstadter felt from his brother-in-law, and the tension of the times forced Hofstadter into another moment of crisis and insight. The similar moment of more than a year earlier just after the Pact had widened into a generally negative stand. He said:

We once fancied that we were hard enuf to cut ourselves off from our class of petty bourgeois intellectuals, that we cd go into the leftwing movement without any illusions or dogmatism and be effective and happy there. We found out tho, that we had been holding plenty of illusions, and now we're not so quick to get enthusiastic abt similar ideas which we have any reason to be skeptical abt.[16]

The ineffectuality of his doubts, expressed earlier in reference to his exit from the Party, had hardened now into a general outlook on life. Although the future belonged to the workers, if it belonged to anyone, Hofstadter said, it did not belong to him.

Also we found out that we could not be effective, that we weren't suited to work with people who were in a party-line frame of mind. When we were in college we were glib and carefree abt converting our friends without taking any thought that we were inducing them to take steps that wd change the whole course of their lives, not necessarily for the better. *That's one responsibility we aren't likely to assume soon again.* We also made the simple discovery that we weren't workers and couldn't be workers, that the workers had no place for us. In short, that we are petty bourgeois intellectuals and that there is a certain inherent alienness between us and the working class. Some people may be able to make the transition, but not us. . . . We aren't tough enuf. . . . We're temperamentally unfit for it, and that is something which can't be reached by argument.[17]

Hofstadter had left his activist stance because he was not comfortable controlling other people's lives. The thought, once joyously nonexistent, of persuading people into Party membership—only to be betrayed—frightened him. In contrast to the blithe young man of nineteen who wrote letters to the student newspaper defending welfare recipients, Hofstadter at the age of twenty-four was much more sober, restrained, and desirous of reflection and analysis rather than action and persuasion. He was in this letter as convinced of his position as he ever was about anything. This was a completely personal statement, unreachable by argument, something felt about his own temperament in disjunction with the movement. The insight—and the identity crisis that it helped to resolve—allowed Hofstadter to turn more fully to his scholarship as an expression of his insights.

All the time he had been arguing politics with his brother-in-law, Hofstadter had also been looking for a dissertation topic, often quite frustrated by the process. He tried several ideas before hitting on his final choice. For a while he wanted to write a biography of Benjamin Wade, until he learned that Wade had burned most of his important papers. Later he thought about Lincoln's Secretary of War, Simon Cameron, but found that someone else had been working on Cameron for fifteen years. By late in March 1940, he had almost decided "to capitulate" and write on "Jedidiah Hockenpfuss, Colonial Antimony Merchant, 1763–1781." This was Felice's slur on a topic that had been suggested by Professor Krout, a subject more respectfully known as Jeremiah Wadsworth who had been a reactionary leader—politician, banker, and insurance salesman—during the American Revolution. His biography was being subsidized by a private group and Hofstadter actually did work on the project for a month before the subsidy and subject petered out. One wonders at such a choice but remembers that Hofstadter had considered writing a remunerative, apolitical task, at least since his attempts at book reviews for the *Herald Tribune* and his one-time desire to become a journalist. It is simply fortunate, both for the integrity of his character and for the on-going flow of historiography, that this project did not work out.[18]

Meanwhile, a seminal idea was developing *en famille* at the Hofstadter/Swados establishment. At the end of October 1939 Felice reported to her brother that she was "now more interested in the irrational than in systems of tought [*sic*] or means of logical activity." She quoted in this regard a "damned good article" by Max Lerner in the *Nation*.[19] There, in addition to discussing the irrational and popular acceptance of ideas, Lerner made a brief, thumbnail sketch of reigning ideas from the seventeenth to the nineteenth centuries, with Darwinism and Marxism indicating the "ascertainable laws of development" in the biological and historical realms, respectively. The great twentieth-century development consisted of the charting of the irrational, Lerner affirmed. To these comments he added that the newest development would play havoc with traditional intellectual history, which had been seen either as the history of ideas in the abstract or as "climates of opinion."

This third approach had been gaining ground. It emphasized "the history of ideas as the expression of broad social and class forces." This approach, represented by Beard and Parrington in the United States, owed much to Karl Mannheim from abroad. It viewed intellectual history as "a succession of defensive and aggressive movements directed toward class and group interests and power relations." "Their assumption," Lerner wrote, "is that both the intellectual apologies for a social order and the intellectual attacks upon it need to be recognized before we can lay bare the social impulsions behind the work of individual thinkers."[20]

No matter what else he may have meant, it is clear that Lerner was attempting at this early point to assess the impact of the sociology of knowledge on the field of intellectual history. It was a new approach to what Marvin Farber had been attempting to do in the field of philosophy. The relation of thinking to biographical, social, economic, and political factors was crucial to a correct understanding of the thought. Its conditioning made it impossible any longer to conceive of a body of thought unrelated to its context.

A month later Hofstadter reported that Felice had been developing a "new idea." It was "studying the use of Darwinism (via Spencer) as a rationalization of capitalism in the late 19th century US." It is not known how far Felice had gone with this idea or what she proposed to do with it for herself. What is known is that in February 1940 Hofstadter was assigned Max Lerner's new book, *Ideas Are Weapons*, to review for the *Political Science Quarterly*. Many of Lerner's basic insights appearing in the *Nation* also appeared in that book and Hofstadter undoubtedly became extremely familiar with them. He also naturally followed closely what his wife was doing.[21]

It is extremely interesting, then, that by June 1940 Hofstadter had appropriated Felice's topic and, with Lerner's new approach to intellectual history and Merle Curti's approval, had begun work in earnest on his Ph.D. dissertation at Columbia. Its tentative title at this point: "The Defense of Property, a Study of Social Darwinism in the U.S. (the 19th Century)." This was, according to Felice, "the kind of book in which all his friends want to have a hand" but "in which," Hofstadter added, "they won't."[22]

The choice of a topic for his Ph.D. dissertation thus represented the culmination of this period of identity crisis in Richard Hofstadter's life. It incorporated the political experiences he had undergone since 1935. It embodied the blend between ideas and socioeconomic forces that Hofstadter had absorbed from the intellectual community around him. It represented his current feeling of alienation from both American Capitalism and revolutionary ideology. At the same time, it represented a completely new research effort on his part. The new work and his particular attitude toward the subject provided the qualities that won it the AHA Beveridge Award and ultimately made it a classic among twentieth-century intellectual histories.

In the original version of *Social Darwinism*, Hofstadter described the ascendant swing of nineteenth-century free enterprise thought. This social philosophy was best represented by Herbert Spencer who applied the basic tenets of Darwin—survival of the fittest and natural selection—to society and social processes in general. Spencer argued that society evolved naturally, that it grew from simpler to more complex forms, and that superior individuals rose to leadership positions if no intervention occurred in these developmental processes.[23]

Spencer's ideas caught on quickly and easily in the United States and were further perpetuated by William Graham Sumner, who used his post as sociologist at Yale not only to elaborate on Spencer's ideas but to rail against regulatory legislation as it came up in Washington.

The theory remained on the "ascendancy" until the 1890's

when the force of reformist thought counterbalanced it and forced its decline. Even before the 1890's several cracks appeared in the surface of this reigning ideology. Lester Frank Ward denied flatly that there were fundamental similarities between the animal world and human society. He laid out a body of social theory amenable to the uses of reform. Pragmatism, as developed by William James and furthered by John Dewey, "controverted" the determinism of Spencer and Sumner. James reasserted the arguments for free will and put life back into the notions of the active nature of the human intellect. In the field of economics by the 1880's, Richard Ely and Simon Patten were reasoning out justifications for a more positive view of state intervention and the regulation of industrial powers. And as sociology developed into social psychology, the issues of determinism and free will were reviewed again.[24]

On a more popular level, Social Darwinism was espoused by Christians and others who questioned the implications of Darwinian evolution for ethical purposes. For these people, competition existed between groups instead of between individuals. This was Darwinian collectivism, which had nearly replaced Darwinian individualism by the 1890's. The outright dissenters to Spencerian thought—those who had denied the theory of individualism all along (reformers such as Henry George, Edward Bellamy, and the early Marxian Socialists like Laurence Gronlund)—joined the stream of Darwinian collectivism from a different starting point. Together these groups, with the reformist academicians, created a groundswell of opinion against Darwinian individualism by the end of the century.[25]

However, the forces of Spencerian thought were not completely quelled before World War I. The reigning ideology also took a popular political form better known as Manifest Destiny. The assumption behind that idea was the superiority of the Anglo-Saxon "race." Pushing across the northern hemisphere, its proponents believed they would populate and control the world. This was the American adjunct to British imperialism. The movement took its impulse from the developing eugenics movement. In the works of Theodore Roosevelt, Admiral Mahan, and Homer Lea, one could see the germs of racist thought. It was the biological argument for militarism. Proponents of this view feared the rise of the Eastern peoples—the "Yellow Peril"; the answer they found: greater militancy among Anglo-Saxons.

But as European War erupted and the preparedness campaign developed in the United States, biological militarism suffered a terrible contradiction. Its argument too closely resembled that of German Teutonic militarism. In the face of this ultimate and embarrassing contradiction, the racism inherent in Anglo-Saxon notions of superiority was dropped. Instead, American propagandists such as William Thayer and the Creel Committee displaced the tenets of Social Darwinism onto German spokespersons—especially unfairly in the case of Nietzsche—in order to develop a good argument against them. Such were the irrational uses of an inverted form of Social Darwinism put to work by propagandists in the time of war hysteria.[26]

Taken as a whole, the story of Social Darwinism in American thought was the story of declension. The force of Spencer's ideas did not decline however, solely because of new ideas, although this was part of the reason. They went out of vogue because the middle class had a change of heart. Here, in his conclusion, one must look closely at Hofstadter's explanation. The ascendancy of Spencerian thought had been due, he said, to the types of business rivalry dominant in the late nineteenth century, to the unprincipled politics prevailing in the United States, and to the need among dominant groups to see their own image in a prevailing cosmic philosophy that justified its behavior.[27] But—and the actual cause for change was expressed very positively by Hofstadter—"nothing is so unstable as 'pure' business competition, nothing is so disastrous to the unlucky or unskilled competitor; nothing . . . is so difficult as to keep the growing numbers of the 'unfit' reconciled to the operations of such a regime."[28] These elements contradicted the principles of Social Darwinism. Spencer's system had given cosmic extension and form to the principle of competition and survival of the fittest. Hofstadter found contradictions within the system that appeared to have operated so smoothly and that, according to Spencer, needed nothing so much as to be left alone. For a system with such failures, was Hofstadter's implication, the only answer was its antithesis: regulation as a way to stabilize economic forces, protection for the unlucky or unskilled, provision of an organ of expression to the "unfit."

Even though annoyingly vague and prolix, Hofstadter was undoubtedly speaking from his own convictions here. He went on:

In time the American middle class shrank from the principle it had glorified, turned in flight from the hideous image of rampant competitive brutality, and repudiated the once heroic entrepreneur as a despoiler of the nation's wealth and morals and a monopolist of its opportunities.[29]

It appeared to him that the intellectual conflict of antithetical ideologies had been resolved by a process of moral repudiation, not unlike—but prior to—the repudiation of the American Communist Party that intellectuals on the Left were experiencing just as Hofstadter was writing. Indeed, the former repudiation had led directly to the movement in which he had first located his political and social existence and so he was directly connected to it.

Once criticized, the whole intellectual edifice came toppling down.

When Americans were once in a mood to listen to critics of Darwinian individualism, it was no difficult task for them to destroy its flimsy logical structure and persuade their audiences that it had all been a ghastly mistake. Spencer and the men of Spencer's generation in America, thought that he had written a grand preface to destiny. Their sons came to wonder at its monumental dullness and its quaint self-confidence, and thought of it ... only as a revealing commentary on a dead age.[30]

Fathers and sons disagreed and a new period of "intellectual transition" arose. Just as Jefferson's world view had gone out of vogue, so had the "flimsy logical structure" of Social Darwinism. But, it must be added, so had the Marxist movement, which also looked, to a later generation, like a quaint edifice in its attempt to be a "grand preface to destiny."

In this work, Hofstadter traced the rise and fall of a major thought system buttressing American Capitalism. He attributed its decline to *contradictions* within the system itself and in its application to the economy. It did not bring order or equity to the human work situation. People—both intellectuals and middle-class consumers of this ideology—became conscious of the contradictions and rebelled against its tenets and implications. In dialectical fashion, a reigning synthesis had been challenged by opposing and contradictory ideas, and a new synthesis had been attained by a combination of old free enterprise philosophy and new reform/regulatory precepts. It is most significant that the contradictions—just as had happened for the German immigrants and their political position in the Democratic Party in his tutorial thesis—of Anglo-Saxon racism caused the final decline of Spencerianism. Reigning ideologies could not withstand the force of their contradictions according to dialectical thought, and history moved because of the force of those contradictions. Hofstadter, although repudiating some (but not all) of his former politics—as we have seen—had *not* repudiated the philosophical underpinnings of those politics. Those underpinnings *were* his unquestioned philosophy of history and they would remain so.

How little, indeed, of his old outlook Hofstadter had shed is revealed in his concluding paragraph of *Social Darwinism*, where he allowed himself some very guarded generalizations.

There is certainly some interaction between social ideas and social institutions. Ideas have effects as well as causes. The history of Darwinian individualism, however, is a clear example of the rule that changes in the structure of social ideas wait on general changes in economic and political life. In determining whether such ideas are accepted, truth and logic are less important than their suitability to the intellectual needs and preconceptions of social interests. *This is one of the greatest difficulties that must be faced by rational strategists of social change.*[31]

The basic principle of Marxist thought—economic causation—had *not* been left behind. Like Marx, Hofstadter still saw change as emanating from the economic sphere of life. But, as in his paper on Wendell Phillips, Hofstadter had now modified that approach, sophisticated it, and turned his attention to the realm of the attendant ideological structure. And, as in his paper on the psychology of slavery, ideas now also had effects. They were causative too, although not as basically so.

The greatest and most recent insight, however (and the reason for his italics here), is the relativity of truth—the all-pervasive power of the applicability of ideas to needs and to interests. For ideas to catch on, they *must* be relevant, cogent, useful—not necessarily logical. "Rational strategists of social change"—Marxists working for a better order—were just now learning new and deeper lessons in this area of relativity and practicability, a lesson learned only slowly after August 1939. It is simply an indication of how ultimately Hofstadter had once held those beliefs—in truth and logic—to observe him summing up *Social Darwinism* in this way.

Hofstadter had accepted Max Lerner's ideas on the new intellectual history and had incorporated the irrational and unconscious elements underlying late nineteenth-century economics. He had successfully articulated the relationship between the economic base and its ideological superstructure. His book was to gain him a reputation and make for him a career. But it was to be vastly misunderstood by many readers. *Social Darwinism* was written out of Hofstadter's own tension between his hatred for Capitalism and its apologists and his repudiation of a vital part of the Marxist social philosophy in which he had put his faith. It was an attempt to reach back into the past and come up with the reigning ideology of Capitalism, as it was formed in the heyday of industrial growth in America, and consider its decline. Actually he had been considering two ideological "revolutions. One was Spencerian; the second liberal. With this second "revolution" in thought—middle class liberalism—the radical movement of the 1930's took exception. Hofstadter had located himself in that radical movement, which had now been forced into decline. By writing *Social Darwinism*, Hofstadter was, implicitly, locating himself in history. He was also—as he had in the past—understanding history through his involvement in the present. It is not surprising, therefore, that in depicting those revolutions in thought, he continued to employ basic concepts from Marxist philosophy: the dialectical notion of change and the intimate relationship between the economic base and ideological superstructure. These would be lasting elements of his work.

NOTES

1. For information on the Dorfman course, Richard Hofstadter to Harvey Swados, September 30, 1939, Harvey Swados Papers, Courtesy

of the Archives of the University of Massachusetts, Amherst, Mass. He added, "Expenses for this year are $5 library fee, but this is only consoling feature." Joseph Dorfman thought Hofstadter might have been influenced by his course, his *Economic Mind*, and his biography of Veblen. Joseph Dorfman to the author, January 18, 1981. Enough attention has not been given to the possibility that Hofstadter gained enormously from the insights of Veblen.

2. Richard Hofstadter, "Some Psychological Aspects of the Slavery Controversy," Unpublished MS, Hofstadter Papers, p. 1.

3. Ibid.

4. Ibid., p. 12.

5. Ibid., p. 10.

6. Hofstadter to Swados, February 8, 1940, Swados Papers.

7. Ibid.

8. Lewis Corey, "Marxism Reconsidered I, II, III," *Nation*, CL (February 17, 1940), pp. 245–48; (February 24, 1940), pp. 272–75; (March 2, 1940), pp. 305–7. For quotation see (March 2, 1940), p. 305.

9. Hofstadter to Swados, March 1940, Swados Papers (emphasis in original).

10. Ibid.

11. Ibid., March 1940 [the second of two].

12. Ibid., October 3 [1940].

13. Ibid.

14. Ibid.

15. Ibid., December 16, 1940.

16. Ibid.

17. Ibid (emphasis added).

18. Ibid., March 1940; May 1941.

19. Felice Swados to Harvey Swados, October 25 [1940], Swados Papers.

20. Max Lerner, "Revolution in Ideas," *Nation* CXLIX (October 21, 1939) p. 435.

21. Felice Swados to Harvey Swados, June 2 [1940], Swados Papers; Richard Hofstadter, "Ideas are Weapons," *Political Science Quarterly* LV (December 1940) p. 621.

22. Felice Swados to Harvey Swados, June 2 [1940].

23. Richard Hofstadter, *Social Darwinism in American Thought, 1860–1915* (Philadelphia, University of Pennsylvania Press, 1945) Chapter I.

24. Ibid., Chapters IV-VI.

25. Ibid., Chapters V, VI.

26. Ibid., Chapter IX.

27. Ibid., p. 174.

28. Ibid.
29. Ibid.
30. Ibid., p. 175.
31. Ibid., p. 176 (emphasis in original).

9

New Beginnings

Hofstadter's dissertation brought him another round of applause at Columbia. His report to his brother-in-law followed the usual tongue-in-cheek style: "Big Me is now Ph.D. with the best exam, they say, in 25 yrs."[1] Relief and pride must have vied for central place in his feelings. But anxiety about a job, especially given his father-in-law's doubts about him, must also have been plaguing Hofstadter by this time.

It was not until the summer of 1942 that those anxieties were assuaged. At that point, undoubtedly through the good offices of his friend Merle Curti, he received a letter from the University of Maryland inviting him to become a member of the faculty there in the fall. Consequently, he and Felice made plans to move. Felice took a leave of absence at *Time*, they made arrangements to leave their belongings in New York, they found a furnished basement apartment in mid-Washington, and Hofstadter began a daily trek from Washington to College Park. The new arrangement entailed getting up at 7:00 A.M., which he grumbled about, taking an overcrowded city bus to the Greyhound station, and catching another bus destined for "Pittsburgh" or "New York," which he took to College Park.[2]

He was pleased with his job, found the students "pleasant and disciplined but not clever," and was impressed with how well they took notes and were quiet in class. He enjoyed assessing his colleagues, several of whom were nondescript and boring, but others of whom became very good friends. He wrote of one in particular, new to Maryland like himself, a member of the Sociology Department, with a manuscript on the sociology of pragmatism. This was a young man from Texas who had "wangled" himself an associate professorship. His name was C. Wright Mills. By October, Felice and Hofstadter had been invited to the Mills' home near Greenbelt and the four had begun enjoying each other, even though Mills was "sadly addicted to sociological jargon."[3]

In addition to his normal undergraduate courses, which included many sections of the introductory American survey course, Hofstadter taught, that first year, a graduate seminar in historical methods and criticism. In the course he had five students: "two girls, two ministers, and a rabbi". He thought they were all "literate and responsive" and that it would be a "pleasure to introduce them to the wonders of research." At the same time, Felice reported that his book, *Social Darwinism in American Life*, would probably not be published until after the war.[4]

Washington was a busy and exciting place to be in the fall of 1942. War preparations were proceeding apace and the city was crowded with newly arrived volunteers and recruits. Felice had decided to take the opportunity of her leave of absence to concentrate on a second major fictional project that she had begun. Accordingly, at first—as she had done in New York—she stayed at home and wrote for long hours, taking walks as recreation, But she could not stay away from the active side of life for long. By the middle of the year she had found herself a part-time job writing copy for the aviation industry. With her usual buoyancy and zest for life, she enjoyed the people, issues, and hectic pace of the scramble to get ready for war. She seemed, indeed, to be in her element, writing up the types of characters she was meeting and sending off her descriptions for her brother's approval.[5]

Hofstadter and his friends went through a variety of attitudes toward the possibility of serving in the Armed Forces. Hofstadter veered back and forth between excitement about getting into the thick of action and disgust with the military and its potential effect on his life. As he watched his brother-in-law, newly graduated from the University of Michigan, enlist in the Merchant Marine, Hofstadter counted on being exempt because he was teaching required courses to newly enlisted Army men. Later he learned that he had been classified as 1A. He appealed that classification on the basis of his status as "essential civilian" and still later was definitively rejected on the basis of his digestive problems and allergies.[6]

Not long after his arrival at Maryland, the friendship with Mills broadened into a lasting, four-way friendship, which included two other new appointees in the History Department. Kenneth Stampp had come to the University of Maryland from Wisconsin, where he had obtained his Ph.D. and worked under William Hesseltine. Frank Freidel, who had been teaching at Shurtleff College in Pennsylvania, had worked as a teaching assistant with Stampp at Wisconsin. These three with Mills formed a close attachment and met regularly for lunch. They agreed on their antipathy toward FDR, their disinclination to acquiesce to their draft boards, American Capitalism, etc.[7]

During the spring of 1943 these four attempted to organize opposition to the administration within the American Association of University Professors (AAUP) chapter on campus. All four were highly discontented with the administrative practices of President "Curly Bird" Byrd, ex-football coach and consummate politician. President Byrd had been making faculty cutbacks. In addition, he had changed the two-semester system to a three-semester system without increases in pay. Now Byrd proposed an increase in teaching load from 12 to 18 hours. At this point, the University had contracted with the Army to teach certain basic courses to new recruits. This was to be a cheap way for the University to do that. Hofstadter and his friends set up a grueling session of questions for the President, the only invited guest at this particular AAUP meeting. The President "wrapped himself in the American flag," asked what the teaching profession was doing complaining about an 18–hour load when others were off fighting, and left the meeting, but not before Hofstadter and his cohorts "pushed thru a resolution to have a faculty investigation of the Army contracts obtained by our school and various others." The four friends clearly made a cohesive, spear heading party with *some* influence at the staid University of Maryland campus, as well as acting as an intellectual oasis for each other.[8]

In March 1943, with wartime activities going on all around

them and with Hofstadter continuing to adjust to his new position, Felice became pregnant. Both parents-to-be were joyous as Felice developed her new physique. At the same time, they realized that the timing was not ideal. Hofstadter continued to plan as if his 1A status would be retained, attempting to light upon some viable but active niche for an intellectual in wartime. If he were drafted, he would be leaving just as the baby was born, not an unfamiliar story for the period. In fact, many of their friends were just then having their children, namely, the Mills and Stampp families. Also, looking to this eventuality, Felice had been urged and had agreed to apply for a Guggenheim Fellowship for study abroad, to be awarded in the spring of 1944 and to allow her to go to Europe the next year. That life abroad was a very real possibility in their minds at this time is clear from some of Hofstadter's more activist comments, such as "I'm awfully tired of teaching stale history to adolescents at a time when the whole world is being torn up. I wd like to see something. If I have to expose myself morally that is too bad." In those days, especially in Washington, life for many seemed very uncertain.[9]

On December 19, 1943, after 21½ hours of labor, Felice delivered a healthy baby boy, whom the couple named Dan. Everyone was enormously pleased. Hofstadter was especially relieved because Felice appeared to have come through the long and difficult labor with flying colors. His comment on her ordeal: "I always say that everything comes hard to Fagel"[10]

But his relief was premature. "Fagel" spent the next month in the hospital, suffering from an "abscess over the spine" and undergoing exploratory surgery, which revealed a "long, embryonic cyst" running up her back which had to be taken out. By January 15, 1944, she had decided to wait six months for the operation, which would not be "serious" but would take a period of six to seven weeks in the hospital. In the meantime, she had an offer of a job from *Newsweek*, representatives from which were pressuring her to return to New York and take up her old career. While tempted, she resisted the pressure, preferring to stick close to her efforts as a "pure" novelist. The new baby, of course, took some extra time as well.[11]

By late spring of 1944, Felice made a new discovery that would answer the *Newsweek* offer she kept putting off. In May or June, she asked Kenneth Stampp's wife, Kay, to feel a lump near her waist. She discovered immediately that she had developed cancer, and the three Hofstadters returned to Buffalo as soon as the spring semester ended. Their financial reserves were slim and their problems were becoming very complicated. They left their newly rented apartment in Hyattsville, where they had moved from central Washington, resigning their books to the care of Kenneth and Kay Stampp, who lived close by, and established Felice as an invalid in her father's new home in Buffalo. The financial, emotional, and familial circumstances dictated such a resolution to this new crisis.[12]

At first it seemed as though the arrangement would be necessary only for the summer. Hofstadter was giving up summer-school teaching and he must have missed the more lucrative salary which such teaching brought, but there was no doubt of the nature of this crisis. It eventually became clear he would also have to take a leave of absence from the University of Maryland for the academic year of 1944–45 as well. Felice, according to her father, could not survive in Washington.

Felice was in enormous discomfort. A day in which she vomited seven times was reported as a good day because she had little pain. She had no energy and needed a special diet, but could hold little or nothing down. She took it with dogged courage. Hofstadter did double duty as her nurse and his son's maid, barely taking time to leave the house once a week. Little is known about Rivi and Aaron at this time, but it is assumed they gave up their emotionalism and stood quietly by, ready to step in and assist if necessary. Dan, grew to be "huge and muscular like a miniature football player, with rough, red, dirty cheeks." He was—most likely—everyone's salvation.[13]

Hofstadter had one consolation during this long, miserable year. It was—as it always would be during the remainder of his life—his work. During that fall of 1944, *Social Darwinism* was published under the auspices of the AHA. Hofstadter sent copies to his friends, with justifiable pride, explaining at one point to Kenneth Stampp that it had been written with some inhibitions, under the iron-clad rules of doctoral theses. And he began work on a new book of essays, writing pieces on Lincoln, Herbert Hoover, and FDR by the middle of the year.[14]

One major episode in the middle of the year distracted him. Back in Maryland, Stampp and Friedel had discovered that Carlton J. H. Hayes had been nominated for the presidency of the AHA. Hayes had served as ambassador to Spain, and the Maryland historians believed him to be an apologist for Franco. The emotional involvement over this nomination, attached as it was to American foreign policy, was high. Stampp and Friedel inquired at AHA headquarters about the procedure for substitution, found they needed 50 or more petition signatures for a new nomination, and managed a campaign to put forward the vice-presidential nominee, Sidney Fay, for president. They sent petitions around and obtained a good number of signatures.[15]

Hofstadter was made aware of this "Crusade," as he called it, and seemed in complete sympathy with the effort from its earliest days. He signed the petition, although requesting that his name not appear alone on a separate page. As time went on, however, he appeared more and more skeptical about the outcome of the effort, informing Stampp that several negative responses from major intellectual historians should "tip you off on how much chance of success you have," and adding, "I bet you Sidney Fay steps in and repudiates the whole thing too."[16]

Hofstadter had also discovered an article on Hayes in the December *Harpers* by Ernest Lindley, a journalist Felice knew. He read it after having signed the petition. It was, he acknowledged, to some degree a State Department apologia, but it seemed to him "to knock the props out from under the Crusade." It presented Hayes as critical of both Fascism and specific policies of the Spanish government while he had been ambassador.[17]

The backsliding on Hofstadter's part caused great consternation among his friends, who interpreted this attitude as motivated by his ambitions to return to Columbia as a faculty member. Several accusations and explanations passed between them, and Hofstadter ended with another of his poignant self-disclosures, writing to his friends:

As for me, for what reasons I can't say just now, I am by temperament wuite [*sic*] conservative and timid and acquiescent. I suppose that at bottom I am a radical only because I can't function intellectually any other way, but not because I have the true flame. You can set this down to true opportunism if you choose. I think you wd be mistaken. It is due among other things to a pervasive inner despair which I doubt that you can very well understand. I say all this by way of analysis, not apology.[18]

Whether such statements were apology or analysis, nothing concrete changed because of the episode. It was too late to re-move Hofstadter's name from the petition. The effort in itself was not successful. Sidney Fay did write to the AHA "deprecating the grounds on which the petitioners had acted" and declining the offer. A written ballot was taken anyway, and Hayes was elected by a vote of 110 to 66. Professor Wesley Gewehr, head of the History Department at Maryland, spoke for the petition-ers. Clearly Stampp and Friedel had gained some ground, if not enough for their ultimate purposes.[19]

This was one of Hofstadter's last statements about his radical leanings. Whoever was "right" on this disagreement over Hayes, the statement is significant in that it reveals what Hofstadter had obtained, personally, from the radical movement of the 1930's. He had found support and space for his mind to operate freely and creatively on the issues with which he came in contact. His was the critical, skeptical mind, the mind that took things apart, the mind that found fault, and the mind that also put things back together in new ways. It had needed that space and support and contrast to middle-class America from which to take off. That mind also grew beyond—or had always been beyond—the restricted, rigidified thinking of orthodox Marxists. It had tried to discipline itself to those restrictions and it had rebelled. Now, it was finding a new niche, professional space and support, from which to operate.

As he worked ahead on chapters for his new book that winter, Hofstadter began to think about publishers. He sent his man-uscript to Reynal and Hitchcock, who "turned it down flat." He then prepared it for the competitive Alfred A. Knopf Fellowship in History and sent it off in the early spring. By the end of May he had been awarded one-half that Fellowship for a publication to be entitled "Men and Ideas in American Politics." The award resolved his immediate financial problems, which he admitted, "were beginning to be like a nightmare to me." It also gave him some writing time, stipulating a 1947 publication date.[20]

The award caused some consternation at the University of Maryland, however. Chairman Gewehr doubted that Hofstadter meant to return the next year. Hofstadter did feel so committed, however, and turned a deaf ear to some overtures from other institutions during his stay in Buffalo in order to fulfill this obligation at Maryland.[21]

In late July 1945 Felice died. It had been a long, tragic illness, with time to become prepared for her death. Nevertheless, Hofstadter must have been drained. He left Buffalo soon after the funeral to take a rest.[22] He appears to have been silent about the tragedy, and one is reminded that he claimed to have amnesia after his mother's death. One is also reminded of his statements after the Nazi-Soviet Pact, which he had been forced into recalling this year. He had characterized himself as having "a pervasive inner despair." He has also been described as a "melancholique" and few of his friends disagree with that description. One friend has attributed this quality to the two deaths of loved ones which Hofstadter sustained at inopportune points in his life. Whatever the case, it appears likely that he emerged with will power and courage in the fall of 1945 and took up his renewed responsibilities at the University of Maryland with quiet fortitude.[23]

Kenneth Stampp has characterized the next academic year as a neutral, coasting one for Hofstadter. It could not have been more. At least his position at the University of Maryland allowed him a connection with the world, neither overstimulating nor dull but supportive and familiar. The decision had been made to leave Dan with his grandparents, Rivi and Aaron. That solution was convenient if not without its problems.[24]

Sometime during that year, Hofstadter received a much coveted offer to teach at Columbia as a member of the History Department. Now no longer under a self-imposed commitment to continue at Maryland, he accepted this offer and planned on returning to the city he and Felice had so enjoyed. His friends were there: Harvey Swados, William Miller, and Mills, who had also been hired by Columbia. There were many reasons to be content. In fact, by May of 1946 Hofstadter was feeling "more in the clear emotionally than I have for a long time." His plans for Dan for the next year had gone awry, he said, but "I will not let it throw me." He had a lot on his shoulders, but one feels a resurrection of the old vitality, prematurely serious perhaps, but quite apparent.[25]

In the summer of 1946, Hofstadter returned to Buffalo to care for his son, now two and one half years old. He stayed there for the most part, spending some time in New York City searching for an apartment. He played tennis with his brother-in-law often. He tried to do some work on Theodore Roosevelt and William Jennings Bryan, subjects of other developing chapters for *The American Political Tradition*, but it was hard going and tedious, and he vowed "no more books for me. That is, after the *next* one." He was still recuperating, still adjusting to life without Felice, as a father alone in the United States in a postwar world.[26]

That summer, first in Buffalo and later again in New York, Hofstadter met Beatrice Kevitt, a widow several years younger than he. They began to see each other on a regular basis and in January 1947 were married. She would bring to their partnership a "sensitivity to style and her exceptional editorial gifts."[27]

These were the turning points for Richard Hofstadter—his coming of age. His life had been full of crises to this point—personal, social, political crises. Now he was no longer a graduate student, no longer an angry, young man. He was, at thirty, beginning to have real successes, quickly becoming a major rising star on the horizon of historical scholarship, publishing his books and winning professional awards. He had suffered enormous losses. But he had surmounted those losses. Now he was to begin a new life in an institution that he admired and with a woman whom he loved. He had returned home, a home that he would never leave again. Although he considered offers from other institutions over the years, he knew New York was his home and allowed the sentiment of loyalty to move and motivate him. He was settling in now, turning his full attention to the opportunities that his profession offered him. Never would his life be quite the same as it had been during his formative years.

Intellectually, as well as emotionally, the period at Maryland formed a new phase for Hofstadter. In addition to his new friends and the different viewpoints they offered, he read Max Weber, whom Mills was then translating. He read Karl Mannheim, whom he later claimed as a primary influence. He read all of Freud, amazing his friend Alfred Kazin by the thorough and systematic study he made of the psychiatrist. Acquaintance with these major figures turned him from the preoccupations of the New York Left and toward new interpretive devices for his historical subjects. But his orientation had been established. It had taken eight years to become established. And it would be difficult or impossible to destroy it.

One good example of the way his interpretative orientation remained with him can be seen by looking just a little further ahead. Hofstadter published *The American Political Tradition* in 1948. Either before or just after that publication date, he started work on a new book. When he did so, he went back, as he had for chapters in *The American Political Tradition*, to materials used in graduate school to pick up some ideas that had been fermenting in his mind. Because of this tendency, the interpretation of the Populists in *The Age of Reform* owes much to the work with Harry Carman and the interest in the social aspects of agricultural history Hofstadter had developed in conjunction with that work. As we have seen, that interest grew up through the fertile, productive year of 1938–39, while Hofstadter put together his papers on Jefferson and Wendell Phillips. It developed by gradually seeing with Phillips the link between slavery in the agrarian South and working conditions in the industrial North.

That interest had also seeped into *The American Political Tradition*. There Hofstadter first devised the concept of the "expectant Capitalist" of Jacksonian America—the entrepreneurial interpretation of the period that he shared with Arthur Schlesinger, Jr. The entrepreneurial interpretation was central to Hofstadter's growing formulation of the ideology of Capitalism. The title of his chapter on Jackson in *The American Political Tradition*, "The Rise of Liberal Capitalism," not only followed out his vision of rampant Capitalism in the early national period, put forward in his article "Parrington and the Jeffersonian Tradition" in 1941, but also indicated his preconceived notion that the ideology—the nascent Capitalistic mind—lurked both beyond the frontier and behind the politically democratic developments of this period.[28]

That "expectant Capitalist" was also linked to the Southern power structure, which Hofstadter had found so central to the abuses of the acreage reduction program of the AAA. That link was made clear in the early pages of his chapter on Jackson, where he described the democrat/aristocrat of the Upper South. Hofstadter wrote:

> Because of the ease and rapidity with which the shrewd and enterprising farmer might become a leader of the community, and hence a gentleman, during the decades when the cotton economy was expanding into the uplands, the upper classes of the Southwest came to combine the quality of the frontier rough necks and the landed gentry. The sportsmanlike, lawless, individualistic, quick-tempered, brawling nature of the first was soon sublimated into the courtly, sentimental, unreflective, touchy spirit of the second.... The difference between the frontiersman's readiness to fight and the planter's readiness to defend his "honor" is not so much a difference of temperament as of method, and there is no better exemplar of the fact than Jackson.[29]

The development of this characterization is extremely interesting, for again one sees Hofstadter observing an inversion. In *Social Darwinism* the middle-class consumers of ideology *controverted* Spencerian ideas into a regulatory ethic. In his paper on Jefferson's ideas, the slow course of a century *strangled* the Jeffersonian ethic and the city mobs *displaced* the old agrarian "people." In the original Phillips paper, Abolitionists *transmuted* proslavery arguments into ideas used by the proponents of radical labor. Here, the brawling nature of the frontiersman was *sublimated* into the touchy spirit of the country gentleman. This is the particularly Hofstadterian phenomenon of change, whereby an attitude of mind subtly transforms into something it was not and one is left with old, recognizable traits in a new context.

The development of this characterization is important also because by "sublimating" the frontiersman into the landed gentry, Hofstadter lost the clear distinction between the two—and some sympathy for both—and he was able to bring the burden of power possessed by the second also to rest on the first, where it did not really belong. It is this characterization and fallacious linkage that appear again in *The Age of Reform*. For there, Hofstadter's vision of the "hard side" of Populism—"the harrassed little country businessman"—is a direct carryover from the Jacksonian "expectant Capitalist." Hofstadter also attributed an important portion of Populist "demonology" to its backward, nostalgic view of the agrarian Utopia supposedly existing "before the development of industrialism and the commercialization of agriculture"—a Utopia that from some perspectives may be seen to have reached its peak in the Southern slave society.

The portrait of the Populists in *The Age of Reform*, then, developed through a long train of insights Hofstadter had been accumulating since his work with Harry Carman. He initially divined that American thought and experience were bound up with its Capitalist economy, that American attitudes were in fact nearly always representative of concepts closely tied to that economy, and that any real change would come only from a major economic upheaval. Because he had been so critical of that economy, because he had put his hopes and faith in the idea of a workers' state—an economy for the people—Hofstadter found it difficult to change this basic interpretive pattern later on. The lessons of his formative years were not easily to be unlearned.

NOTES

1. Richard Hofstadter to Harvey Swados, May 21, 1942, Harvey Swados Papers, Courtesy of the Archives of the University of Massachusetts, Amherst, Mass.

2. Kostelanetz, "Indomitable Skepticism," p. 169; Felice Swados to Harvey Swados, September 1942; Hofstadter to Harvey Swados, October 1942, Swados Papers.

3. Hofstadter to Harvey Swados, October 1942.

4. Ibid.; Felice Swados to Harvey Swados, March 24, 1942, Swados Papers.

5. Felice Swados to Harvey Swados, October 14, 1942, October 23, 1942, Swados Papers.

6. Hofstadter to Swados, March 31, 1943, July 15, 1943, August 19, 1943, Swados Papers; Hofstadter to Merle Curti, April 25, 1944, Merle Curti Papers, Wisconsin Historical Society, Madison, Wisc.

7. Kenneth Stampp, Personal interview with the author, April 2, 1981.

8. Stampp, Interview, April 2, 1981; Hofstadter to Harvey Swados, August 19, 1943, Swados Papers.

9. Hofstadter to Harvey Swados, August 19, 1943; Felice Swados to Harvey Swados, February 16, 1944, Swados Papers.

10. Felice Swados to Harvey Swados, December 20, 1943; Hofstadter to Harvey Swados, December 23, 1943. All in Swados Papers.

11. Felice Swados to Harvey Swados, January 15, 1944, February 16, 1944, Swados Papers.

12. Stampp, Interview, April 2, 1981.

13. Felice Swados to Kenneth Stampp, December 4, 1944, Letters to Stampp Courtesy of Kenneth Stampp, Berkeley, Calif.; Felice Swados to Harvey Swados, September 12, 1944, September 16, 1944, September 24, 1944, September 26, 1944, November 22, 1944, Swados Papers.

14. Hofstadter to Stampp [Fall 1944].

15. Stampp, Interview, April 2, 1981.

16. Hofstadter to Stampp [December 1944]. There are four letters that Kenneth Stampp has retroactively dated December 1944. For quotation here, see the second of these.

17. Ibid.

18. Ibid.

19. *American Historical Review* L (April 1945) pp. 663–64.

20. Hofstadter to Stampp, May 30, 1945, July 10, 1945.

21. Ibid., May 30, 1945.

22. Ibid., August 1945.

23. Alfred Kazin has stated, "he was of course . . . a great melancholic . . . very often humorists are very melancholy people." William Keylor, Interview with Alfred Kazin, Columbia Oral History Project, [1972] Columbia University, New York, N.Y., p. 6; H. Stuart Hughes has also observed: "the crucial element in Dick's biography" was the death of his mother. "I think the sad cast of his attitude dates from that, which was reinforced by the death of his first wife." And he adds to the statement made by Kazin: "My image of an evening of the Hofstadter's is of animated conversation going on, in which his second wife, Bede, was a leader, with Dick participating only intermittently, not by any means tuning out, very much following everything, very much appreciating everything . . . then occasionally coming in himself with one of his celebrated comic acts. . . . He was a natural mimic and a natural clown in the sense of a background of sadness, which would be enlivened by [something that] was a specific act or episode, an emergence from the sadness in a bravura performance, and then the sadness taking over again." William Keylor, Interview with H. Stuart Hughes, COHP, n.d. [1972], p. 6.

24. Stampp, Interview, April 2, 1981.

25. Hofstadter to Curti, May 18, 1946, Curti Papers.

26. Hofstadter to Stampp [June 1946].

27. Stampp, Interview, April 2, 1981; Stanley Elkins and Eric McKitrick, "Richard Hofstadter: A Progress," in Elkins and McKitrick, eds., *The Hofstadter Aegis* (New York, Knopf, 1972) p. 308.

28. Arthur M. Schlesinger, Jr., "Richard Hofstadter," in Marcus Cunliffe and Robin Winks, eds., *Pastmasters* (New York, Harper and Row, 1969) pp. 278–315.

29. Richard Hofstadter, *The American Political Tradition* (New York, Vintage Books, 1948) pp. 46–47.

PART II

Introduction

Many of the elements of Hofstadter's early, implicit theory of change remained with him as he continued to write history through his life. Of his nine major studies, three stand out as full-blown works depicting the salient points of American experience. They illustrate well the development and elaboration of his earlier dialectical form. *The Age of Reform* (1955) was to earn him the reputation with which he lived for the rest of his life. *Anti-intellectualism in American Life* (1962) was written over a long period, starting before *The Age of Reform* was finished. It responded to some of the same stimuli. It was in many respects Hofstadter's most personal piece of work. *The Idea of a Party System* (1969) capped Hofstadter's career and developed a theme which had been central to his work but had been left unexplicated. The dialectical structure in these books indicates how Hofstadter retained and developed the philosophical underpinnings of Marxism even as he eschewed the surface political elements of the theory.

As has been seen, the term "dialectic," though problematical, developed widespread usage during the 1930's and is used advisedly. It is a term that, by the 1940's, Hofstadter himself used un-self-consciously in notes to himself or in offhand comments about the nature of life. We have seen him use it with reference to Wendell Phillips's thinking about slavery and labor. Later he came to use it ever more casually. Referring to the Salzberg

Seminar in American Studies, in which he participated during the summer of 1950, for instance, Hofstadter said, "The situation ... had a dialectic of its own which forced us to be self-consciously ... American." At about the same time, he wrote, "But skill in dealing with the human context of ideas is in large part a by-product of self-evaluation, in which alone the full personal urgency and the psychological dialectic of ideas can be felt." It was a term which others of his generation shared and which was at times used by others to describe his work. By the 1960's, it was used in a loose and amorphous way, sometimes simply as a synonym for "tension." But the term has a background of its own and because it is both problematic and used advisedly, it will be worth while investigating it.[1]

There are two major definitions of "dialectic." Both mirror the more basic historical uses of the term. The first reads: "the art of critical examination into the truth of an opinion ... logical argumentation or disputation." In the Middle Ages, for instance, this definition denoted a type of argument used to debate the questions of Christian scholasticism, especially in the French universities. It was the attempt to take apart an opponent's argument by dissecting his propositions and offering alternative proposals—"the critical examination into the truth of an opinion."[2]

The second definition reads: "an interpretive method, originally used to relate specific entities or events to the absolute idea, in which some assertable proposition (thesis) is necessarily opposed by an equally assertable and apparently contradictory proposition (antithesis), the mutual contradiction being reconciled on a higher level of truth by a third proposition (synthesis.)" This definition does more to describe changing human institutions and comes from Georg Wilhelm Hegel.[3]

Hegel used the concept, as we have seen in Felice's M.A. thesis, as the basis for his vision of a dynamic universe and to indicate a triadic principle of movement that characterizes both the individual process of knowing and the development of "History." This is a process of "reaction"—a procedure by which the individual obtains contradictory insights and adds them to previous knowledge to form a more comprehensive whole, or stage, of knowledge. In the union between two opposites or contradictory ideas, another process also takes place—the process of "sublimation." This involves preserving something in a less immediate state than originally was the case and merging it, later, into a higher, or more complex, whole. In the original process of pulling apart the elements making up the thesis, "sublimation" occurrs to keep the thesis partially intact while the antithesis develops. In the formation of a new synthesis, also, the process of "the negation of the negation" occurs. The thesis is negated by the contradictory antithesis and a second negation of the antithesis occurs in order for it to recombine with its opposite, the thesis, in a new, higher form. For Hegel's theory of knowing, there is always something incomplete, partial, or one-sided about *any* stage, attitude, or interpretation. The truth, he said, "lies only in the whole." In terms of individual knowledge, then, the dialectic is a critical method, a method of clarification and understanding, a "formal [structural] cause." And it works for the social world as it does for individuals. As a whole it is the " 'logic' of movement."[4]

When Marx and Engels took hold of Hegel's ideas, they "stood this orientation on its head." For them, the dialectic operated according to a materialist orientation. Instead of the impetus toward freedom and "Spirit" postulated by Hegel as the purpose of the logic of movement, Marx and Engels pictured man as an economic, material being, identified by his or her work function in society. The way in which human beings produced their means of subsistence and the relationships created out of those means defined history and made change possible. Change itself, however, was no less dialectical than Hegel had pictured it. Social contradictions originated in the realm of work and its organization, rather than in the world of ideas or Spirit, as Hegel had imagined. Marx carried the dialectic into the field of social tensions, which, he said, developed in every epoch between the controlling and the controlled classes. His insistence on violent revolution as the only path toward true social change derived from this assertion.[5]

In Russia, those followers of Hegel and Marx carried on the philosophy of dialectical materialism and influenced Lenin, who added his own notions of Party leadership and imperialism to Marx's views about contemporary revolution. It is this modified version of the dialectic—as it had come to be conceived by Marxists in the 1930's—that influenced Hofstadter's philosophy of history.

There is a pattern, then, in Hofstadter's books, which is dialectical in nature and by which he viewed social change. This pattern has sometimes been taken as simple irony. Since Hofstadter was adept at describing moods and the discrepancy between expected and actual results—which is irony—this interpretation is understandable. But if one searches his work carefully for an answer to the question of how change actually came about for Hofstadter, one discerns this repetitious pattern. A fatal, originally buried, or invisible quality or characteristic rises to the surface in people's minds and eventually emerges as a glaring inconsistency or contradiction, fatally harmful to the original balance. This may be seen as the process of "reaction" in purely Hegelian terms.

The contradictory quality or tendency arises out of the changes in the economic base. It in turn affects the outlook of the group and their normative judgments about how life should be lived. This outlook becomes a set of social expectations derived from and dependent upon the community and a shared cultural background. It is eventually projected into the public arena in a political movement. It is opposed by an older expectation, more closely tied to a former economic reality. The opposing tendencies may involve a conflict between ideal values inherited from the past and concrete needs arising from the environment. In the ensuing political confrontation, there is a shift of assumptions, often manifested by a realignment of political forces, themselves representative of the original economic concerns. The shift also often entails a new coalition or the co-optation by one group of another's primary goals. In effect, a new set of assumptions acceptable to a sizable minority or a majority is created.

The pattern amounts to a kind of theory of political behavior. It may be viewed in microcosm—as short term and internal to a period or group—or in macrocosm—through a long period of time and external to a particular period or movement but descriptive of society as a whole. The process is found in Hofstadter's depictions of Populism and Progressivism in *The Age of Reform*, in his depictions of politics and twentieth-century intellectuals in *Anti-intellectualism in American Life*, and in the Founding Fathers' resistance to the idea of legitimate opposition in *The Idea of a Party System*. For purposes of brevity, I have chosen to present the use of this structure with regard to Populism in *The Age of Reform*, politics in *Anti-intellectualism* and the Founding Fathers in *The Idea of a Party System*.

NOTES

1. Richard Hofstadter, "The Salzburg Seminar, Fourth Year," *Nation* CLXXI (Octoter 28, 1950) p. 391; Richard Hofstadter, "Charles Beard and the Constitution," in Howard K. Beale, ed., *Charles A. Beard* (Lexington, University of Kentucky Press, 1954) p. 86.

2. *The Compact Edition of the Oxford English Dictionary*, I (New York, Oxford University Press, 1971) p. 715.

3. *Random House Dictionary of the English Language* (New York, 1967) p. 657.

4. John Herman Randall, *The Career of Philosophy, II: From the German Enlightenment to the Age of Darwin* (New York, Columbia University Press, 1965) pp. 310–314. For quotations see pp. 310, 312.

5. Karl Marx, "The Communist Manifesto," in Robert Tucker, ed., *The Marx-Engels Reader* (New York, W. W. Norton Company, 1972) p. 331 ff.; Marx, "Estranged Labor" in *The Economic and Philosophic Manuscripts of 1844*, in the same volume, pp. 56–67.

10

Populism: The Progressive Dialectic

With the change of the economic foundation the entire immense superstructure is more or less rapidly transformed. In considering such transformations the distinction should always be made between the material transformation of the economic conditions of production ... and the legal, political, religious, aesthetic or philosophical ... forms in which men become conscious of this conflict and fight it out. Just as our opinion of an individual is not based on what he thinks of himself, so can we not judge of such a period of transformation by its own consciousness; on the contrary, this consciousness must rather be explained from the contradictions of material life, from the existing conflict between the social forces of production and the relations of production.
—Karl Marx, Preface to *A Contribution to the Critique of Political Economy*

Hofstadter's analysis of Populism in *The Age of Reform* focused on the dual nature of the mind of the American farmer. It began with a chapter on "The Agrarian Myth and Commercial Realities." Hofstadter contended that Populism as a political movement rested on a double legacy from the period 1815–60 and before. Two clusters of attitudes coexisted harmoniously in the early, preindustrial years of nationhood, he maintained. Together they made up the original thesis of the American agrarian mind. One cluster arose out of the Jeffersonian prediction about how American life would evolve. It consisted of the image of

independent, self-sufficient yeoman farmers populating the hills
and valleys of the new continent, living in freed)m, equality,
and comfort in contrast to the constricted lives of the r European
forebears. The image originated among European agrarian aris-
tocrats—the Physiocrats in France, a "learned agricultural gentry
in England"—who idolized country life and bulwarked their
privileges with allusions to the classical masters of pastoral poetry. At first it was accepted and promulgated among like classes
in America. Eventually it became a "mass creed." It embodied
among other ideas a natural rights theory of labor—"the fundamental right to labour the earth." In the 1890's, when Populism arose, this image constituted one side of the collective mind
of the rural political movement, the "soft" side.[1]

The "hard" side of the Populist mind originated in the widespread and mundane motive for emigration to America: the
desire to better one's lot, to get rich quick, to move ahead socially
and materially. This side of the rural character was not so much
formed and guided by the frontier, as Frederick Jackson Turner
had argued, as it was influenced by the vicissitudes of the international market. Its orientation was eastward, instead of westward, and it was particularly susceptible to optimistic forecasts
of increased return from investments. Thus, it adapted speedily
to the innovations of mechanized farming, land speculation, high
mobility rates, and the lure of a cash crop—those aspects that
marked the westward movement in the United States. In contrast
to the community-based and land-limited economic circumstances of European agriculture, American farmers responded to
the lure of open land with the cult of individualism and the
motive of high profits.[2]

Before 1815 and industrialization, these ideas coexisted peace-
fully. They formed the core of a set of integrated attitudes that
united the peoples of a new nation. They made up a value system
which operated, in the terms of dialectical change, as the social
and intellectual thesis of a new culture. In this thesis, commercial
impulses were harnessed by the agrarian ideal. However, as immigration increased and as the vast quantities of arable land
came to be considered in terms of what their produce might
bring in the expanding industrial market, both in the East and
in Europe, the fine balance between these attitudes began to

shift and a conflict between them arose. Commercial realities impelled the farmer to drop the original version of the stable, family-farm idea based on self-sufficiency in favor of a high-profit, quick-return ethic.

At the same time as this actual shift in values was occurring, however, the farmer, so Hofstadter says, tightened his grip on the old ideal and began the process of its ossification. As the profit motive tightened its grip on him, the farmer tightened his own grip on the old view of the city as the center of all evil and of evil as stemming from the predatory nature of business. "Oddly enough," says Hofstadter, "the agrarian myth came to be believed more widely and tenaciously as it became more fictional."[3] Once the gap between myth and reality began to be felt, it was only a step to the perception of victimization. Hofstadter continued his analysis:

The agrarian myth encouraged farmers to believe that they were not themselves an organic part of the whole order of business enterprise and speculation that flourished in the city, partaking of its character and sharing in its risks, but rather the innocent pastoral victims of a conspiracy hatched in the distance. The notion of an innocent and victimized populace colors the whole history of agrarian controversy and indeed the whole history of the populistic mind.[4]

It is Hofstadter's primary point that this ossified aspect of the old ideal both motivated and characterized the Populist movement *and* provided its limitations. What I wish to point out is Hofstadter's assumption of a kind of double dynamic. As commerical realities exerted their pressures on the old ideal, it would have been simpler to picture the yeoman farmer submitting to the new reality with its concomitant values. That the farmers did not come up with a new world view to match their commercial reality is due to Hofstadter's own historical perception of the relationship between the farmers' minds, attached to an increasingly unrealistic vision from the past, and the farmers' human behavior, responding to the economic exigencies of the moment with the typical Smithian inclination to "truck, barter, and exchange." Here is the first complete example of unresolved tension. It is a matter of technological innovations thrusting new self-images on men, while men—attached to the past—tenaciously cling to old values that do not match the new self-images.[5]

The decline of the old value system was not within anyone's control.[6] And, inadvertently, the farmer himself contributed to its decline by accepting the exigencies of commercial farming. Thus, the original synthesis fell apart through the fatal contradiction of its parts. The farmer "had innocently sought progress from the very beginning, and thus hastened the decline of many of his own values."[7] By allowing progress and profit to become equated, the farmer had fatally loosened the control of the idea over the reality. Unbalanced, the two came into conflict, one striving for recognition, the other hardening into an outmoded ideology. The result became the "harassed little country businessman, who worked very hard, moved all too often, gambled with his land, and made his way alone"—the very opposite of the originally idealized yeoman or villager.[8] The tension between ideal and reality led to hypocrisy in the "harassed little country businessman"—a hypocrisy that would not allow him to admit that the profit motive had won its battle with freedom and self-sufficiency. This was the unresolved conflict between opposing and contradictory tendencies in the private, psychic realm of the farmers' minds before the advent of Populism.

The conflict was also expressed in the public sphere. Symbolic of the increasing discrepancy between yeoman myth and commercial reality—and proof of the inadequacy of the Frederick Jackson Turner interpretation—was a piece of legislation like the Homestead Act. Turner's interpretation had pictured the Populist revolt as brought about by the closing of the frontier and the frustrations among farmers resulting from that closing. Hofstadter's point is that the broadening of the international market and the cycles of an international Capitalist economy more truly caused the Populist revolt. Actually, more land was settled after 1890 than before. Closely connected to Turner's theory was the contemporary acceptance of the Homestead Act at its face value. As Hofstadter assessed it:

The conception that the end of free or cheap land was primarily responsible for precipitating discontent implies that the existence of such land had been effective in alleviating it, and suggests that the effects of the Homestead Act up to about 1890 were what had been hoped for at the time of its passage.[9]

But the effects had been exactly contrary to the original expectations. And those expectations stemmed directly from the Jeffersonian vision. Said Hofstadter:

The fathers of the Homestead Act and the fee-simple empire had acted upon a number of assumptions stemming from the agrarian myth which were out of date even before the act was passed. They trusted to the beneficence of nature, to permanent and yeomanlike nonspeculative settlement; they expected that the land really would pass without cost into the hands of the great majority of settlers; and they took it for granted that the native strength of the farmer would continue to rest upon the abundance produced on and for the farm.[10]

The farmers suffered from the same illusion as had Jefferson, according to Hofstadter's interpretation of the latter from his graduate school days. Here, with the perspective of hindsight, Hofstadter was able to comment on the blindness of the farmers. They "knew not what they did," acting on assumptions already "out of date." The picture is one of a community that was naive, trusting, credulous, and blind. Because assumptions did not match reality, the effects turned out to be exactly contrary to the original expectations.

As it worked out, the Homestead Act was a triumph for speculative and capitalistic forces, and it translated cheap or free land into a stimulus for more discontent than it could quiet. The promise of the Homestead Act was a lure for over-rapid settlement in regions where most settlers found, instead of the agrarian utopia, a wilderness of high costs, low returns and mortgages.[11]

Thus, even the Homestead Act contributed to the inexorable progress of "commercial reality," and people—little people— were caught in the middle of the inevitable cultural lag between economic forces and mental expectations, even in the public realm of national legislation. With these shocks, the agrarian mind found itself in the throes of adjustment to the processes of industrialization.

The farmers were beset by other, external elements as well. Natural forces—drought, wind storms, insects—took their toll. They were exploited by interest groups, railroad magnates, bankers. They were caught in the cycles of the international market.[12] All these external actors increased the tension between the two sets of values warring for dominance in the farmer's mind. In the end, it was the combination of this internal, psychic tension and the force of external factors that caused the farmers to take action and move into the political realm. Men were becoming conscious of the change in the relationship between their own position in society and the "forces of production."[13] Whereas in the preindustrial thesis the farmers had occupied a leading and emulated position, by 1860 they recognized that the speculators, the bankers, and the railroad magnates had passed them by in terms of power, prestige, and status.[14]

As the Populist political movement took shape, certain aspects of the agrarian myth hardened and soured even further in the minds of some of its articulate members. These aspects of the Populist mind Hofstadter has coined collectively a "demonology." They looked, for instance, he said, to the past for a golden age of plenty in which the small farmers had not been exploited or harassed by the financial powers. They saw a clear-cut division between the predator and the innocent victims of their society, between the robbers and the robbed, between the malicious and the innocent. They pictured history as a personalized act of aggression by an international conspiracy against the little "wounded" yeoman. They rhetorically identified the Jew with the predatory money interests of the city and centered on him as "Shylock." They were haunted by the fear and suspicion of strangers, and they thus easily turned jingoistic. These were the marks of both nativism and isolationism. The Populists—on their "soft side"—adopted them all.[15]

The demonology—this newly unbalanced set of values that projected evil onto the cities, the Jews, the strangers, and the money interests—worked as a dynamic, increasing the tension that would have lessened if the farmers could have moved out of their old habits of mind. And although Hofstadter did not deliberately point it out, the element of paranoia in their thought served to show how the preindustrial synthesis had disintegrated into its antithesis. The farmer now faced economic dependency instead of self-sufficiency. He faced the fetters of indebtedness instead of financial independence. Instead of stability, he faced the vicissitudes of an international market. But it is Hofstadter's primary point that the causes for these problems lay not in external factors alone, but in the semiconscious internal state in which the farmers sensed the diminution in status brought on by changing economic circumstances but were powerless truly to act in their own best interests. Out of this frustration, they developed a reaction formation, in which the city, whose treasures they would have preferred to share, became the menacing monster of the novelist Ignatius Donnelly's fiction. The original agrarian myth helped them in the process. In the end, the farmers blinded themselves to their current reality by hardening and clinging to the original agrarian ideal and by refusing to let their minds grow with economic reality.

By the 1880's and 1890's, however, they did know that they had to organize politically for self-protection. It was just this political action that resolved the conflict between the soft and hard sides of the farmer Populists and brought them into a new age. The political Party itself was divided into two opposing factions. "Purists," like Tom Watson and Henry Demarest Lloyd, worked out a balanced platform for measures like aid to farm credit and government ownership of communications. But opposing them, a group of old-time, grass-roots veterans were fed up with the failure of the grange movement and "hungry for success." These individuals, like General Weaver, the 1892 candidate for President, and Herman Taubeneck, the *permanent* national chairman, were ready to sacrifice crucial planks of the platform for a sure-winning coalition. In addition, the Party desperately needed money. When the elements representing wheat and cotton interests came into contact with silver interests, they committed a fatal error and took up the silver issue as the leading plank of the Party. They did so to attract votes but ran into direct competition from the Democratic Party. When the Democrats, on their part, put forward a staunch silverite, the Populists found themselves backed into a corner from which they were forced to endorse Bryan. By doing so they committed "suicide," killing themselves off just as they had begun to live.[16]

In this ultimate political maneuver, the two factions within the Party came to represent the inevitable conflict between the "principled" and the "practical" elements. On the one hand, the Watsons and the Lloyds were determined and steady in their desire for long-term, radical innovations based on federal support for farming. On the other hand, the Taubenecks and Weavers were eager to strike a broad coalition and obtain success before anything.

It is Hofstadter's uncanny sense for irony—which becomes the dialectical structure when put into the motion of sociopolitical change—that is behind his observation that just as it had to kill itself before it began to live, so also through defeat the Populist Party saw success. The issues the "principled" elements had enumerated in their original platform—the income tax, railroad regulation, the initiative and referendum—were becoming the platform of a new coalition. This new coalition, formed between old Populists of the Lloyd stripe and formerly uninvolved urban reformers, placed the issues proposed by the Populists squarely in the forefront of a new political era. A new synthesis, Progressivism, was being born out of the disintegration of the old, preindustrial synthesis. The commercial farmers helped to create it by finally letting go of the agrarian myth. Instead, they came to realize fully that they had more in common with other aspects of commercialism than they had had with the old yeoman farmer, that business could teach them invaluable techniques for controlling or manipulating the market, and that they could obtain what they wanted from government by the use of methods devised by the newly developing corporations. Their minds had come into conjunction with the economic process.[17]

Through the device of a third-party political movement, then, the farmer-Populists had been able to goad, prod, and activate "a capacity for effective political indignation" after the waste and corruption of the post-Civil War era. Hofstadter, with the benefit of hindsight, asserted that such prodding and agitation were the only necessary functions of third parties in the United States— that winning was not their goal. But by so asserting he had also placed the Populists in the perspective of the larger sweep of history. Third-party agitation provided the dynamic for resolution of the split in the farmers' minds, as well as the impulse for the resolution of the tension between ideal and commercial reality.[18]

A full dialectical cycle was completed with the Populist third-party venture as a catalyst between the preindustrial yeoman thesis and the new Progressive synthesis. Marx's dictum had been worked out for nineteenth-century American society and one is reminded again of the words he wrote in 1859:

No social order ever disappears before all the productive forces for which there is room in it have been developed; and new, higher relations of production never appear before the material conditions of their existence have matured in the womb of the old society.[19]

There is an epilogue to Hofstadter's story of Populism: It is the twentieth-century conclusion to the nineteenth-century background. It was a fact for Hofstadter that the political crisis of Populism did not substantially affect the farmer. Populism marked the death of the agrarian myth, yes, but it did not substantially affect the economic trends that were of longer duration and greater impact than the political movement. Hofstadter treated the changes in the American farmer's economic position in the second section of his last chapter on Populism; that section was entitled "The Golden Age and After" and it is of especial importance here. There was irony in the fact, Hofstadter thought, that just after their defeat by the industrial forces of the Republican Party in 1896, the farmers enjoyed a period of greater prosperity than ever before.

Thus, the "final" victory of industrialism over the farmer was ironically followed by the golden age of American agriculture, to which agricultural interests later looked back nostalgically when they were defining a goal for the nation's farm policy.[20]

Why? Because of the new lessons the farmers had been incorporating from business. Hofstadter gave lip-service to the changing economic circumstances: the market shift from Europe to the American urban East, the new stability that the shift brought for staple farm products, and the resulting rise in prices. But his major point was that the farmers themselves contributed to the prosperity by curtailing the volume of their production, by withholding surpluses, by developing cooperatives, by using trained scientific experts, by developing lobbying techniques— by accepting, in short, the lessons taught them by corporate Capitalism.[21]

Taking the whole analysis up to his own time, Hofstadter observed that between 1815 and 1955 there had been a major reversal between dependent and independent elements in the American economy. Whereas before 1815 rural American farmers—who were in the majority—could be said to have "fed" the isolated islands of urban America, by the mid-twentieth century, the farmers—now a definite minority—could be said to *be* fed by the large urban populations. That they were so "fed" was the result of the new political and economic synthesis of the twentieth century. As they dwindled in numbers, Hofstadter pointed out, the rural elements had been forced to drop another of the staple ideas of the agrarian myth: that of majority rule. In preindustrial, Jeffersonian days, it appeared that the yeoman farmers would outnumber urban populations for many years. With the shift in demography of the late nineteenth and early twentieth centuries, however, farmers had been forced to make a connected shift in political assumptions.

The ideologists of agrarianism had appealed to majority rule and to the idea that there is an inherent and necessary relation between agrarianism and democracy. The political efforts of farmers had been infused with a strong suspicion of organized power. Now, as the agrarian sector of the economy shrank, farmers ceased to think of majority rule and began to rely increasingly upon minority action—indeed, in the end, upon minority rule. For minority rule was the salvation of the prosperous farmers. One of the most striking features of twentieth-century American politics has been the way in which the farm population has *gained* in political striking power with its relative losses in numbers, growing more cohesive, more vocal, and more effectual almost in proportion as it has been progressively outnumbered.[22]

The culminating feature of this gain in favor—in "striking power"—was the principle of parity, a "claim," Hofstadter maintained, "upon federal policy that no other single stratum of the population can match."[23] By parity—the supported price structure paid for by the urban population buying the produce of the farmers—the agricultural community was now subsidized, or "fed", by those very urban elements the Populist demonology had so vilified. By one of those strange inversions, not unknown to Marx and Engels, or to Hofstadter at an earlier age, "the American city itself ... saved the American farmer."[24]

In macrocosmic dialectical form, Hofstadter had moved the farmer from the pathos of the Populist demonology to the price supports and favored status of twentieth-century "parity." Economic changes in the "relations of production" had forced changes in ideology and in political status. Old values and new needs had clashed. The conflict had taken political form. And its resolution had established a new congeries of relationships. It is little wonder that Hofstadter concluded his section on Populism in *The Age of Reform* with the following reflection: "The dialectic of history is full of odd and cunningly contrived ironies, and among these are rebellions waged only that the rebels might in the end be converted into their opposities."[25]

NOTES

1. Richard Hofstadter, *The Age of Reform* (New York, Vintage Books, 1955) pp. 23–36. For quotations see pp. 25, 28.

2. Ibid., "The Farmer and the Realities," pp. 36–46.

3. Ibid., p. 30.

4. Ibid., p. 35.

5. For the quotation from Smith, see Adam Smith, *An Enquiry into the Nature and Causes of the Wealth of Nation*, in David Riede and J. Wayne Baker, eds., *The Western Intellectual Tradition* (Debuque, Iowa, Kendall-Hunt, 1980) p. 124.

6. Hofstadter, *Age of Reform*, p. 35.

7. Ibid.

8. Ibid., p. 46.

9. Ibid., pp. 53–54.

10. Ibid., p. 57.

11. Ibid., p. 55.

12. Ibid., pp. 54–57.

13. Karl Marx, "Preface," in *A Contribution to the Critique of Political Economy, 1859*, in Marx, *Selected Writings in Sociology and Social Philosophy*, T.B. Bottomore, tr. (New York, McGraw-Hill, 1964) p. 52.

14. The discussion of status anxiety comes early. Hofstadter said: "Rank in society? That was close to the heart of the matter, for the farmer was beginning to realize acutely not merely that the best of the world's goods were to be had in the cities and that the urban middle and upper classes had much more of them than he did but also that he was losing in status and respect as compared with them." *Age of Reform*, p. 37.

15. Ibid., Chapter II, "The Folklore of Populism," pp. 60–93.

16. Ibid., pp. 94–109. This is the substance of what Hofstadter has called "Success through Failure."

17. For the realization about business, text at note 21.

18. The third-party function was very important for Hofstadter. See *Age of Reform*, pp. 60, 97.

19. Marx, "Preface," 1859, p. 52.

20. Hofstadter, *Age of Reform*, p. 109.

21. Ibid., pp. 110–16.

22. Ibid., p. 115 (emphasis in original).

23. Ibid., p. 119.

24. Ibid., p. 110.

25. Ibid., p. 130.

11

Power and Intellect: The Dialectic of American Democracy

On first glance it appears that *Anti-intellectualism in American Life* is a linear and relatively straightforward account of American rejection of theory, system, and high culture in several areas of life, some of which provide significant elaborations of undeveloped material first presented in *The Age of Reform*. On more careful investigation, however, one finds embedded in the evolution of attitudes in this book a dialectical structure. The structure, when it appears, is similar to but often more completely crystallized than it had been in *The Age of Reform*. More often in the later book Hofstadter was deliberate in its use.[1]

Anti-intellectualism in American Life was only *ostensibly* a study of the history of primitivism and folk wisdom. At some points, Hofstadter, owing to his own inherent bias, reverted to telling the story of the intellectuals rather than their opposite numbers. More specifically, it was the rapprochement between intellect and the seat of governmental power that fascinated him. It was just when this connection became his focus that Hofstadter's use of the dialectical structure to convey his sense of change became apparent. Conversely, the structure was not apparent when he discussed religion, business, or education, although within his reflections on specific aspects of these fields, he did make dialectical-like linkages. The use of the dialectical structure to present change in the political arena, then, tied this book to *The Age of Reform* and indicates the continuing pattern to Hofstadter's work as a whole. Furthermore, his reversion to the dialectic in a field in which he was clearly on familiar ground—and very closely engaged—is also evidence that the structure itself arose out of a deep-seated aspect of his intellectual assumptions.

Section III of the book, entitled "The Politics of Democracy," includes three chapters: "The Decline of the Gentleman," "The Fate of the Reformer," and "The Rise of the Expert." One is immediately aware that although Hofstadter had dealt with figures like James Davenport and William Tennant—anti-intellectuals both—instead of someone like Jonathan Edwards in his chapters on religion, in the chapters where the subject was politics, his focus and point of view were those of Jefferson and John Quincy Adams. Necessarily Hofstadter did not limit himself to these two; his purpose—one of them—was to present a cultural dialogue between opposing points of view. He was constrained, therefore, to present the opposition. But in contrast to the chapters on religion, where no "intellectualist" religious figures appeared at all, in these chapters on politics where intellectuals did appear, the sympathies of the historian are quite apparent.

A three-part pattern underlies the tension between opposing and contradictory tendencies in this section. At certain specified points, that tension has been resolved and a synthesis achieved. In "The Politics of Democracy," a harmoniously balanced government, in which no great strains appeared, developed when intellect and power were in rapprochement. When the forces of primitivism, egalitarianism, or power politics had taken over, the synthesis became subject to corruption, disarray, and strain. As with the mind of the intellectual, which Hofstadter described in his introduction to this book and which was peculiarly poised between playfulness and piety, so the government in which intellect and power were reconciled was a newly harmonious synthesis where internal contradictions had not yet come into play. Hofstadter developed those points of synthesis over time.

Between 1787 and the mid–1790's, a period of equipoise existed in American political leadership.

The intellectual as ruling-class gentleman was a leader in every segment of society—at the bar, in the professions, in business, and in political affairs. The Founding Fathers were sages, scientists, men of broad cultivation . . . who used their wide reading . . . to solve the exigent problems of their time.[2]

Hofstadter has introduced his thesis—a thesis not without its internal contradictions. Strong evangelical, anti-intellectual forces had already developed. Noticeable in the election of 1796 and culminating in the election of 1800 an additional quality appeared: disrespect for political standards arising from the controversy over revolution in France. Some people were "playing politics with little regard for decency or common sense" and "political controversy . . . degenerated into demagogy." Jefferson was criticized for possessing "the characteristic traits of a philosopher" which amounted to "timidity, whimsicalness, and a disposition to reason from certain principles . . . an inertness of mind, a wavering of disposition." The equipoise in government had rested on the qualities of character, courage, and prescience among gentlemen-politicians. The opposition represented the antithesis to these qualities, both in the dialectical and ordinary meaning of the term. The most striking quality of this opposition consisted of an egalitarian ethos, which in its furthest reaches required destruction of the privileges on which the gentlemanly qualities rested.[3]

The egalitarian ethos was expressed by one William Manning, a New England farmer writing political tracts in 1798 when feelings were running high. Manning had attempted to elucidate the purpose of education in a republic. He wished, he said, to spread learning as widely as possible but at the same time to cut out higher education, which operated solely for the self-interest of the very rich. "To Manning learning and knowledge were of interest mainly as class weapons." For Manning social equality took precedence over cultural quality.[4]

Jefferson was able to speak to these sentiments, even though he did not symbolize them. He was also able to appeal to the interests of evangelical religious elements, which, in spite of his espousal of rationalism, he preferred to the orthodox and established sentiments of the Federalists. Thus, intellect and power were firmly joined once again through a process of political coalition familiar to the reader of *The Age of Reform*. Jefferson had effected a working political synthesis, he had combined the gentlemanly qualities of the Founding Fathers and the egalitarian sentiments of the Mannings and the evangelicals, which had threatened the original balance of power.[5]

While the gentlemen of the Virginia Dynasty continued to hold the reins of power in Washington, the egalitarian attitude became a groundswell of "Populistic" opinion. But it was one of those additional ironies of historical movements that the groundswell did not also incorporate the values of tolerance and freedom. Although one might have expected the parties opposed to a narrow, elitist set of attitudes to adopt a major concern for tolerance and freedom, this was not what happened. Instead, according to Hofstadter, "Populistic" egalitarians and Federalists found themselves on common ground.

The shabby campaign against Jefferson, and then the Alien and Sedition Acts, manifested the treason of many wealthy and educated Federalists against the cultural values of tolerance and freedom. Unfortunately it did not follow that more popular parties under Jeffersonian or Jacksonian leadership could be counted on to espouse these values. The popular parties themselves eventually became the vehicles of a kind of primitivist and anti-intellectualist populism hostile to the specialist, the expert, the gentleman, and the scholar.[6]

The combination of tolerance and freedom *with* courage, prescience, and character represented the only real basis for an active life of the mind, as Hofstadter was to point out in his concluding chapter to *Anti-intellectualism*. But as yet no such rapprochement had taken place. In Jacksonian America, egalitarianism proved as stifling to intellectual needs as elitist intolerance had been to Populistic needs. Not only the Party in power but the opposition possessed its internal strains.

As the groundswell rose, Hofstadter observed of the situation: "Something was missing in the dialectic of American populistic democracy." That democracy had not allowed itself an avenue for the development of leadership. Where would it come from? It would arise from within, spontaneously, from an "inborn, intuitive, folkish wisdom." Thus, the egalitarian anti-intellectuals answered the "artificial" educational proposals of the gentlemen, offering their counterpart to William Manning's educational brief. Originating in the sphere of education—where values were most deeply rooted—Hofstadter was presenting here the developing clash between two antithetical social groups who held directly antagonistic ideals about the nature and function of the mind in public life.[7]

The articulation and confrontation of these values took place in the 1824 and 1829 elections, where the completion of the dialectical cycle took place. Adams's plan for a national cultural capitol at Washington, based on European models, was defeated by "the native vigor and native style" of Jackson, who had military, masculine, and pioneering charm. By 1828 Adams represented a "kind of leadership which had outlived its time." His type had become "obsolete," while Jackson embodied "what . . . [America] would become."[8] The abstracted qualities which each of these two men symbolized for the American people set up a competitive, antithetical alignment that would be repeated.

The issue was posed to the voters mainly as a choice between aristocracy and democracy. But as the two sides fashioned the public images of the candidates, aristocracy was paired with sterile intellect and democracy with native intuition and the power to act.[9]

That pairing foreshadowed the future. A resolution had been effected between "intuitive, folkish wisdom" and the power of public office. It was a political synthesis that began the alienation of the intellectuals and formed the source of later beliefs that they could not work within a system that so favored anti-intellectual and anti-cultural prejudice.

It was not Hofstadter's main point, however, that a cultivated group of political leaders lost power to a popular party, but that the anti-intellectual values of the egalitarians infiltrated, undermined, and demoralized the old set of attitudes themselves within the minds of the gentlemen. That is, the gentlemen adopted values antithetical to those they had espoused at the beginning of this period, and it was not an external challenge that resolved this phase of the "decline" but an internal one occurring in the name of power and displayed in political behavior between 1828 and 1840.

The story of Davy Crockett's switch in allegiance from Jackson to the Adams/Clay men points up the incorporation of the new values in the minds of the old elite. As the party of opposition, the Adams/Clay men took a new interest in political techniques. "There was a premium on men who could keep touch with the common people and yet move comfortably and function intelligently in the world of political management and business enterprise."[10] Among those most closely in touch with the common people was Crockett.

For Hofstadter, Crockett served as symbol of all that egalitarian and anti-intellectualism meant: the frontier, militarism, manly qualities, and practicality. Crockett's behavior and the use of his image by political factions represented the tension between the old and new sets of values and the learning process occurring in the ranks of the Adams/Clay politicos. For Hofstadter, Crockett symbolized the intrusion of the new values into the minds of the old gentlemen.

The issue precipitating Crockett's withdrawal from the "Populistic" Party and his entry into the Gentlemen's Party—and thus the abandonment of that party's old values—was Polk's land bill. Polk wanted the federal government to contribute land from the western districts to Tennessee for the purposes of higher education. Crockett, who represented the squatters in those western districts, made an argument like that of Manning in 1798, saying:

This College system went into practice to draw a line of demarcation between the two classes of society—it separated the children of the rich from the children of the poor. The children of my people never saw the inside of a college in their lives, and never are likely to do so.... If a swindling machine is to be set up to strip them of what little the surveyors, and the colleges, and the warrant holders, have left them, it shall never be said that I sat by in silence, and refused, however humbly, to advocate their cause.[11]

Again, the issue of education formed the basis for polemical contention between political forces, this time within the same Party.

The Adams/Clay men had learned their lesson, however, and

realizing what the split in ranks over this issue could mean to them, they took advantage of the opportunity, approached Crockett, and succeeded in persuading him of the validity of their own views. Hofstadter reported the situation, indicating just how important Crockett had become to the gentlemen as a symbol of values formerly alien to them.

To the Adams/Clay men, always under severe pressure from the Jackson forces, the split in the ranks of the Tennessee Jacksonians came as a gift from heaven. Before long, the astute opposition organizers, realizing that to have a pioneer democrat in their ranks would give them a magnificent counterpoise to Jackson, approached Crockett and took advantage of his alienation from the Jackson men in his state and his longstanding personal resentment of the President to bring him around to the opposition.[12]

The old gentlemen had learned the art of political machination and had devised scheming and crafty ways to manipulate individuals for the self-serving interests of politics and to move into areas of discord through their own cupidity—all of which, so it appears, had been adopted from the "Populistic" elements. The old values of courage, character, and prescience were on the wane.

The transferral of allegiance by Crockett is an arresting episode in American political history. Hofstadter's special use of it is meant to show the adoption by the gentlemen of a set of values they had originally vigorously opposed. The exigencies of political battle and the experience of being on the outside in the power game had forced them to adopt the tactics of their opponents. That the egalitarian and primitivist values were indeed dominant is illustrated by the choice of Harrison as Presidential candidate in 1840. Harrison appealed to the same elements as Crockett had: He was a "hero of early Indian campaigns," he could be interpreted as a backwoodsman, he had lived in a log cabin. Addresses in the House of Representatives attacked Van Buren on the basis of his "regal splendor ... [in] the President's palace." Even Daniel Webster felt compelled to deny that he was an aristocrat, lamenting the fact that he was not born in a log cabin. By such assertions, "the Whigs tried to assure their victory

by using against him [Van Buren] the same techniques of bal-
lyhoo and misrepresentation that the Jacksonians had used against
John Quincy Adams twelve years earlier." Thus, "by 1840 the
conquest of the Whig Party by the rhetoric of populism was
complete." The Adams/Clay men had succeeded in getting their
man elected at the expense of their own original values.[13]

The dialectic of attitudes had completed a full cycle from the
gentlemanly synthesis of 1787. In this example, the process was
composed of a series of smaller cycles that showed increasingly
the hold of the egalitarian attitude on the minds of the gentlemen. Jefferson had not needed to move very far from his original
position to incorporate the pietists in 1800. The balance was still
on the side of the gentlemanly values. Egalitarian politics provided a greater challenge than the pietists alone, however, and
the synthesis of 1828 established a new balance. The unpopular
and "obsolete" Adams had been roundly repudiated by the Jacksonians whose primary concerns focused on anti-intellectual
egalitarianism. That ethos continued to grow in appeal until by
the new synthesis of 1840 it was clear that the old set of attitudes
had completely capitulated to the force of popular politics, not
only in the external arena of partisan warfare but in the internal
realm of men's minds. By succumbing to the insidious pressure
of power politics, the old gentlemen had ended by doing exactly
what they had set out to avoid. Not only did they behave according to the principles of the Jacksonians but they also *believed*
in those principles, thus abandoning their original commitment
to the disinterested search for truth or enlightenment and the
idea that it was necessary to apply this belief to the political
process. The egalitarian ethos had crowded out the ethos of
gentlemanly, and even Puritan, virtue; in the end the gentlemen
themselves had contributed to that process. Like the Populists
in *The Age of Reform*, "the gentleman as a force in American
politics was committing *suicide*."[14] The term is apt. Hofstadter
means here self-immolation, just as he did when he used this
term in reference to the Populist decision to go for silver in 1896.
Deliberately, if semiconsciously, they chose to destroy themselves
and, like the Populists, for the same reason: votes.

The egalitarian, anti-intellectual synthesis in politics stayed
put, in Hofstadter's opinion, until the advent of Progressivism.

But long before 1901 internal contradictions took active shape and the old debate was reinvigorated. The gentlemen had gone to the brink of death, as it were, looked over the abyss, and pulled back. Slowly they regrouped. By 1872 they had formed a new position. Jackson had brought with him the creed of rotation in office, a policy based on the egalitarian desire to share all forms of property. Basing their movement on the issue of courage, character, and prescience in power, the gentlemen took hold and fastened upon the question of civil service reform, pitting themselves against the professional politicians, arguing for "purity and excellence in ... governmental practice."[15]

This was a realignment of the old Jacksonian battle. On the one hand, there were the gentlemen taking their cues from England and pushing for institutional reforms that would reinstate the criteria for appointment that had existed in the 1790's: competence, public repute, and personal integrity. On the other hand, there were the firmly ensconced professional politicians, who feared the "decadent" European, model and the class system upon which it was based and pointed to the impractical, unmanly, and unpatriotic scholars who stayed home while other "gallant" youths went off to "breast the storm of war."[16]

Thesis and antithesis worked themselves out in a cultural dialogue. The gentlemen heaped the epithets of "ignorant, vulgar, selfish, and corrupt" on the professionals, holding up their own idea of purity for contrast. The professionals answered by asking: Are you qualified for the reality of politics? Are you capable of asserting yourselves? Are you *manly* enough to fight in the ruthless, materialistic, "real" world?[17]

Although the Pendleton Civil Service Act of 1883 successfully climaxed the campaign waged by reformers, they had been badly handicapped in the longer run by the stigma of effeminacy. It is Hofstadter's opinion that such sociopolitical opposition between antithetical sets of values become resolved through the political process, especially through the election of a Presidential figure who adequately symbolizes and synthesizes those sets of values. For the Mugwumps, rapprochement—or synthesis—between the values of the intellectuals or reformers and the professionals or business people did not occur until the rise to prominence of Theodore Roosevelt. Here, finally, was a figure

who could overcome the stigma of effeminacy in the person of
an intellectual and an aristocrat—a well-born son of the Eastern
elite who also rode horses, led brigades, and "roughed" it in the
West.[18] The dialectical pattern had made another full cycle, Roosevelt symbolizing a new balance between character and intuition, prescience and primitivism, reflection and action.

The new synthesis created a resolution between the needs of
democracy—now restated in complex modern industrial terms—
and the values of the intellectual as expert and as social critic.
In contrast to his interpretation of Progressivism in *The Age of
Reform*, Hofstadter maintained in *Anti-intellectualism* that expertise and social criticism were newly recognized as the only possible
methods for dealing with the "larger aggregates of power built
up in the preceding decades," that now the forces of intellect
were not drawn backward and blinded but put to active service
for democracy, and that in Progressivism an experimental attitude toward government prevailed. The Progressives now pre-
figured the New Deal rather than looking backward toward the
Mugwumps, as they had been shown to do in *The Age of Reform*.[19]

The relationship between intellect and power remained balanced throughout the Progressive period. Although sometimes
tenuous, the nature of the twentieth-century rapprochement did
not change. Although it was formed by the concrete circumstances and personal qualities of various administrations and
incumbents, the Presidencies of Theodore Roosevelt, Woodrow
Wilson, and Franklin Delano Roosevelt and the campaign of
Adlai Stevenson all represented the premise that the intellectual
as expert was a necessary adjunct to twentieth-century democratic government. When it came to John F. Kennedy, who was
able to fill the image gap left by Stevenson, the old manly "vir-
tues" were effectively recombined with "courage, character, and
prescience." Thus, Hofstadter left his reader with the resolution
of a new synthesis as well as an indication that the American
attempt to combine intellect and democracy had come full circle
from the tradition of the Founding Fathers—and in fact had
been successful.[20]

From the perspective of the larger sweep of history, then,
Hofstadter had reinterpreted the traditional periods by a dialectical focus on the alienation and rapprochement of intellec-

tuals and political power in America. The early balance between the needs of democracy and the values of the gentlemen was slowly undercut in the political arena and in the gentlemen's minds by the egalitarian ethos. When in full control of government, the egalitarians institutionalized themselves by the practice of the spoils system. During this period, when they were out of power, intellectuals regrouped and agitated for civil service reform, while poking holes in the egalitarian synthesis, finally weakening it, and gaining strength themselves.

Out of the midst of this agitation, Theodore Roosevelt developed an approach that united the best of two alien value systems and established a new balance with intellect again the dominant principle. That type of balance was continued throughout the Democratic administrations of the twentieth century. Because of the continuing and increasing need for the advice and contributions of intellectuals as experts in the post industrial world, the Progressive synthesis had lasted.

From the thesis of the Founding Fathers, then, which in its furthest reaches remained in men's minds until 1840, through its egalitarian antithesis, which with the exception of the early Republican Party retained power until 1901, to the synthesis of the Progressive definition of the intellectual, Hofstadter had structured his discussion of politics in macrocosmic dialectical terms.

The "Politics of Democracy" is really a history of intellectuals, the roles they have assumed in relation to political power, and the opposition they have encountered and sometimes created. It is a history of intellectuals as social and political types—as was *The Age of Reform* and Hofstadter's earlier book *The American Political Tradition*. It is the history of the particular way in which those social and political types embodied attitudes widely diffused and sometimes of great age within the population in general.

In most of the other sections of *Anti-intellectualism in American Life*, the point of view and the evidence belong to those elements of the American populace that furthered the purposes of evangelism, primitivism, or practicality. There is therefore a tension between those sections and "The Politics of Democracy." The political section seems to be a history within a history. The tension developed, it appears, because of Hofstadter's subliminal assumption that the political arena was the focal point in which social attitudes from many other areas of life are finally expressed. As political leadership often symbolized many of the ideals that people cherished, so the political process itself served as a forum for the articulation and clash of attitudes that had much deeper and longer-lasting roots than any one campaign or ephemeral political movement could encompass. "The Politics of Democracy" was more important to Hofstadter than any other section of this book because while other spheres of life may have served as sources for the attitudes under consideration, the political process served as the stage on which those attitudes and values finally directly confronted one another. In this assumption, Hofstadter again showed his debt to Marx, who had indicated the social basis of politics.

Behind politics existed, for Marx, an array of social and economic factors—"the social relations of production"—that had to be taken into consideration in any effort to change the political structure of the "state." Hofstadter, in *Anti-intellectualism in American Life*, attempted to bring a wide-ranging assortment of anti-intellectual attitudes to bear on the political process in America. This is why "The Politics of Democracy" appears to be a history within a history and is such a centerpiece to this book. To bring the social factors to bear on that political process, Hofstadter had brought back into play some old Marxist techniques and assumptions, not only about the nature of the sweep of history, but about the nature of the structure of society as well.

NOTES

1. For an observation of the dialectical structure of this book, see David Riesman, review of *Anti-intellectualism in American Life*, *The American Sociological Review*, 28 (December, 1963) pp. 1038–1040.

2. Richard Hofstadter, *Anti-intellectualism in American Life* (New York, Vintage Books, 1962) p. 145.

3. Ibid., pp. 146, 147.

4. Ibid., pp. 151–54, especially p. 153. For quotation see p. 152.

5. Ibid., p. 150. This was a "curious political alliance, based upon common hostility to established orthodoxy" according to Hofstadter.

6. Ibid., p. 151.

7. Ibid., p. 154.

8. Ibid., p. 158.
9. Ibid., p. 160.
10. Ibid., p. 161.
11. Ibid., pp. 163–64.
12. Ibid., p. 164.
13. Ibid., pp. 164–65.
14. Ibid., p. 165.
15. Ibid., p. 181.
16. Ibid., p. 183.
17. Ibid., p. 185–186.
18. Ibid., pp. 191–96.
19. Ibid., pp. 197–98. The rapprochement between egalitarian and elite is nicely if abstractly put in the phrase "the type of man who had always valued expertise was now learning to value democracy and ... democracy was learning to value experts."

20. This is the major point of "The Rise of the Expert." Hofstadter gave much time to LaFollette whom I have not included because he did not seem to serve as a synthetic figure, as Presidential incumbents did. For Kennedy see pp. 228–29: "Kennedy was all authority and confidence and he appealed to their desire that intellect and culture be associated with power and responsibility." Thus, Kennedy bridged the gap, as Jefferson and Teddy Roosevelt had also been able to do.

12

Anti-Party Bias: The Dialectic of Thought and Action

> The production of ideas, conceptions and consciousness is at first directly interwoven with the material activity and the material intercourse of men, the language of real life. ... Consciousness can never be anything else than conscious existence, and the existence of men is their actual life process. If in all ideology men and their circumstances appear upside down as in a *camera obscura*, this phenomenon arises from their historical life process just as the inversion of objects on the retina does from their physical life-process.
>
> —Karl Marx, *German Ideology*

In *The Idea of a Party System,* Hofstadter reflected his lifelong intense interest in the manifestation of ideas through the political process.[1] Here he traced the idea of legitimate opposition from its contrary, the anti-party bias of eighteenth-century British political philosophers, through the process of early American political behavior. The book is a study in irony because of the tension between thought and behavior. The tendency in early American thought about political parties led to the conclusion that they were useless, divisive, and evil. At the same time, the tendency in behavior showed that they were a necessary part of political life in a republic. The story became, then, one of how an early bias against parties was worn away by the challenges of action in the world of political exigency.

Because Hofstadter was treating the Founding Fathers once

again—the forerunners of Mugwump ideas—one finds in this book new treatments of elements from both *The Age of Reform* and *Anti-intellectualism in American Life*. Most of the book is an enlargement of the first chapter of "The Politics of Democracy." And the request for freedom and tolerance for opposing ideas, which he made most strongly at the end of *Anti-intellectualism*, he made here the subject of historical analysis and exposition. Having reviewed the dialectical tension between Jefferson and his opponents in the election of 1800 in *Anti-intellectualism*, one is not surprised to find the re-creation of those tensions writ large in *The Idea of a Party System*. The book is, with its close attention to the attitudinal side of political preconceptions, both more penetrating in historical insights and less comprehensive in its range of vision than its parallel section in *Anti-intellectualism*.

Hofstadter treated the central paradox that: "party government [was] instituted by anti-party thinkers."[2] The purpose of his study was to pull apart this assertion and demonstrate its truth. The original thesis, then, in this book consisted of the legacy of anti-party thought inherited by the Founding Fathers from their eighteenth century British predecessors. The thesis was plagued by three types of contradictions. Internally—in the purely intellectual sphere—there were "glimmerings" of the notion that parties resulted from human nature and were thus inevitable. This was a logical contradiction found in the writings of a very few political thinkers—among them Madison. Externally, practical issues challenged the efficacy of the notion of unity that the anti-party bias implied. As early as the Constitutional Convention, for example, various divisions occurred over the inclusion of a Bill of Rights. Later various groups became polarized over the issues posed by the French Revolution. These particular challenges elicited restatements of the anti-party principle. Alongside of these particular issues went the long-term actual development of Federalists and Republicans, under the noses but against the principles of the major protagonists in the drama. Throughout these changes in reality, the idea that parties were evil and to be avoided maintained its grip on the minds of the Fathers. It was Hofstadter's intention to portray *both* levels—that of thought and that of behavior—at the same time.

For Hofstadter, the inapplicability of the idea was even more important in this book than it was in his other books. The old assumption that opposition was illegitimate did not synchronize with the political reality of the new nation. The gap between the two was wide and unbridgeable—or appeared so to the historian with hindsight. But the idea died a long, slow, and painful death. It was Hofstadter's intention to show the death of the idea—or the dissolution of the thesis—through its continued inapplicability in the crises of the early Republic.

The first of those crises came when the Constitution was adopted. The anti-party thesis dominated even the creation of the document. The Fathers had been extremely careful to provide explicit checks on the various political bodies that they created in the Constitution. The purpose—well known—was to balance one branch of government against another so that no one branch would gain undue power *and* so that no one class in society would dominate another. The point in terms of parties, however, was that "the Fathers hoped to create not a system of party government under a constitution but a constitutional government that would check and control parties."[3]

Thus, the very intention of the Constitution had been to effect the anti-party idea. The Fathers had believed that if they created enough avenues for political expression within the structure of government itself, the citizens would not need to create other bodies of political opinion and expression. Unchecked parties had, so they thought, created havoc in earlier Republics—Greek and Roman. Checked, permanent parties, operating under their own indigenous notions of loyalty, order, and discipline, were barely comprehensible. The Fathers' eyes were turned backward.[4]

Madison expressed the first doubt in an otherwise deeply held belief system. In the *Federalist* #10 he voiced the idea that parties were founded in "the nature of Man." Later when he and his friends were forming an actual opposition in 1792, he took his thinking a step further, writing of one party operating as a check on another. Here, Hofstadter thought, appeared a "glimmering" of the view to be developed later by another group of political participants. On balance, Madison agreed with the others that "factions" would only undermine the liberty of the Republic. With the inherent contradiction in these ideas, on the eve of the first real political crisis of the Republic, Hofstadter found a "profound if fertile ambiguity" in the thinking of the Fathers. The original thesis had encountered some opposition in intellectual terms.[5]

With the actual challenges of running a government, the anti-party idea was put to the test. At the culmination of each crisis, the idea again regained ascendancy. But the cumulative effect of the crises *and* the actual appearance—and then disappearance—of factions was to weaken the old British preconception fatally. The idea maintained its grip on the Fathers' minds but *not* on their behavior. Through Washington's handling of the Whiskey Rebellion, through John Adams's treatment of the threat of war with France, through the transferral of power from Federalists to Republicans in 1801, and through the war with England in 1812, the anti-party bias was mouthed by the leading figures of the era at the same time as they actively developed policies and principles that opposed one another.

When the Whisky Insurrection occurred, Washington connected it with the pro-French political Democratic clubs and he took the opportunity in his farewell address to reiterate the case against parties. He voiced the same argument heard during the debate over the Constitution. Republican institutions provided vehicles enough for the articulation of political views. The people had the opportunity to elect their representatives; they did not need to form auxiliary political bodies. Washington also saw himself as standing above party, as representing the common interests and welfare of the citizenry, not as a partisan leader. Hofstadter concluded that Washington had led the move to prevent the development of parties, but also concluded with Joseph Charles: "had he been successful in this ... it is most doubtful that representative government in this country would have outlived him for long." Again, from the perspective of hindsight, Hofstadter commented on the blinded nature of men, who were unable to grasp the slow, evolutionary institutional needs and changes of society and thus worked counter to the historical processes of which they were so intimately a part.[6]

The threats of war with France, the XYZ Affair, and the resulting criticism of John Adams and his foreign policy culminated in the Alien and Sedition Acts and served to provoke the most severe crisis to date for the young Republic. The stability and existence of the Republic were threatened from two directions. On the one hand were cries from the high Federalists who hoped a war with France would quash criticism and allow them to return to power. On the other hand, the Republican traffic with agents from France threatened to embroil the United States in European entanglements that would prove uncontrollable.

The whole question of opposition in a threatened and very fragile new nation was a real one. The effort to quell opposition, in the form of the Sedition Acts, had an ironic outcome. The Acts were not successful because the opposition to Federalists' war-mongering came from an increasingly organized "Party" that the government could not silence short of force. The government could not use force because an armed militia, outside of wartime conditions, would not be tolerable to the people. Adams, for his part, felt no less above the interests of party than had Washington; therefore, he would not aid the more partisan elements of his own Party in their efforts to silence the opposition. So, ironically, it was ultimately the "effort to 'destroy faction' " initiated by the high Federalists that culminated in the very unpopular Alien and Sedition Acts, and that in turn caused the Federalists not to "quash criticism" but to lose the election of 1800. They had, as had the Populists in 1896, overstepped their limits and destroyed their balance. Hofstadter was prompted to conclude with an inimitable summary:

The French crisis took the country through an extraordinary cycle of party preponderance. Having begun so auspiciously for the Federalists, with its promise of the complete eclipse of their opponents, it fractured their party, lost them vital public support, and brought them to a full stop before the doughty intransigence of their President.[7]

This microcosmic dialectical cycle had proceeded from the thesis of unity under Federalist hegemony, through the antithesis of complete "fracturing," to the synthesis of Adams's anti-party *and* anti-war outlook.

By the election of 1800, the real march of events in the new political environment had brought the two factions into direct opposition. "The pragmatic pressure of political conflict" had forced party development,[8] and the transferral of power became a supreme test of the strength of the nation. The thesis of unity was again being challenged—and was eventually positively resolved. Hofstadter set himself to explaining the major historical question: "Somehow we must find a way to explain the rapid shift from the Dionysian rhetoric of American politics during the impassioned years 1795 to 1799 to the Apollonian political solution of 1800–1801."[9] The explanation he found is informative. The ideal challenged by reality reasserted itself.

For the very reason that the preconception of the anti-party bias was important, the spirit of conciliation was high in both Parties at the point of the delicate transfer of power to the "other" Party in 1801. Political parties had not yet become legitimate. Therefore, both Federalists and Republicans continued to act as if they were above the fray of political battle. They acted the part of disinterested statesmen. The Jeffersonians applied "the gentle means of conciliation and absorption" by deliberately retaining highly qualified Federalists in office.[10] Hamilton, for his part, when forced into the difficulty of having to decide between Burr and Jefferson, showed balance and good judgment. That decision provoked from Hofstadter one of his most revealing statements on life and history.

There are moments of supreme illumination in history when the depth of men's beliefs in their own partisan gabble has to be submitted at last to the rigorous test of practical decision. For about eight years the Federalists had been denouncing Jefferson and his party ... [with] Jacobinism, atheism, fanaticism, unscrupulousness, wanton folly, incompetence, personal treachery, and political treason. Now this atheist in religion and fanatic in politics was to be quietly installed in the new White House, by courtesy of a handful of Federalist Congressmen, and ... there was also not a man to raise a hand against him.[11]

The loud voices of divisive Party rhetoric were abandoned at the necessary moment for older, deeper-seated values of conciliation. The phenomenon marked a new synthesis in which the eighteenth-century anti-party idea operated to make a smooth transition possible. Although future reality lay in another direction, here the force of old ideas operated to make a practical problem soluble. If Adams's adherence to anti-party doctrine had helped balance the Federalist synthesis against the crises of politics, so Jefferson's—and ironically Hamilton's—similar adherence helped to balance the Republican synthesis. With the successful transferral of power, the intellectual thesis of antiparty thought had successfully combined with its opposite, the reality of party politics, to produce a new Administration "completely" committed to comity and the highest good of the commonweal.

Eventually cracks developed in the new thesis too. By the very loss of Federalist power—and eventual disintegration as a faction—the Republicans also lost the benefits of a critical opposition. They faced new challenges from abroad and out of necessity abandoned their traditional principles of economy, decentralization, and low military profile. In fact they replaced those principles with "the whole range of Hamiltonian policies."[12]

The embargo offered the first challenge in the series of crises that led Jeffersonians away from their original principles. On this issue Hofstadter's phrasing is particularly revealing. He summed up the effect of the issue by asserting: "The embargo unseated the wits of Republicanism, brought out its starkest internal contradictions, caused it to turn against its own principles, and tainted the shining image of its moral and intellectual leader."[13] Unintended consequences followed challenges to men's ideas from the real world of politics. But even more than irony in this statement, one is aware of the observation on Hofstadter's part of a pivotal moment in time when "the antithesis . . . [turned] on its axis." Here the embargo provided the fulcrum for change, the policy around which other issues took on new meanings, and also provided the beginning of the process whereby Republicans transformed themselves into "the exponent of a kind of neo-Federalism."[14] The "pragmatic pressure of political conflict"—now not intranational but international—had forced the Republicans into becoming what they had set out to combat. This is a dialectical cycle within the larger dialectic of thought and action.

The rhetoric of anti-party thought continued despite reality, however, until by the Administration of Monroe it was all but purified out of existence. For Monroe, "conciliation would be achieved on firm Republican terms." Parties, he argued, arose out of defective governments, not out of human nature. America, being a Republic, was in principle perfect, and harmony—

not discord—would prevail here. These thoughts extended to the furthest possible point the bias against party in "a type of mind which could not accept strife as a permanent condition of civic existence." It was—as other such extensions had been for Hofstadter—the ossification of an idea and therefore the death knell of its existence. Monroe had attempted complete unity, complete conciliation, with his eyes fixed on the old Federalists. He had not opened his eyes to the need for structural changes in the new environment of the nineteenth century.[15]

As Monroe continued to look backward, then, a new generation arose to fill the gap between need and value. Almost as if they had sneaked in a side door while the backs of the Virginia Dynasty were turned, this group arose out of a new environment, from a different social background, and with new ideas. The group, presented in a social detail that was notably lacking in the descriptions of the Founding Fathers—who indeed had been painted only in intellectual and political colors—formed the real functional antithesis to the original anti-party mentality. It was the Albany Regency that first developed a real Party theory, not on paper or in the academy but in the practical thick of local and partisan politics.

Martin Van Buren, as representative of the new type, was born the son of a tavernkeeper, as were several of his cronies. He practiced law, without benefit of higher education, in Columbia County, New York. "His political conduct was . . . [thus] shaped by the experience of a quarter of a century pleading at the bar."

He adopted a mode of address that relied upon friendly and rational persuasion, a feeling for the strengths and weakenesses [sic] of others, a spirit of mutual accomodation, and a certain relish for the comedy of human encounters of the sort one sees daily in the county courthouse or the country tavern.[16]

He became known for the friendly-adversary relationships that he developed and maintained with political and legal opponents. He took in stride the combative, competitive, "rough" side of politics. In direct contrast to the high "honor" espoused by the Founding Fathers, he never developed the assumption that his dignity or personal principles were at stake, an assumption that had led to so much acrimony and bitterness between Federalists and Republicans. At the same time, he became a devoted and staunchly loyal Republican, never veering from total support for the political organization he had at first adopted.[17] In short, he was the personal antithesis to the Founding Father social type.

Van Buren clashed and broke politically with DeWitt Clinton over the War of 1812. Until the end of Clinton's life in 1828, Van Buren worked against Clinton's form of "high" Republicanism, based on family and wealth. He also worked against the "fusion policy" promoted by Monroe and reminiscent of the absorption techniques of Jefferson after 1800. And he took advantage of the example of anti-party thought in John Quincy Adams to formulate both a rationale and a Party plan for defeating Adams in 1828. By that year, Van Buren "had succeeded in bringing the strong partisan spirit of the Bucktails and the Albany Regency to the national scene, and in making the New York organization and its doctrine an object of national attention."[18]

The doctrine itself consisted, at base, of a new ethic. It involved Party unity, sacrifice of personal careers to common interest, an anti-personal approach to politics, a democratic but business-like attitude toward the everyday work of Party affairs, decision making that issued from members in Party conclave, discipline, hard work, patience, endurance, and camaraderie. These were, in many ways, contradictory qualities to those set forth by the gentlemen of early American politics. But in practice, Van Buren had grown up within the ranks of the Republican Party and emulated the figure of Jefferson, so they also represented a very real synthesis of the old and the new approach to politics.[19]

Even more importantly in terms of the cause for change, new aspects of the political environment of the country called for a new ethic. New states, nominating conventions, electors chosen by popular vote, an enlarged suffrage all demanded Van Buren's changed approach.

The election of 1824 made the situation clear. John Q. Adams, in his attempt at total disinterest and personal purity, represented the souring and imbalance of the old approach. He provided a foil and an impetus for the Van Buren forces. Monroe and Adams had their eyes fastened so fixedly on the eighteenth-century that they did not perceive present imperatives. Into the gap between reality and theory moved Van Buren, offering a new, more viable synthesis to meet the problems of a new age. His forthright policy of legitimate opposition finally closed the gap between theory and reality. With the election of Jackson in 1828, a new synthesis was established in which thought and action were finally synchronized and the anti-party bias laid to rest.

The dialectic in *The Idea of a Party System* served Hofstadter well. It allowed him to clarify the distance between the exigent political reality of the new Republic and the intellectual legacy of British political philosophy. It allowed him to present an unworkable idea that governed the minds of the principal figures, while he also showed the strains, as politicians working under the limitations of that idea met the challenges of foreign policy and conflicting opinion groups within the new nation. It allowed him to picture the antithetical intellectual and behavioral elements developing outside the limelight of the Virginia Dynasty's dominating point of view. It allowed him to present that antithesis in the social and practical terms that facilitated its synchronization with new nineteenth-century political problems. It allowed him to see it as growing up with and developing out of the native experience rather than tied to the legacy of European thought about politics. And it allowed him to present it as the other side of the picture he had painted of the same period in *Anti-intellectualism in American Life*. In other words, legitimate opposition originated in just those anti-intellectual elements that had retarded progress in the earlier book. Now, an ideological factor from the legacy of the ruling classes created a *camera obscura* in which those classes thought according to one set of principles and acted according to another. When the generation, which had grown up apart from that legacy but within the native environment of the new nation, finally established itself, it ceased "to see through a glass darkly" and began to see "face to face."

NOTES

1. Hofstadter labeled himself a historian of "political culture" rather than a historian of either politics or ideas in his 1960 interview with David Hawke. It is also important to recall that this book was written

in response to the new interest in the early 1960's in political developments of the third world where opposition was often thought to be "a dangerous and inadmissible luxury." Richard Hofstadter, *The Idea of a Party System* (Berkeley, University of California Press, 1969) pp. 3–5.

2. Ibid., p. 54.
3. Ibid., p. 53.
4. Ibid., p. 51. The Fathers were reading classical political thinkers like Aristotle and Machievelli, who discussed political form but gave little attention to parties.
5. Ibid. Madison's ideas are discussed on pp. 64–73; for the 1792 idea see p. 81; for Hofstadter's comment see pp. 67–68.
6. Ibid., pp. 91–102. For the Charles quotation see p. 102.
7. Ibid., pp. 102–11. For quotation see pp. 110–111.
8. Ibid., p. 84.
9. Ibid., p. 130.
10. Ibid., p. 127. Also see p. 155 where Jefferson is quoted as saying, "The way to effect it [unity] is to preserve principle but to treat tenderly those who have been estranged from us, and dispose their minds to view our proceedings with candour."
11. Ibid., pp. 138–39. For Hamilton's decision see pp. 136–40.
12. Ibid., p. 172.
13. Ibid., p. 177.
14. Ibid., p. 172.
15. Ibid., pp. 194–98, 18. For quotation see p. 194.
16. Ibid., p. 215.
17. Ibid., pp. 216–19.
18. Ibid., pp. 221, 231–38. For quotation see p. 238.
19. Ibid., pp. 223–26.

13

Conclusion

Any fully comprehensive treatment of the thought of Richard Hofstadter would require a complete biographical account of all his successive periods. I have attempted to treat fully the first such period—a phase of Hofstadter's intellectual development that is necessary but only partially sufficient for a complete understanding of this person, intellectual, and historian. Further biographical study will undoubtedly reveal other layers of influences and applications that speak to different problems in the work of Richard Hofstadter. I have tried to indicate what the next phase—that at the University of Maryland—entailed as far as intellectual influences went. It is quite clear, however, that no further work would yield understanding of a layer quite so basic as that of the phase treated here.

One confusing aspect of Richard Hofstadter's life and carrier is that he wrote on many widely ranging subjects and refused to be pigeon-holed as a specialist in one particular period of American history. Some have argued on this basis that Hofstadter's attention span was short, that he was superficial, and that he jumped from topic to topic because he could not do otherwise. Rather than requiring of Hofstadter a method that he did not follow, it seems better to look for unity in his work from another angle. I believe that unity is at least partially indicated by the answer to the question of how Hofstadter viewed change. It will be helpful to review some of the steps that occurred on the way to resolving that question.

Hofstadter's cultural ethnic, and social inheritance helped create receptivity to Marxian thought in the 1930's. From the small and independent Republic of Cracow, full of local pride and the spirit of autonomy, to the turbulent Lower East Side of New York—where the drama of first- and second-generation Jewish assimilation was most dramatically played out, from the German roots of his mother's family to the marginality of his father's position, a multiplicity of factors contributed to Hofstadter's fascination for politics, feeling for the complex structure of society and change, and preoccupation with the American past.

His own experiences growing up in the booming Buffalo of the 1920's—cheerleading while the stock market crashed in October 1929, watching the bread lines form around him after 1930, observing the effects of the overproduction that had seemed so innocent and buoyant at first—all these gave him an initial, first-hand experience of the unexpected consequences inherent in the American socioeconomic laissez-faire structure. When he encountered a committed group of radical intellectuals at the University. the stimulation of their discussions filled needs for him, not only intellectually, but socially, culturally, and even familially. He was able—through the student movement—to take his education in his own hands and make of it a truly lived experience. He was able to establish an identification procedure that would stay with him the rest of his life.

He was also, able, eventually, to combine ego, libido, and social role in an integrated way that made sense at many levels. He formed a group of close friends. He married. His professional life stemmed from this identity. He also cemented the cultural inheritance of his father and established himself on the fringes of American society, by choice. He found certain intellectual preconceptions, attitudes, and styles that he shared with his friends: a critical, argumentative, verbal turn of mind, the sense that politics was a viable mechanism for social change, and an inner tension between alienation and ambition.

During these undergraduate years, he developed from the boy who wrote "The Skeleton in The Closet," with its contradictory impulses and its use of a seminal type of anti-hero in a creative, dramatic form, to the college student, a major in history and philosophy, who wrote a tutorial thesis with materials from the Congressional Record to test the economic factors of homestead and the tariff as causative in the election of 1860. Even this early the seeds of his later orienation toward history were apparent. His humor, his ability to portray internal tensions, his fascination with economic causation all were contributing factors in the development of his mature writing.

In New York, he grew from an excessive dependence on the logical resources of his mind to a more integrated approach. When Hofstadter was heavily involved with the "scientific" and deductive thinking of the Communist Party, his two major faculties—logic and imagination—were not effectively combined. His study of the social problems inherent in a major economic program of the current AAA showed his excessive reliance on statistics and calculation—a tendency that one must assume paralleled the thinking of friends and colleagues on the Left.

As he grew emotionally and intellectually, however, he took greater risks in his academic efforts and dared to bring in elements of the imaginative play of his mind. As we have seen, his work benefited from that greater freedom and he was to move ahead successfully on that basis. In fact, Hofstadter's historical scholarship did not show the salient points of his mature work—did not gain breadth and depth—until the academic year of 1938–39 when he worked with Merle Curti for the first time and began Ph.D. work. When he was able, through the sympathetic ear of a like-minded mentor, to try out the historical principles that were part of his everyday world view, he began to see (1) inversions in history (2) incongruities between the American economic environment and certain ideas such as French Physiocracy, and (3) the relationship between American Capitalism and the ideas that it spawned. The new integration involved an application of the principles of the dialectic to history and showed for the first time the salient traits of his later structure. Without this work and the integration brought about through the good offices of Merle Curti, he might have remained on the level of his tutorial or M.A. thesis, attempting to impose with statistics and logic alone the "science of society." Whatever happened in that year of intensive academic involvement—which was also a year of political insight and crisis—was crucial to Hofstadter's development as a historian.

We have also seen his continuous interaction with Felice Swados after the fall of 1934 and their joint debt to the philosophical preconceptions of Marvin Farber. Their relationship is a knotty, complex, intimate, and psychological problem too complicated for full exploration here. However, one may note several evident points.

Felice preceded Hofstadter in several important areas: work with the NSL, study in the Philosophy Department at the University of Buffalo, formation of a group of congenial friends, involvement with the topic of Social Darwinism. But the influences also went in two directions. He was the source of an article she wrote on Negro health in the antebellum South. She also seems to have followed him to the *Herald Tribune* for book reviews. And as he became established in graduate school, his were the dominant political ideas expressed in their correspondence.

Felice seems to have needed an authority—in the form of a figure, or a system, or an institution—on which to rely. This is not out of keeping with her own authoritative attitude and the streak of authoritarianism in her family seen in her father. It was indicative of her mind that, when she changed later, she announced it in definitive terms without explanation, development, or context. Writing to her brother, she said:

Which brings me to telling you of the great revolution in my own thought: although I still believe that reason conquers all, I am now more interested in the irrational than in systems of thought or means of logical activity.... Farber had taught me that man is a thinking machine but that is a dirty lie and it took me four years to unlearn it. Now I am much more concerned with feeling and emotion and maybe that may make me a better writer."[1]

This was written while Felice was attempting to put together a novel and move from her position as editor of a scientific column in *Time* to more imaginative, creative writing. One cannot imagine the author of the "bedbug letter" expressing himself in such terms. Hofstadter's was an independent, a uniquely original, and creative mind from the start, capable of absorbing and applying "systems of thought" but not yielding to them. If this was true intellectually, it is hard to conclude that he was ever really dominated by Felice in any other way. But at the same time, she led him into a life that he might never have experienced so intensely if it had not been for her. For better or worse, she was a determinative influence in his life.[2]

Hofstadter and Felice were immersed in the controversies of their day. One of the most pressing concerns, as several original participants have observed, was the correctness of the philosophy of historical materialism. Both Hofstadter and Felice were directly engaged in this debate. The subject was discussed throughout the pages of journals to which they subscribed, such as *Science and Society*. It was a household topic for subscribers to the *New Masses*. For at least the entire first year that the couple lived in New York—the winter of 1936–37—Felice attempted to publish an article on dialectical materialism in *Science and Society*. That article undoubtedly derived from her M.A. thesis. She corresponded at some length with one of the editors of the journal, D. J. Struik, a professor of mathematics at the Massachusetts Institute of Technology and later editor of a volume of Marx's and Engels's correspondence. She also held long conversations about the relationship between the natural world and the dialectic with a friend who was studying physics and considering the applicability of those principles to the sciences. That friend reports that both he and Hofstadter were more skeptical than Felice. At the same time, however, Hofstadter himself wrote a paper on the dialectic for one of his classes at Columbia. Alfred Kazin remembers Hofstadter sitting outside the main reading room of the New York Public Library writing the paper. The philosophy simply dominated the era in which they all came of age. It formed a continuous background conversation to Hofstadter's academic pursuits. It was an integral part of his political commitments and moral principles. Even members of an older generation, such as Merle Curti, seriously discussed it as an analytical tool for historical interpretation. There can be little doubt that the philosophy of dialectical materialism helped to define Hofstadter's life at this time.[3]

After August 1939, as we have seen, while others moved away from their involvement with the Left, Hofstadter did *not* break away from his political and philosophical orientation in the severe sense true of others. His alienation from American Capitalism remained intense. He began to go beyond Marx in his criticisms of American society. When he went to Maryland in the fall of 1942, he met there others who shared his point of view. Nowhere in this period is there any indication that Hofstadter reembraced the traditional American values of liberal democracy. But he was able to maintain his rejection of American values at the same time as he *also* rejected the political logic that had led him to the Communist Party. The double negativity left him, as he said, with "nowhere to go," and contributed to his feeling of marginality.[4]

He did not snap back, as others did, perhaps because he inherited the matter-of-fact and dogged qualities of his maternal grandmother, perhaps because he had no illusions to begin with. For whatever reasons, having stepped into the abyss of criticism and alienation, he continued there. To have stepped back from that critical stance would have meant giving up everything he had decided was important to him. The process of involvement in left-wing politics had been fully experiential; it had become an entire life-style. Retaining those lessons of criticism and detachment was a matter of psychic integration—not only of intellectual gamesmanship. One understands Alfred Kazin's choice of images in his epitaph on Hofstadter in this regard. That choice entailed speaking of Hofstadter not as historian or even as intellectual but as passionate human being, who had approached despair and pulled back from it by an effort of the will. In the days after the announcement of the Nazi-Soviet Pact, Hofstadter and Kazin were writing together at the New York Public Library. Kazin was working on *On Native Grounds*, Hofstadter on *Social Darwinism*. In those days, Hofstadter was going through the moments of intense insight we have noted: insight into what the left-wing movement had meant for him and what consequently Soviet perfidy also meant. Kazin, as well as anyone, knew what was happening with Hofstadter in those days.

When Kazin came to write of his own times in *On Native Grounds*, he wrote of the dialectic as a tool of literary criticism best used when applied figuratively. Hofstadter, responding from Maryland to Kazin's work with warmth and appreciation when it was ready to be published, wrote, "Your characterization of the radicalism of the '30's there is one of the best things of its kind I have seen." Kazin had also referred to the dialectic as a "guiding thread" rather than a "ready-cut pattern on which to tailor historical facts." For this reference he used Engels, as Felice had used him in her discussion of the irony of history and of crisscrossing patterns of individual intentions among individual human wills. This must have been a favorite passage for those people at that time.[5]

In his mature work, the dialectical structure functioned for Hofstadter as a kind of "logic of movement" through which to depict a changing society. Balance, harmony, and equilibrium were momentary states achieved for single instants in the march of time, and contradictions, tensions, strains, and blindnesses marked the major portion of human life. Almost always there was for Hofstadter a yawning gap between ideas about the nature of life—always firmly anchored in past institutions—and the present, pressing, challenging reality. That gap seems reminiscent of the sense of disconnection felt by Hofstadter and people like him after the Nazi-Soviet Pact. Then there was the shock of realization that expectations did not match reality and that people—those who "believed"—had been blind. In Hofstadter's histories, external political and economic reality called for a solution in their own terms, but people's minds most of the time were averted from the realities in front of them. This was true of the Populists, the Founding Fathers, the Mugwumps, and others, as it had been true of many in the 1930's.

The gap between reality and ideas, needs and values, is tied to a basic assumption about the social order that Hofstadter had retained from his Marxist outlook. He continued to assume the existence of an economic process that marches inevitably, powerfully, and inexorably forward. That base, in the United States, was made up of Capitalism in all its many manifestations—in his later books as it had been in his early papers. Arising from that base, but tied to it, were the legal, political, social, religious, and intellectual pursuits of Americans. These were caused by the base and expressive of the base, but changed *more slowly* than it did. The discrepancy in the rate of change caused the cultural gap that made people blind to the realities of their own contemporary economic and social orders. The relationships between base and "superstructure" then were intricate and finely balanced. Their essential nature did not change through Hofstadter's work. That set of relationships explains why politics was, for him, a forum for the expression of more deeply seated attitudes and states of mind.

The cultural gap also takes on significance itself as a causal factor because of the very nature of the dialectic. Although people see only "darkly," they do see partially and are at times able to resolve some of their difficulties for short periods of time. But the tension between what people understand and what they need to understand exists in a nearly continuous way because in the dialectic, as Hegel had postulated, "If we understand it, we pass on to take account of what is left out."[6] Hofstadter, always operating with the benefit of hindsight, was able to point to what had been left out. In fact, he has testified to just this perception as one of the major lessons of history for him, personally. "An awareness of limitation is one of the things I get from history, and what I hope to find in histories of others."[7]

It is also necessary to point out that Hofstadter in time moved away from explicit inclusion and treatment of the economic "base." In his early papers as a student, he treated it most directly—if not completely explicitly. As he developed in sophistication and finesse, he added elements to his history and causation became more complex and multiple. In this way, he himself, during the course of the 1940's, exemplified the development from Progressive simplicity among historians to counter-Progressive multiplicity and complexity. By *The Age of Reform*, the cause for change was the process of industrialization itself. For both Populists and Progressives, the challenge to their thinking arose from a threat of another social group that had more wealth, power, prestige, or status than they. These "other" groups occupied their particular positions because they were more in tune with the industrialization process than either Populists and Progressives. To arrive at a synthesis or a resolution of pressing problems, each political movement was forced to put itself in alliance with the business ethic, if not directly as a political coalition than at least indirectly by adopting its attitudes and points of view.

In his later work, Hofstadter lost his grip on the powerful and inexorable force of the industrialization process. That process appears in neither *Anti-intellectualism in American Life* nor *The Idea of a Party System*. The dialectical structure of change, however, remained, as we have seen. Change was caused in *Anti-intellectualism* by the tug of ideas, assumptions, and attitudes. Although syntheses were clear, it was the elastic tension—the internal contradictions—of each set of assumptions (both for politicians and for intellectuals) that Hofstadter treated. The subject of the book as a whole was the fundamental opposition between the purposes of democracy—equality and justice for all—and the purposes of intellectual endeavor—quality, refinement, insight, purposeful planning. Although the dialectic did mark his history here, his main purpose was to comment on the classical problem of the role of the intellectual, particularly in relation to governmental power. What he said in this regard allowed the Marxist influence a back-door entrance, for the ossification of ideas was the basic danger to forward movement and ossification in ideological terms originally meant for Marx a hardening of the mind in channels conditioned by an earlier stage of production. As has been pointed out, Hofstadter believed totally in the necessity of freeing the mind of its binding fetters from the past. This was the *only* way to effect a conjunction between human intellect and the demands of the economic and social order.[8]

In *The Idea of a Party System*, one also misses the sense of economic causation. Perhaps this was due to the fact that Hofstadter focused on the period before the Industrial Revolution proper. Perhaps not. Whatever the answer, the external challenges arose entirely from the political realm, both domestically and in the area of foreign policy. The established pattern was again repeated. Old ideas did not meet the need posed by new realities; thus, new ideas formed in response to the new reality, but also clashed with the old ideas and tension or ambivalence developed in the minds of people and caused an imperfect conjunction between mind and reality. Hofstadter had stepped partway into the social structure and was looking at it from a magnified perspective more closely sighted than he had ever attempted before or did afterward.

Hofstadter had, then, through his joint convictions about the structure of society and the structure of change, implicitly answered the question Beard raised in 1933. He had "given ... [his history] consistency of structure by a deliberate conjecture respecting the nature or direction of the vast movements of ideas and interests called world history." The pattern Hofstadter found events to be making in history was cyclical in nature but essentially directionless. It operated from a number of different directions. From this perspective, Hofstadter seems to have rejected utterly the Progressive faith in progression in history.

The dialectic also serves to uncover some larger interpretive features of Hofstadter's work—features that have been obscured because of his elusive and subtle literary tendencies. It is an outstanding element in Hofstadter's history that those who met the needs of the emerging economic and social order—Capitalists, plutocrats, his "structural" reformers—were not often treated directly. They were present in his histories but mainly as foils against which his actors could proceed—unsuccessfully.

Several illustrations arise from *The Idea of a Party System*. Although the focus in that book was the anti-party idea, Hofstadter made it quite clear that the idea itself served to hold back real adaptation, real innovation, real coordination of values and needs. He had, in a sense, misled the reader. By focusing so single-mindedly in his first two chapters on the history of the anti-party ideology, he had approached his subject *as if* that ideology were the causative factor, which in fact he thought it was not. Not only was the ideology deemed not causative in this book, it was actually retardative. So why did Hofstadter as a historian deal with it at all? Did he not want to show how American society moved ahead?

The anti-party bias of the Founding Fathers operated as one vehicle for their gentleman-like qualities of disinterest. These made the transfer of power in 1801 smooth. It was this disinterest, too, that Hofstadter criticized so harshly in *The Age of Reform*. It was one of the qualities the Progressives inherited directly from their Mugwump fathers, and that, in *Anti-intellec-tualism*, the Mugwumps inherited themselves directly from the Founding Fathers. This honorable disinterest and its concomitant qualities were a subject of recurrent critical concern for Hofstadter in one form or another over a long period of time. The prevailing and dominant ideas of this "Yankee" type—the ruling class in America for most of its history—were usually retardative and not causative.

At first glance, the anti-party bias of the Founding Fathers seems an unimportant component of their intellectual heritage, a bias that was dysfunctional in the new environment. Eventually, it was outmoded and disappeared. But when it is considered in the context of his other treatments of the same social type, it becomes apparent that Hofstadter *continually* viewed this Yankee social type as a negative force in Americn history, and that the anti-party bias, which was really one part of a whole dominant Yankee ethos, was part of a crucial, continuing critical concern for Richard Hofstadter.

The Founding Fathers-Mugwump-Progressive as a type, then, was pervasive throughout Hofstadter's work. If one asks, in this regard, who it was who opposed this group through American history, one comes up against the "foils" pointed out above. Within the examples cited, several answers appear: In the early period, it was the Party politicians like Van Buren—common people with practical goals; in the later period, it was immigrants and their bosses, whose system more nearly matched the needs of late nineteenth-century cities; from the political perspective, it was those who wanted to change things "structurally," the Tom Watsons and Henry Demarest Lloyds and the Upton Sinclairs and Gustavus Myers. These were the people who wanted to make major institutional changes, to move away from private ownership, away from "the rights of property, the philosophy of economic individualism, the value of competition." These were, in effect, the anti-heroes of American history.

Whenever Hofstadter perceived a "glimmering" of real forward movement, one now begins to realize, he put that glimmering in terms *opposed* to the Founding Fathers-Mugwump-Progressive ethos. Real desirable forward movement in terms of social groups and in terms of the synchronization, of needs and values was put in terms opposed to the main line of American development, opposed to the directions indicated and proposed by its Anglo-Saxon leadership.

Real forward movement did not seem possible very often in American history for Richard Hofstadter. To the extent that people did accept the values of that Anglo-Saxon leadership, real forward movement was retarded. From this point of view, the statement of unity among the American people, which Hofstadter made in 1948 in the introduction to *The American Political Tradition*, indicated nothing positive. Unity by itself, as we have seen in his early papers, indicated only passive acceptance of the dominant group's moral, economic, and social code—or of the inevitable nature of history. It did not indicate anything that Hofstadter believed was morally preferable. *The Idea of a Party System* appears to have been the capstone to Hofstadter's life work because there he was attending in close-up style to opposition—both as a value and as an institutional feature of American life—as a positive good.

Opposition was the positive good in Hofstadter's social lexicon as well as in his political one—opposition not within established lines, but in and for itself. Since the Yankee approach had both dominated and retarded American history, opposition to this "ruling class" was a positive social benefit. America had backed its way into modernity by giving up parts of this dominant ethos a bit at a time—the anti-party bias by 1828, self-sufficiency and family independence by 1896, some of the guilt complexes and personal responsibility of the Progressives by the "experimental" New Deal. Real forward movement did not come with unity or through the dominance of the American Yankee. Real forward movement came through the intrusion, the incorporation, the *synthesis* of foreign attitudes, politics, and social types with the dominant ones.

It is not a given truth that historians must choose topics they like or of which they approve to research and develop. Richard Hofstadter was addicted to criticism and refinement of his critical perceptions. He was forever choosing topics to address that did not appeal to him. He has, in fact, been called a misanthrope. This was not the case. He was simply able, through a native perspicacity, to deal incisively with what were elements essentially foreign to his own background and experience. Hofstadter himself neither participated in the Yankee ethos nor had roots very deep in native soil. His own background, as we have seen, was that of his anti-heroes: immigrant, politician, intellectual-agitator. This fact makes a difference for understanding his history.

The dialectical form, then, gave a logic of movement to Hofstadter's history, but did not give it a single direction. Hofstadter's was a cyclical pattern and that pattern itself linked the socioeconomic order and the life of the mind. Ideas, for Hofstadter, were conditioned responses to an established order—not unreflective or mechanistic, indeed sometimes extremely articulate and clever, but inextricably connected nonetheless. They were more expressive than they were instrumental, although they did help to make changes in the challenging external environment.[9]

Change came, then, through politics, which was the forum for expressing deeply held beliefs related to an older order. The tension between current reality and new *and* old ideas made up the dialectical pattern, which itself had no determined direction. It is here, at the final and ultimate question for historians, that Richard Hofstadter differed most from the Progressive point of view. Because the American experience had been completely monopolized by the Capitalist order, because Hofstadter could not identify with that order, the history of that order could not be "progressive" in the old optimistic sense.

It is not insignificant that when Hofstadter came to write *The Progressive Historians* and created, in full-length portraits, three biographical and historiographical accounts of men who had been enormous influences on his own work, he revealed in contrast how he thought history worked. In discussing Parrington's architectonic sense of structure, for instance, Hofstadter wrote: "Its disadvantage hangs on the fact that history itself does not take place architectonically, but with a fluid dialectic of its own. It is capricious, asymmetrical, organic, rather than geometrical." Discussing Beard's dualism in *An Economic Interpretation of the Constitution*, he wrote: "Rather than an exceedingly complex jumble of special interests, he fell into a trap from which a consistent use either of Bentley or of Madisonian pluralism might have saved him."[10] Here is the well-known presentation of the view of complexity and ambiguity with which Hofstadter is so often associated—and which is true enough. Shall we, then, leave it at this, that Hofstadter's ultimate answer to Beard's challenge in his 1935 AHA address was an indication of chaos and disorder?

Not quite, for Hofstadter said more about Beard. Pointing out the most salient aspects of the Progressive ethos in and through which Beard operated in the early years of the twentieth century, Hofstadter asserted that Marxist ideas were slowly permeating the intellectual atmosphere, even in the highest academic circles. E.R.A. Seligman's book, *The Economic Interpretation of History*, best represented that permeation. Seligman presented the modification of economic causation that Engels had developed in "letters that have become classics of the Marxist canon." By the 1890's when Engels wrote these letters, he had come to view the economic force not as the "only causal agent in history" but as one that operated with other agents deriving from the superstructure and was, only in the final analysis, decisive. Beard, Hofstadter maintained, endorsed Seligman's and Engels's views as "axiomatic."[11]

Seligman detached the economic interpretation of history from Marx's Socialism and prescriptive teleology, thus making economic causation acceptable and compatible with Progressive pluralistic ideas about the state, asserted Hofstadter. At the same time, this "urbane but somewhat denatured version of the economic interpretation of history" was the Socialists' main contribution to Progressive thought.[12]

Later, in discussing Beard's moral ambiguity toward the idea that actual financial interests motivated the Founding Fathers' positions toward the Constitution, Hofstadter maintained that many public issues were "charged with moral import" and that it was not necessary for any historian to "force himself into a posture of moral neutrality about . . . [those questions]" but that, without setting himself or herself up as a moral authority, the historian by his or her choices and arrangement of materials was always "trying to provide a sense of the requirements and limitations of social situations, of the effect that actions and decisions have had upon large numbers of people."[13] Moreover, Beard's stress on motives in the Constitution had detracted from the more important historical question of the "interplay between what was intended and what was actually achieved."[14] Then, precisely at the point at which he had most thoroughly and deliberately considered Beard's own preconceptions and the existence of irony in history, Hofstadter again footnoted Engels's letter to J. Block, written in 1890. Reaching back into his own past for the 1935 edition of the Marx and Engels correspondence to find a reference point for his last discussion of the primary historiographic influence on his life, Hofstadter wrote:

There is a splendid passage in one of Engels' clarifications of historical materialism that is appropriate here: "History makes itself in such a way that the final result always arises from conflicts between many individual wills, of which each again has been made what it is by a host of particular conditions of life. Thus there are innumerable intersecting forces, an infinite series of parallelograms of forces which give rise to one resultant—the historical event. This again may be viewed as the product of a power, which taken as a whole, works unconsciously and without volition. For what each individual wills is obstructed by everyone else, and what emerges is something that no one willed."[15]

Engels had been in the process of redefining the elements of historical materialism. What he had come up with formed the base for classical Marxist philosophical scholarship in the 1930's. Felice had used this letter to indicate the ironies of history in her M.A. thesis and to introduce her discussion of the "laws of society." What better or more complete rephrasing of the dialectical process did Hofstadter need to put forward his own sense of inherent contradictions and the tensions between reality and ideas?

The fact that Hofstadter's structure remained such a deeply embedded part of his history and the probable reason for his eschewing talk of theory in history were expressed in a letter he wrote Alfred Kazin around 1940. He said there:

One thing that's very important: don't class me with the genus historicus. I suppose you're right that they look down their noses at genus literarius, but I am really a suppressed litterateur who couldn't make the grade just writing good prose and had to go into history. Unlike my brethren

I look up to writers, and I'm fearfully afraid of them, all of them, from competent journalists to literary critics.[16]

This affirmation of literary self-hood puts Hofstadter in the category of a writer who would and could have used the dialectic as a "guiding thread" rather than a "ready-cut pattern"—a writer who would have found it natural to apply the subtle insights from the intensive growth period in his youth to the subjects of his maturity without explicating them. The structure which underlay those insights has gone unremarked and their implications for Hofstadter's work unappreciated. Those implications, in part, make Hofstadter one of the foremost popularizers of Marxist categories among historical circles and perhaps the number one link between the Old Left and the New.

NOTES

1. Felice Swados to Harvey Swados, October 26, 1939, Harvey Swados Papers, Courtesy of the Archives of the University of Massachussetts, Amherst, Mass.

2. Kazin has argued that she did dominate him and that Hofstadter did not emerge as a historian until the publication of *The American Political Tradition*. See Chapter 6.

3. For *Science and Society* articles on the dialectic, a representative, unsystematic sample, see Antonie Pannekoek, "Society and Mind in Marxian Philosophy, "*Science and Society* I (Summer 1937) pp. 445–53; J. D. Bernal, "Dialectical Motion and Modern Science," II (Winter 1937) pp. 58–66; Corliss Lamont, "Socialism and Inevitability," Communications, II (Fall 1938) pp. 512–14; Ralph Winn, "Dialectics and General Principles," Communications, II (Fall 1938) pp. 520–26; J. B. Haldane, "A Dialectical Account of Evolution," I (Summer 1937) pp. 471–86; Felice Swados to Harvey Swados, January 25, 1937, October 10, 1937; Marvin Chodorow to the author, May 17, 1982; Alfred Kazin, Official interview, Columbia Oral History Project, p. ll.

4. Kenneth Stampp, Personal interview with the author, April 2, 1981. Stampp emphasized that *The American Political Tradition* was written from this perspective.

5. Richard Hofstadter to Alfred Kazin, November 16, 1942, Courtesy of Alfred Kazin; Alfred Kazin, *On Native Grounds* (New York, Reynal and Hitchcock, 1942) p. 413.

6. John Herman Randall, *The Career of Philosophy II: From the German*

Enlightenment to the Age of Darwin (New York, Columbia University Press, 1965) pp. 310–14.

7. Richard Kostelanetz, "Richard Hofstadter: Historian's Indomitable Skepticism," in Kostelanetz, ed., *Masterminds* (New York, Macmillan, 1967) p. 118.

8. See Richard Hofstadter, *Anti-intellectualism in American Life* (New York, Vintage Books, 1962) final chapter.

9. Stanley Elkins and Eric McKitrick, "Richard Hofstadter: A Progress," in Elkins and Mckitrick, eds., *The Hofstadler Aegis* (New York, Alfred A. Knopf, 1973) p. 302. They say: "It was this which came to preoccupy him: the varying conditions under which mind itself has been obliged to function in this culture." And further: "His attention was forever being drawn to the way in which people who professed given ideas actually behaved and to the circumstances which may have rendered such ideas attractive to them." It is this trait that I feel developed from Hofstadter's first encounter with Marxism.

10. Richard Hofstadter, *The Progressive Historians* (New York, Vintage Books, 1968) pp. 188, 401.

11. Ibid., p.198.

12. Ibid., pp. 196–200. For quotation see p. 200.

13. Ibid., p. 229.

14. Ibid., p. 230.

15. Ibid., n. 2.

16. Hofstadter to Kazin, n.d. [1940], Courtesy of Alfred Kazin.

Bibliography

UNPUBLISHED SOURCES

Manuscript Collections

Amherst, Mass. The University of Massachusetts. Harvey Swados Papers.
Buffalo, N.Y. The Buffalo and Erie County Historical Society. Julius
  Pratt Papers.
New York, N.Y. Columbia University. Rare Book and Manuscript Li-
  brary. Harry Carman Papers.
New York, N.Y. Columbia University. Rare Book and Manuscript Li-
  brary. Richard Hofstadter Papers.

Interviews

Adler, Selig. Buffalo, N.Y. March 26, 1981.
Chodorow, Marvin. Stanford University. May 17, 1981.
Goodfriend, Betty. Acoustical Society of America. May 26, 1981.
Kazin, Alfred. City University of New York. November 19, 1980.
Miller, William. West Redding, Conn. May 29, 1981.
Pratt, Julius. Medford, N.J. May 27, 1981.
Riesman, David. Harvard University. September 20, 1980.
Sanes, Irving. Buffalo, N.Y. March 26, 1981.
Stampp, Kenneth. University of California at Berkeley. April 2,3, 1981.

Theses and Other Papers

Goodwyn, Lawrence. "Hicks, Hofstadter, and the Continuing Legacy of Consensus Historiography." Paper presented at the 1982 meeting of the Organization of American Historians, Philadelphia, Penn., April 1, 1982.

Hofstadter, Richard. "The Tariff and Homestead Issues in the Republican Campaign of 1860." Tutorial Thesis, University of Buffalo, May 1936.

————. "The Southeastern Cotton Tenants Under the AAA, 1933–1935." M.A. Thesis, Columbia University, June 1938.

Swados, Felice. "Two Types of Materialism: A Comparison of the Mechanical Materialism of Holbach and the Dialectical Materialism of Marx and Engles." M.A. Thesis, Smith College, 1936.

PUBLISHED SOURCES

Newspaper and Periodicals

Buffalo Bee. University of Buffalo, Buffalo, N.Y. September 1933—December 1936.

Nation. New York, N.Y. 1937–1939.

New Masses. New York, N.Y. 1932–1937.

Student Advocate. Greenwood Reprint Corp. January 1936—March 1938.

Student Review. Greenwood Reprint Corp. September 1931—December 1935.

Books by Richard Hofstadter

Social Darwinism in American Thought, 1860–1915. Philadelphia, University of Pennsylvania Press, 1945.

The American Political Tradition. New York, Alfred A. Knopf and Random House, Vintage Books, 1948.

The Age of Reform. New York, Alfred A. Knopf and Random House, Vintage Books, 1955.

Anti-intellectualism in American Life. New York, Alfred A. Knopf and Random House, Vintage Books, 1962.

The Progressive Historians. New York, Alfred A. Knopf and Random House, Vintage Books, 1968.

The Idea of a Party System. Berkeley, University of California Press, 1969.

America at 1750: A Social Portrait. New York, Alfred A. Knopf and Random House, Vintage Books. 1971.

Books—General

Aaron, Daniel. *Writers on the Left.* New York, Avon Books, 1965.

Adler, Selig, and Connolly, Tom. *From Ararat to Suburbia.* Philadelphia, Jewish Publication Society of America, 1960.

Avineri, Schlomo, ed. *Marx's Socialism.* New York, Lieber-Atherton, 1973.

Beale, Howard K. *Charles A. Beard.* Lexington, University of Kentucky Press, 1954.

Beard, Charles A. *An Economic Interpretation of the Constitution.* New York, Macmillan Co., 1913.

———, and Beard, Mary. *The Rise of American Civilization.* New York, Macmillan Co., 1930.

Becker, Carl L. *Every Man His Own Historian.* New York, F. S. Crofts, 1935.

Bell, Daniel, ed. *The Radical Right.* New York, Doubleday, Anchor Books, 1964.

Cantor, Milton. *The Divided Left.* New York, Hill and Wang, 1978.

Cowley, Malcolm. *The Dream of the Golden Mountains.* New York, Viking Press, 1980.

Curti, Merle. *The Social Ideas of American Educators.* New York, Scribner's Sons, 1935.

———. *The Growth of American Thought.* New York, Harper & Brothers, 1943.

Deutscher, Isaac. *The Prophet Outcast, Trotsky: 1929–1940.* London, Oxford University Press, 1963.

Diggins, John P. *Up From Communism: Conservative Odysseys in American Intellectual History.* New York, Harper and Row, 1975.

Draper, Theodore. *American Communism and Soviet Russia.* New York, Viking Press, 1960.

Elkins, Stanley, and McKitrick, Eric, eds. *The Hofstadter Aegis.* N.Y., Alfred A. Knopf, 1974.

Erikson, Erik. *Childhood and Society.* New York, W.W. Norton & Co., 1950.

Forcey, Charles. *The Crossroad of Liberalism.* New York, Oxford University Press, 1961.

Hartz, Louis. *The Liberal Tradition in America.* New York, Harcourt, Brace, & World, Inc., 1955.

Higham, John. *Reconstruction of American History.* New York, Humanities Press, 1962.

————.*Writing American History*. Bloomington, Indiana. Indiana University Press, 1970.

Horton, John Williams, Edward T., and Douglas, Harry S., et. al. *The History of Northwestern New York, Vol. I: Buffalo and Erie County*. New York, Lewis Historical Publishing Company, 1947.

Howe, Irving. *World of Our Fathers*. New York, Harcourt, Brace, Jovanovitch, 1976.

————, and Coser, Lewis. *The American Communist Party*. Boston, Beacon Press, 1957.

Jay, Martin. *The Dialectical Imagination*. Boston, Little, Brown & Co., 1973.

Josephson, Matthew. *Infidel in the Temple*. New York, Alfred A. Knopf, 1967.

————. *New York Jew*. New York, Random House, Vintage Books, 1979.

Kazin, Alfred. *On Native Grounds*. New York, Reynal & Hitchcock, 1942.

————. *Starting Out in the Thirties*. Boston, Little, Brown & Co., 1962.

————. *A Walker in the City*. New York, Harcourt, Brace & Co., 1951.

Lasch, Christopher. *The Agony of the American Left*. New York, Random House, Vintage Books, 1969.

————. *Haven in a Heartless World*. New York, Basic Books, Inc., 1977.

Marx, Karl, and Engels, Frederick. *Correspondence 1846–1895*. Edited by Dona Torr. New York, International Publishers, 1934.

————. *Selected Writings in Sociology and Social Philosophy*. Translated by T. B. Bottomore. New York, McGraw-Hill Co., 1956.

————. *The Marx-Engels Reader*. Edited by Robert C. Tucker. New York, W. W. Norton & Co., 1972.

Morton, Marion. *The Terror of Ideological Politics*. Cleveland, Case Western Reserve University Press, 1971.

Myers, Constance Ashton. *The Prophet's Army: Trotskyists in America 1928–1941*. Westport, Conn., Greenwood Press, 1977.

Leopold, Richard. *The Growth of American Foreign Policy*. New York, Alfred A. Knopf, 1962.

Pole, Jack Richon. *Paths to the American Past*. New York, Oxford University Press, 1979.

Pells, Richard. *Radical Visions and American Dreams*. New York, Harper & Row, Harper Torchbooks, 1973.

Randall, John Herman. *The Career of Philosophy, Vol. II: From the German Enlightenment to the Age of Darwin*. New York, Columbia University Press, 1965.

Riepe, Dale, ed. *Phenomenology and Natural Existence: Essays in Honor of Marvin Farber*. Albany, State University of New York Press, 1973.

Riesman, David. *The Lonely Crowd*. New Haven, Conn., Yale University Press, 1950.

————. *Constraint and Variety in American Education*. New York, Doubleday Anchor Books, 1958.

Rogin, Michael Paul. *The Intellectuals and McCarthy: The Radical Specter*.
Cambridge, M.I.T. Press, 1967.

Schlesinger, Arthur M., Jr. *The Age of Roosevelt, Vol. II: The Coming of
the New Deal*. Boston, Houghton Mifflin Co., 1958; Sentry Edition, 1965.

Skotheim, Robert A. *American Intellectual Histories and Historians*. Princeton, N.J., Princeton University Press, 1966.

Swados, Harvey. *Nights in the Garden of Brooklyn*. Boston, Little, Brown,
& Co., 1960.

————. *Standing Fast*. Garden City, New York, Doubleday & Co., 1970.

Thomas, Hugh. *The Spanish Civil War*. New York, Harper & Bros., 1961.

Treadgold, Donald W. *Twentieth Century Russia*. Chicago, Rand McNally
& Co., 1959.

Trilling, Lionel. *The Liberal Imagination*. New York, Viking Press, 1950.

Warren, Frank. *Liberals and Communism: The Red Decade Revisited*. Bloomington, Indiana University Press, 1966.

Wechsler, James. *The Age of Suspicion*. New York, Random House, 1953.

————. *Revolt on the Campus*. Seattle, University of Washington Press,
1973.

Wise, Gene. *American Historical Explanations*. Homewood, Ill., Dorsey
Press, 1973.

Wish, Harvey, ed. *American Historians: A Selection*. New York, Oxford
University Press, 1962.

Book Reviews and Articles by Richard Hofstadter

Book Reviews

E. Merton Courter, ed. *Georgia's Disputed Ruins*. *New York Herald Tribune
Books* (April 18, 1937): 14.

Vida D. Scudder. *On Journey*. *New York Herald Tribune Books*. (April 18,
1937): 3.

Isaac Goldberg. *Major Noah, American-Jewish Pioneer*. *New York Herald
Tribune Books* (April 25, 1937): 19.

Georgia Harkness. *The Recovery of Ideals*. *New York Herald Tribune Books*
(June 6, 1937): 13.

A. H. Murray. *The Philosophy of James Ward*. *New York Herald Tribune
Books* (July 11, 1937): 10.

Everett E. Edwards, comp. *The Early Writings of Frederick Jackson Turner*.
Political Science Quarterly LIV (December 1939): 638–39.

Dwight L. Dumond. *Anti-slavery Origins of the Civil War in the United*

States. Pennsylvania Magazine of History and Biography LXIV (April 1940): 284–85.

Max Lerner. *Ideas are Weapons. Political Science Quarterly* LV (December 1940): 621.

Richard W. Leopold. *Robert Dale Owen. Mississippi Valley Historical Review* XXVII (March 1941): 638–39.

Maurice R. Davie. *Sumner Today: Selected Essays by William Graham Sumner, with Comments by American Leaders. New England Ouarterlv* XIV (December 1941): 774–75.

Articles

"The Tariff Issue on the Eve of the Civil War." *American Historical Review* XLIV (October 1938): 50–55.

"William Graham Sumner, Social Darwinist." *New England Quarterly* XIV (September 1941): 457–77.

"Parrington and the Jeffersonian Tradition." *Journal of the History of Ideas* II (October 1941): 391–400.

"William Leggett, Spokesman of Jacksonian Democracy." *Political Science Quarterly* LVIII (December 1943): 581–94.

"U. B. Phillips and the Plantation Legend." *Journal of Negro History* XXXIX (April 1944): 109–24.

Articles on Richard Hofstadter

Cremin, Lawrence A. "Richard Hofstadter (1916–1970): A Biographical Memoir." Pittsburgh, Pennsylvania, National Academy of Education, 1972.

Elkins, Stanley, and McKitrick, Eric. "Richard Hofstadter: A Progress," in *The Hofstadter Aegis.* Edited by Stanley Elkins and Eric McKitrick. New York, Alfred A. Knopf, 1973 pp. 300–367.

Garraty, John A. *Interpreting American History: Conversations with Historians, I.* New York, Macmillan Co., 1970 pp. 145–60.

Gillam, Richard. "Richard Hofstadler, C. Wright Mills, and 'the Critical Ideal.' " *The American Scholer,* 47 (1977–78): 69–85.

Hawke, David. "Interview: Richard Hofstadter." *History* 3 (September 1960): 135–41.

Howe, Daniel Walker, and Finn, Peter Elliott, "Richard Hofstadter: The Ironies of an American Historian." *Pacific Historical Review.* 43 (1974): 1–23.

Kazin, Alfred. "Richard Hofstadter, 1916–1970." *American Scholar* XL (Summer 1971): 397–403.

Lasch, Christopher. "On Richard Hofstadter." *New York Review of Books* (March 8, 1973): 7–13.

Pole, Jack Richon. "Richard Hofstadter, 1916–1970," in *Paths to the American Present*. New York, Oxford University Press, 1979. pp. 335–37.

Schlesinger, Arthur M., Jr. "Richard Hofstadter," in *Pastmasters*. Edited by Marcus Cunliff and Robin Winks. New York, Harper & Row, 1969. pp. 278–315.

Singal, Daniel Joseph. "Beyond Consensus: Richard Hofstadter and American Historiography," *American Historical Review* 89 # 4. (October, 1984): 976–1004.

Woodward, C. Vann. "Richard Hofstadter 1916–1970." *New York Review of Books* XV (December 3, 1970): 10.

Articles—General

Amberson, William R. "The New Deal for Share-Croppers." *Nation* CXL (February 13, 1935): 185–88.

Corey, Lewis. "Marxism Reconsidered I, II, III." *Nation* (February 17, 1940): 245–48; 272–75; 305–7.

Hicks, Granville. "On Leaving the Communist Party." *New Republic* C (October 4, 1939): 244–45.

Kristol, Irving. "Memoirs of a Trotskyist." *New York Times Magazine* (January 23, 1977): 42ff.

Kunitz, Joshua. "Seeds of Counter Revolution." *New Masses* (October 27, 1936): 11–13.

Lerner, Max. "Revolution in Ideas." *Nation* CXLIX (October 21, 1939) 435–37.

Letters to the Editor

Allen, Jay, et al. "To the Active Supporters of Democracy and Peace." *Nation* CXLVIII (August 26, 1939): 228.

Hook, Sidney, et. al. "Manifesto." *Nation* CXLVIII (May 27, 1939): 626.

Index

About the Author

SUSAN STOUT BAKER is an Assistant Professor of History at the University of Utah, Salt Lake City.